How to Pass

SECOND EDITION

HIGHER

History

Simon Wood

**HODDER
GIBSON**

AN HACHETTE UK COMPANY

The Publishers would like to thank the following for permission to reproduce copyright material:

Acknowledgements
The publishers are grateful for the use of material on **p.9** taken from the SQA Higher History Course Specification © Scottish Qualifications Authority.
p.158 extract from Andy MacPhee, *The Scottish Wars of Independence, 1286–1328* (Hodder Gibson, 2010); **p.158** extract from *Scotland: a New History* by Michael Lynch published by Pimlico. Reproduced by permission of The Random House Group Ltd. © 1992; **p.169** extract from James E. Handley, *The Irish in Scotland* (John S. Burns, 1964), reproduced with permission of Cork University Press; **p.169** extract from Simon Wood, *Migration and Empire 1830–1939* (Hodder Gibson, 2011); **p.170** extract from Allan Macinnes, Marjory Harper and Linda Fryer (eds), *Scotland and the Americas, c.1650–c.1939* (Lothian Print for the Scottish History Society, 2002); **p.182** extract from A. Dickson and J.H. Treble, *People and Society in Scotland: Volume III, 1914–1990* (John Donald Publishers Ltd, 1992), reproduced with permission of Birlinn Ltd via PLSclear; **p.182** extract from I.G.C. Hutchison, *Scottish Politics in the Twentieth Century* (Palgrave, 2001), reproduced with permission of SNCSC.

Photo credits
p.36 © TopFoto; **p.45** © Trinity Mirror / Mirrorpix / Alamy; **p.60** © Georgios Kollidas - Fotolia; **p.67** © Hulton Archive/Getty Images; **p.78** © Hulton Archive/Getty Images; **p.87** © Chronicle / Alamy; **p.96** © Illustrated London News; **p.105** ©Library of Congress, Prints & Photographs Division, U.S. News & World Report Magazine Collection, LC-DIG-ppmsc-01269; **p.116** © Gamma-Keystone via Getty Images; **p.122** © CORBIS/Corbis via Getty Images; **p.135** ©World History Archive / TopFoto; **p.140** ©NATIONAL ARCHIVES/AFP/Getty Images; **p.154** Public Domain/http://commons.wikimedia.org/wiki/File:The_Battle_of_Stirling_Bridge.jpg[05Feb2015]; **p.157** Public Domain /http://commons.wikimedia.org/wiki/File:Battle_of_Bannockburn_-_Bruce_addresses_troops.jpg[05Feb2015]; **p.164** © Scottish Life Archive, National Museums of Scotland; **p.168** © Photos.com/Getty/Thinkstock; **p.174** © The Print Collector / Heritage Images / TopFoto; **p.176** © Lt. Ernest Brooks/ IWM via Getty Images.

Orders: please contact Bookpoint Ltd, 130 Park Drive, Milton Park, Abingdon, Oxon OX14 4SE. Telephone: (44) 01235 827827. Fax: (44) 01235 400454. Email education@bookpoint.co.uk Lines are open from 9 a.m. to 5 p.m., Monday to Friday, with a 24-hour message answering service. Visit our website at www.hoddereducation.co.uk. If you have queries or questions that aren't about an order, you can contact us at hoddergibson@hodder.co.uk

© Simon Wood 2019
First published in 2015 © John Kerr
This second edition published in 2019 by
Hodder Gibson, an imprint of Hodder Education
An Hachette UK Company
211 St Vincent Street
Glasgow, G2 5QY

Impression number   5   4   3   2
Year   2023 2022 2021 2020

Cover photo © Paplauski Vital – stock.adobe.com
Illustrations by Emma Golley at Redmoor Design; Barking Dog Art Design and Illustration; and by Aptara, Inc.
Typeset in CronosPro-Lt 13/15 by Aptara Inc.
Printed in India

A catalogue record for this title is available from the British Library.

ISBN: 978 1 5104 5242 8

SCOTLAND EXCEL

We are an approved supplier on the Scotland Excel framework.

Schools can find us on their procurement system as:

Hodder & Stoughton Limited t/a Hodder Gibson.

MIX
Paper from responsible sources
FSC™ C104740
www.fsc.org

Contents

Introduction

This book gives specific advice about nine of the most popular topics at Higher History. In total there are nineteen possible topics to study but many of the topics attract very few students. The nine covered in this book are by far the most popular topics studied by more than 10,000 candidates who sit Higher History every year.

This book will help you to achieve your best possible result in the Higher History examination by telling you all you need to know about the exam and the assessments you are likely to take. You will find valuable information about the topics you are learning and advice on how to write the History assignment.

It tells you *how* to learn and *what* to learn. By working your way through this book you will find it easier to understand and write, both extended responses (essays) and answers to the three different types of source based questions.

Finally, there are also many 'Hints & tips' written by some of the most experienced examiners and markers in Scotland.

Higher History

From 2018 the Higher History exam will be made up of two exam papers that are both 1 hour 30 minutes long. The different exam papers examine different skills. The **British, European and world history** paper will examine your ability to write two extended responses, more commonly known as essays, on British, European and world history. The **Scottish history** paper will examine your knowledge and ability to interpret presented sources on Scottish history. The British, European and world history paper will be out of 44 marks and the Scottish history paper will be out of 36 marks.

As well as the exam there is a History assignment. This is an independent piece of research where you choose the issue to answer and write up a response in a 1 hour 30 minute write-up. You are allowed to take in one side of A4 with a Resource Sheet to help you with your response. The assignment is worth 30 marks. Therefore Higher History is out of 110 marks in total.

How to be a better learner

Before you start revising all the information you have to know for the exam, have you thought about how efficiently you learn? Do you spend hours just reading notes over and over again? Revise for a while then ask yourself some serious questions. How much of your revision can you really remember an hour after you have finished? How much can you remember the next day? The next week?

The following activities are just some examples of ideas that will help you to revise for any subject, not just History.

But why bother doing different things?

Think about this

If you always do what you have always done, then you will always get what you have always got.

If you really want to improve then things have to change. They will not change just because you want them to. You have the power to make a difference to yourself.

The pyramid of efficiency

This pyramid diagram shows on average what a person will remember 24 hours after a 'learning experience' if they do nothing to reinforce it. For example, if you sit and read over information and then do nothing to reinforce that reading then after 24 hours you will have forgotten 90 per cent of the information you read. That is not the best way to use your time.

After 24 hours you will remember ...

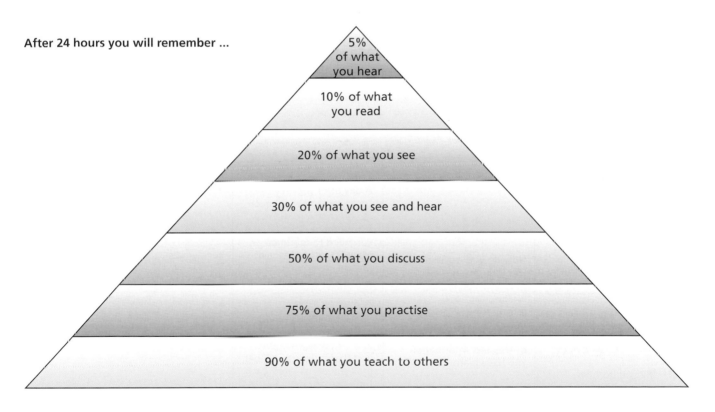

This pyramid shows what percentage of new information an average person would remember (or retain) after 24 hours if they used the methods of learning shown here – *and* if that person did nothing to reinforce the learning during the following 24 hours

On the other hand, if you try to explain clearly what you have recently revised to a friend then you are using your learning for a purpose. That means you can expect to remember over 75 per cent of what you revised. The same is true if you just record your thoughts or information onto your phone, or other digital device. So it makes sense to think about *how* you intend to learn.

The 'I really know this!' test

Think of a place you know really well. It could be a room in your house, a shop or street, or a quiet place you like.

From your memory, describe, list or draw in detail all the things you can see in your place. Try to be as detailed as you can, list things such as colours and patterns and where everything is in relation to everything else.

Next time you go to that place take your list with you. When you get there you will recognise instantly every single detail – but do those details appear on your list? I bet they don't.

Remember: The point is that recognising lots of detail is not the same as knowing it.

Now think about your revision. If you read over the same book or notes again and again you will feel you know the material but you are really just recognising your notes. Without the prompt of your notes in front of you, can you really be sure you know the information well enough to use it in an exam?

On the next few pages, you will find tips and ideas for making your revision more effective and maybe even more enjoyable.

How do you know what to revise?

Your brain works best when it has a definite puzzle to solve, so try these steps.

3

A day after your revision, try to remember as much as you can from the new learning box. That is what you need to reinforce, so remember the colour of the new learning box and think what you wrote in it.

Check back to remind yourself what you wrote in the new learning box and then try to remember it all sometime later. Each time you do that you reinforce your new learning.

2

Now do your revision – and this time you have a purpose. You are now looking for **new** information. When you have finished this session of revision, write a new list of the new information you have learned.

Now shade each list in a different colour. That will make each list easier to see in your mind's eye.

1

Decide on a focused topic or question from the section you have been studying.

BEFORE you do ANY revision on this topic, write a list of all that you already know about the subject. It might be quite a long list, but you only need to write it once. It shows you all the information that is in your long-term memory. So now you know what you **do not** have to revise – you already know it! And now you know what you **do** have to revise!

Stop and review

Here's another idea to help your learning.

1 When you have done no more than five minutes of revision, stop!
2 Write a heading in your own words which sums up the topic you have been revising.
3 Write a summary in no more than two sentences of what you have revised. Don't fool yourself. If you cannot do it, or do not want to do it, why not? Don't ever say to yourself, 'I know it but I cannot put it into words.' That just means you don't know it well enough! So if you cannot write your summary, then revise that section again, knowing that you must write a summary at the end of it.

Your brain now knows exactly what it has to do. You will learn much more effectively.

We guarantee your revision will suddenly improve!

Use technology

Why should everything be written down?

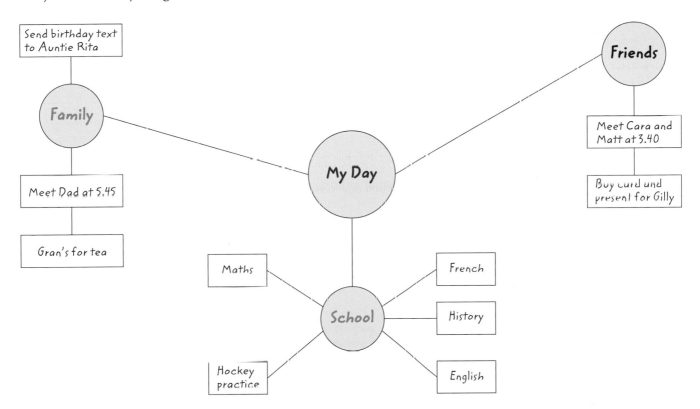

Have you thought about 'mental' maps, diagrams, cartoons and colour to help you learn? And rather than write down notes, why not record your revision material?

What about having a text message revision session with friends?

Why not make a video diary where you tell the camera what you are doing, what you think you have learned and what you still have to do?

You could share these things with your friends. Keep in touch with them about how and what they are revising through Facebook or other social media sites.

They deserve a laugh. Nobody said revision had to be boring. And after you gain the results you want you can watch the videos again and wonder why you got so stressed in the first place!

Make electronic files

Many of you will use notebooks full of blue or black ink writing. Many of the pages will not be especially attractive or memorable. But it's making material memorable that is most important.

Most people have access to a PC, iPad or Mac. *Use it to help you.*
- Start by opening up a new file for each topic you are revising, for example, 'what the Western Front was like for Scottish soldiers in the First World War '.
- Then you could start by summarising your class notes. Your typing might be slow but it will get faster and nobody can write badly when typing.
- Next you can add different fonts and colours to make your work stand out. But the *most important* thing is that you can easily copy across relevant pictures, cartoons and diagrams to make your work more attractive and *memorable*.

If you don't know how to find images use Google Images and make your choice. By doing so you are immediately using your brain to search for relevant items to your topic and that requires you to use your understanding. Ask your friends if you're not sure how to do these things. Trade with them some of the advice from this book!

Story boards

Everyone can draw stick people and many people are really good sketchers.

Many people are also visual learners, so putting a story into images can really help you to remember information. Choose a part of your course to revise and think how you could simplify it into a set of cartoon scenes that tell the main story.

Pictures or words

There is a lot of advice given But the ideas map below shows many different ideas o   your revision more effective and enjoyable.

To make you really think about the ideas on the map draw it yourself.

Add colour, perhaps colour-coding revision methods that you *have* tried, *will* try and *might* try and also those you really do not want to do.

Then add as many new ideas about how to revise as you can. Once again you are forcing your brain to be active. Try to add as many new ideas to the map as possible.

How you will be assessed

Chapter 1

The examination

British, European and world history exam paper

The basics

The British, European and world history paper is assessed by extended responses, which are often referred to as essays. This exam paper has two sections: Section 1 on British history and Section 2 on European and world history. You will need to answer one essay from the British section and one essay from the European and world section. Each essay is worth 22 marks so the overall mark for this paper is 44.

The British section of the paper has five periods of history to choose from. You only have to study one of these periods. You will answer *one* question on *one* part only.

The parts or topics are:
- Part A: Church, state and feudal society, 1066–1406
- Part B: The century of revolutions, 1603–1702
- Part C: The Atlantic slave trade
- Part D: Britain, 1851–1951
- Part E: Britain and Ireland, 1900–1985

Each part has six key issues. Each of these issues is developed with a detailed description of content. You must write one extended response from a choice of three questions in the British section. Each question will be about one of the key issues.

An example of this is the following, Part D: Britain, 1851–1951, which is developed through studying the following six key issues.
1 An evaluation of the reasons why Britain became more democratic, 1851–1928
2 An assessment of how democratic Britain became, 1867–1928
3 An evaluation of the reasons why some women were given the vote in 1918
4 An evaluation of the reasons why the Liberals introduced social welfare reforms, 1906–14
5 An assessment of the effectiveness of the Liberal social welfare reforms
6 An assessment of the effectiveness of the Labour reforms, 1945–51

The exam paper will sample three of these six issues. These three questions will obviously vary for each year. To be safe and have a choice of questions in the exam, you must study at least five of the key areas. This will ensure you will have a choice of at least two essays in the exam.

Your extended response must deal with an issue-type question that asks you to use your knowledge to construct an argument and make a judgement based on questions that start with a number of question stems. These stems are:
- To what extent was …
- How important was …
- 'Quotation.' How valid is this view?

To answer each question successfully you will need to have good knowledge of the historical event or topic. However, this is not enough on its own. You also must be able to analyse and evaluate these historical events. This is where careful reading of the question is vital. Your ability to answer the issue in the question is what matters.

Your extended response (essay) is worth 22 marks.

In the European and world section, there are nine topics to choose from. Like the British section, each topic is structured around six key issues. You only have to study one of the European and world topics. You will have to write one extended response from a choice of three questions in the European and world section. Each of these questions is also worth 22 marks.

The layout of this section is very like the British section apart from the topics. There are nine parts in this section. You will answer one question on one part only.

The parts or topics are:
- Part A: The Crusades, 1071–1204
- Part B: The American Revolution, 1763–1787
- Part C: The French Revolution, to 1799
- Part D: Germany, 1815–1939
- Part E: Italy, 1815–1939
- Part F: Russia, 1881–1921
- Part G: USA, 1918–1968
- Part H: Appeasement and the road to war, to 1939
- Part I: The Cold War, 1945–1989

Each part has six key issues. Each of these issues is developed with a detailed description of content. You must write one extended response from a choice of three questions in the European and world section. Each question will be about one of the key issues.

An example of this is the following, Part I: The Cold War, 1945–1989, which is developed through studying the following six key issues.

1 An evaluation of the reasons for the emergence of the Cold War, up to 1955
2 An assessment of the effectiveness of Soviet policy in controlling Eastern Europe, up to 1961
3 An evaluation of the reasons for the Cuban Missile Crisis of 1962
4 An evaluation of the reasons why the US lost the war in Vietnam
5 An evaluation of the reasons why the superpowers attempted to manage the Cold War, 1962–79
6 An evaluation of the reasons for the end of the Cold War

The exam paper will sample three of these six issues. These three questions will obviously vary for each year. To be safe and have a choice of questions in the exam, you must study at least five of the key areas. This will ensure you will have a choice of at least two essays in the exam. The style of questions is the same as in the British section.

Remember that you will have to answer one extended response (essay) in both the British and the European and world sections. That makes two extended responses in total. Each extended response is worth 22 marks, so Paper 1 is out of 44 marks in total.

How is the extended response marked?

How the marks are allocated in the extended response helps you to construct the answer.

To be successful you must:
- structure your answer correctly
- use relevant knowledge in your answer
- analyse and evaluate the information to answer the question.

Structure – the introduction

The introduction is awarded up to **3** marks. To ensure you get **3** marks you need to do three things.

1 Your introduction must include at least two sentences of context. This means you must set the historical scene by explaining the 'back story' of the essay. It is a good idea to have specific details of events or themes here as good context is rewarded.
2 You need to give a line of argument. Now, this will depend upon the question that is asked. The easiest way to do this is to use the words of the question directly in the argument. So, if a question asks, 'How important were the reports of Booth and Rowntree in causing the Liberal reforms of 1906–14?' a relevant line of argument might be, *'The reports of Booth and Rowntree were very important in causing the Liberal reforms of 1906–14, but other factors also need to be looked at.'* This is a clear line of argument that directly addresses the question posed, but also introduces the idea that there are other factors to look at.
3 You will need to outline other factors that are relevant and have importance in helping you to answer the question. Introduce other

factors in a new sentence or sentences. You will need to mention at least three other factors or themes to show that you understand the issues in the essay. This will help the examiner as they will see how the essay will develop.

A good introduction is well worth taking time over. It shows the direction that the essay is going to take and will settle you down and give you confidence before you develop the main part of the essay. It will also give you a guide to refer to if you get halfway through the essay and wonder what comes next. Examples of successful introductions are illustrated in both the British and the European and world sections of this guide.

Structure – the conclusion

The conclusion is worth up to **3** marks. To ensure you get **3** marks you must do three things.

1 Your conclusion must be based on the information you have developed in the main body of the essay. You must not introduce new information in the conclusion.
2 You must come to an overall judgement that answers the question posed. This judgement must mention the different factors you have mentioned in the main body of the essay and compare them to each other. This comparison should provide a relative judgement between the factors showing which is more or less important and why this is.
3 You must support your judgement with evidence that you have developed in the main body of the essay.

Examples of successful conclusions are illustrated in both the British and the European and world sections of this guide.

Knowledge

There are **6** marks given for the use of accurate and relevant knowledge in the main part of the essay. Your knowledge must be relevant to the question asked and you must use the information to help you answer the question. For example, if a question asked how democratic Britain was by 1918, relevant knowledge on the franchise would be to say that by 1918 women aged over 30 who were graduates or married to a householder had gained the vote in national elections, but women under this age could not vote. Reading the question carefully is important here, as irrelevant information is not awarded any marks. Good essays will contain much more than 6 marks of accurate and relevant knowledge because detailed knowledge is essential for success in developing analysis and evaluation.

Analysis

Up to **6** marks are given for analysis of the accurate information you have described.

Basic analysis

Up to **3** marks are given for basic analysis. You get these marks each time you make a simple comment that makes a basic judgement about your information. In a question about why women got the vote in 1918, a comment may be made such as, 'The WSPU campaign was very important in women gaining the vote in 1918 because their violent campaign made the issue of votes for women front page news and therefore a major political issue.' The important aspect of this sentence is that there is a reason why the WSPU's campaign was important. Make comments like this three times in your essay and you will get 3 marks.

Analysis plus

There are **3** more marks available for developing your analysis. There are several ways to do this, but one simple way is to introduce counter-analysis. This is where you add in debate or discussion of the relevance of a factor. To continue the example above, a further comment might be, 'However, it can be argued that the WSPU campaign actually held back the campaign for the vote as the government could not be seen to give in to violence.' If you extend your argument with this sort of discussion three times, then you can gain an extra 3 marks.

The other way to develop argument is through linking factors together with relevant argument. For example, you could link the argument above with another factor: 'It could be argued that the WSPU campaign actually held back the campaign for the vote as the government could not be seen to give in to violence, whereas the campaigns of the NUWSS, which were law-abiding, did begin to persuade politicians that women should have the vote.' This is linking argument rather than building evaluation, as this is a link between factors rather than a supported judgement between factors that supports an argument. Evaluation is explained below.

Evaluation

There are up to **4** marks awarded for the way in which you evaluate the knowledge to answer the question posed. Evaluation is where you make judgements on the factors that are relevant when answering an essay question. Build these judgements across all the factors you discuss to construct an argument that answers the question posed.

For an essay on why women were given the vote in 1918, several factors will be looked at, including the campaign of the WSPU, the campaign of the NUWSS, the impact of the First World War, social change and the example of other countries. Each factor will need to be evaluated and some judgement made as to its relative importance, depending on the question asked. So, if you were arguing that social change was the most important reason why women gained the vote, the following evaluation may be made on the NUWSS: 'The NUWSS had a very important role in women gaining the vote in 1918 as they managed to persuade many MPs that women should get the vote and introduce legislation in parliament. However, the steady social and political progress made by women during the nineteenth century was more important. Women had made steady progress in employment and education, as well as local politics, which made it difficult to argue they were not fit to vote.' This is evaluation as a judgement is made on the factors and it is linked to a line of argument that you have introduced. If developed across an essay, this can gain you an extra 4 marks.

Beware!

The biggest problem with essay writing happens when people write descriptive essays or try to repeat an essay they did well in class. You must react to the wording of the question in your essay. The quality of evaluation and analysis is what makes a successful essay. If this is carefully linked to the question asked, then you will do well.

A question of timing

It is very important to keep an eye on time in the examination. You will have 1 hour 30 minutes to complete the British, European and world history paper, so spend up to 45 minutes on each essay. It is far better to complete two essays of a similar length than one long essay and one short essay. Two consistent essays will always score more than one good and one poor essay.

Checklist

For extended response questions:

☞ **Introduction** is made up of context, line of argument and factors and is worth 3 marks.

☞ **Knowledge** is made up of relevant and accurate descriptions and is worth 6 marks.

☞ **Analysis** is made up of relevant comment arguing about the importance of individual factors and is worth 3 marks. If this is developed by identifying counter-argument or links between arguments a further 3 marks are available.

☞ **Evaluation** is made up of relevant argument that directly answers the question posed, makes supported judgement on individual factors and builds across the essay. This is worth 4 marks.

☞ **Conclusion** is made up of making a relative judgement between the factors you have developed in the main body of the essay that answers the question posed and is worth 3 marks.

Summary !

* You have two exam papers, each 1 hour 30 minutes in length.
* The British, European and world history paper asks you to write an extended response (an essay) from a choice of three questions for each part of the course you have studied. You must write two essays, one for each topic area.
* The Scottish history paper assesses the Scottish topics and asks you to explain events and assess presented source material. One question is knowledge based and three questions ask about presented sources.

The Scottish history exam paper

The basics

There will be five different topics in the Scottish history exam paper. You will have learned about one of the five topics.

- Each topic will have four questions.
- Each topic will have four sources on Scottish topics.
- Each topic will be out of 36 marks overall: two questions will be out of 8 marks and two questions will be out of 10 marks.
- Three of the questions will relate to the presented sources and one question will assess your knowledge of part of the course.

Sources

At the most basic level sources are divided into the categories of primary and secondary. You will probably be familiar with these terms. A primary source was produced at the time an event in the past was happening or by someone who experienced the event and then wrote about it at a later date. Secondary sources are written by people, normally historians, well after the event, but they are about the past. The sources that you will study will be written.

The important thing to remember is to make judgements on the presented sources in light of your understanding of the period you have studied. Your assessment of the source(s) is valid as long as you can properly justify it based on the available evidence. All of the questions require the application of accurate recalled knowledge and you should remember to use it when supporting your answer. Recalled knowledge can be used to extend and explain points from the source as well as supply new information not included in the source, but relevant to answer the posed question. The 'Explain' question will not have a source so you will have to use remembered information for the entire answer.

The Scottish history exam paper

Section 3 is a source-based part of the examination paper that assesses important periods from Scotland's past.

You will be studying one of the following topics.

- Topic A: The Wars of Independence, 1249–1328
- Topic B: The age of the reformation, 1542–1603
- Topic C: The Treaty of Union, 1689–1740
- Topic D: Migration and empire, 1830–1939
- Topic E: The impact of the Great War, 1914–1928

How will this section of the exam paper be structured?

Each of the options studied provides illustrative examples of content to be covered in each area of mandatory content. The following is the outline for The impact of the Great War, 1914–1928.

Topic E: The impact of the Great War, 1914–1928	
Key issues	**Description of content**
1 Scots on the Western Front	<ul><li>voluntary recruitment</li><li>the experience of Scots on the Western Front, with reference to the battles of Loos and the Somme</li><li>the kilted regiments</li><li>the role of Scottish military personnel in terms of commitment, casualties, leadership and overall contribution to the military effort</li></ul>
2 Domestic impact of war: society and culture	<ul><li>recruitment and conscription</li><li>pacifism and conscientious objection</li><li>Defence of the Realm Act (DORA)</li><li>changing role of women in wartime, including rent strikes</li><li>scale and effects of military losses on Scottish society</li><li>commemoration and remembrance</li></ul>
3 Domestic impact of war: industry and economy	<ul><li>wartime effects of war on industry, agriculture and fishing</li><li>price rises and rationing</li><li>post-war economic change and difficulties</li><li>post-war emigration</li><li>the land issue in the Highlands and Islands</li></ul>
4 Domestic impact of war: politics	<ul><li>the impact of the war on political developments as exemplified by the growth of radicalism, the ILP and Red Clydeside</li><li>continuing support for political unionism</li><li>the crisis of Scottish identity</li><li>the significance of the Great War in the development of Scottish identity</li></ul>

The other four descriptors follow a similar structure of key areas and descriptions of content.

Question types: Introduction

There will be four questions assessing your skills in Scottish history. The wording of the questions is standard and will be used across all topic areas examined. The question stems are given below. Three of the questions relate to the presented sources. The final question is a knowledge question that is based purely on what you can remember about the period. There are four questions, so the entire course will be assessed in some way. As you can see from the above illustration there are four key areas. Each key area will be assessed in some way. Next to the key areas are descriptions of key content the exam board expect you to have covered.

1 Evaluate the usefulness of Source ...   8 marks
2 How much do Sources X and Y reveal about different interpretations of ...   10 marks
3 How fully does Source ...   10 marks
4 Explain ...   8 marks

These types of question assess your ability to:
- evaluate a source and what it tells us about a historical event
- analyse differing interpretations of a historical event
- judge how much a source tells us about a historical event
- explain the causes or impacts of a historical event.

Each question demands a particular approach and level of knowledge to be successfully completed.

Answer The Question (ATQ)

The biggest problem that examiners see with source work is candidates who do not *Answer The Question*. Many candidates simply select information from the presented sources and/or their own knowledge, but fail to comment on it in any way. If you do this you will get some credit for selecting the correct information (assuming you do), but you will not get the high marks YOU want.

To succeed, each question needs to be answered directly. The answer that merely provides relevant facts from the source and recall is not answering the posed question directly, even if the evidence selected is relevant to the question, and will not achieve high marks.

Question approach
1 Source evaluation question

This question is worth 8 marks. This question will relate to one of the areas identified in the description of content identified in each course descriptor, so it will ask about a narrow, specific area of the course content. The evaluation question is a basic question for historians looking at source material. Historians have to develop the ability to be critical with the evidence they are faced with. It is important not to accept evidence just because we are told it is useful. The time when a source is produced is important, as is who is telling us the information. The content is also very important as it can give us the view of the author. Also, what is not there is important. All sources you look at will only give you part of the picture of the event. Historians must, therefore, evaluate the usefulness of a source for the study of a particular topic. The question stem will, therefore, always be as follows: 'Evaluate the usefulness of **Source A** as evidence of …'

So, for the 'Evaluate the usefulness' question you will need to explain whether or not the source is **useful** in explaining an event or development. Remember, you need to ATQ!

Remember, a source for this sort of question can only give us **part** of the picture (historians write *books* explaining developments and events), so a source is only going to be able to tell us part of the answer.

Good practice

A sentence that says, '*Source A is useful for explaining … as it shows us … but it does not tell us the whole story …*' is providing an **evaluation**. The marker knows from this sentence that you know there is a bigger picture than the source is telling.

Bad practice

If, on the other hand, you say, '*Source A describes developments … but it does not tell us about …*', you are **simply describing** the source and gaps. You are not answering the question directly.

Underneath each question in the exam paper there is a prompt to help you. It tells you what the examiners are looking for. For the 'Evaluate the usefulness …' question the prompt is as follows:

In reaching a conclusion you should refer to:
- *the origin and possible purpose of the source*
- *the content of the source*
- *recalled knowledge.*

How are answers to this question marked?

The full 8 marks can be achieved in a number of combinations of source provenance, content and recalled information.

The marks for each of the features are achieved in the following ways:

Evaluation of provenance (where a source comes from)

Up to 4 marks may be given for making evaluative points about *authorship, type of source, purpose* and *timing*. For 4 marks to be given some explanation is needed as to why these features of the source are useful. This will depend on the particular source you are evaluating. You need to manage your comments to fit the particular source and question.

You need to make up to four points in the following way:

Source A is written by …, which is useful in studying … because …

Source A is a … type of source, which is useful for studying … because …

The level of detail given in the reason is key to getting marks here.

Evaluation of content

Up to 2 marks can be achieved for the interpretations of the parts of the source you consider are useful in terms of the question. For full marks to be given, each point needs to be mentioned separately and its usefulness explained.

Sources will contain three separate points of content that will gain credit; they will also contain material that will act as distracters, so be careful when selecting the information. Make sure that the information you use is relevant in answering the given question.

So, again, you need to make relevant evaluation of the content in the following way:

Source A describes …, which is useful in finding out about … because it shows …

You will need to do this up to twice.

Evaluation of relevant recall

Up to 3 marks are achieved by the application of relevant and developed recall. Recall can be through developing the points in the source further, or the introduction of new knowledge that the source does not contain. This has to be developed in terms of the question for marks to be given.

So, again, you need to make relevant evaluation of the gaps in knowledge that the source does not cover.

However, Source A does not tell us about …, which was an important effect/impact/part of …

You will need to do this up to three times.

Checklist

When answering evaluation questions you should:

☞ come to a judgement on the usefulness of the source in terms of the overall question
☞ comment on the usefulness of the origin, authorship, type and purpose of the source
☞ identify the main relevant points made in the presented source and comment on the usefulness of these
☞ identify areas that extend the points in the source or that are not mentioned in the source, but relate to the question.

2 The two-source interpretation question

This question is worth 10 marks. This question will relate to one of the areas identified in the description of content identified in each course descriptor, so it will ask about a narrow, specific area of the course content. The two sources will each contain three points of interpretation, relating to causes, consequences or analysis of developments. Remember, people disagree and agree about events. Two people can watch exactly the same football match and agree about the game. They will probably both support the same side. If two people support different sides they are likely to disagree about events on the pitch. You may get two people who agree on some bits of the game, but disagree on others.

The interpretation of differing views is an important skill for a historian to master. Views about important historical events differ. People in the past were no different to people today. For example, an English chronicler and a Scottish chronicler will probably have very different views of the Battle of Bannockburn. Historians can also differ in their interpretation of events. It is important to develop the skills that can identify these differences. In order to encourage you to identify the differences between two sources the question stem will be as follows: 'How much do Sources A and B reveal about differing interpretations of …'

For the interpretation question you will need to explain the differing interpretations of the historical event or impact illustrated by the source. Six marks are available for this part of the answer. This can be gained in a number of ways. Each source will contain three points relevant to the issue identified in the question. The points from the source will need to be interpreted. This means you have to identify them and then explain them in your own words. You can also pick up marks for identifying the overall interpretation or focus of the source.

Six more marks are available for points of interpretation that have not been covered by the two sources. So, as you can see, you have 12 marks available so you can get the full 10 marks in a number of ways.

Remember you need to ATQ!

Underneath each question in the exam paper there is a prompt to help you. It tells you what the examiners are looking for. For the 'How much do Sources A and B reveal about differing interpretations of …' question the prompt is as follows:

Use the sources and recalled knowledge.

How are answers to this question marked?

There are 10 marks allocated to this question as previously mentioned. Up to 6 marks are available for explaining the differing interpretations of the two sources and up to 6 marks are available for identifying interpretations that the two sources have not covered. You will have to make a clear judgement on how much the two sources show about differing interpretations of the historic events described in the sources. Source points will need to be explained and any recall you use will have to be linked to the answer with relevant explanation.

So, good practice may be to:

Make an overall judgement: *Sources A and B show very different interpretations of …*

Identify the overall viewpoints of the two sources: *Source A suggests that … whereas Source B feels that …*

Interpret the views of the first source: *On the one hand Source A says …, which shows/explains …*

Interpret the views of the second source: *On the other hand Source B differs when it says …, which shows/explains …*

Bring in recalled knowledge: *However, Sources A and B leave out important points about … For example, the sources make no mention of … which is an important reason/cause/effect of …*

Checklist

When answering two-source interpretation questions you should:

☞ come to a judgement as to the extent to which the source interpretations reveal differing interpretations of the historic events being described

☞ interpret the significant views illustrated in each source to show the differing interpretations

☞ bring in recall to show you understand that there are different interpretations that the sources do not cover.

3 The 'How fully' question

This question is worth 10 marks. This question will relate to one of the four main key issues identified in each course descriptor, so it will ask about a broad area of the course content. This question tests your ability to relate a source to your broader knowledge of a period. A historian needs to place sources in their timeframe. Awareness of the broad events that surround a source is vital if a historian is to be fully informed about events. The presented source will tell you part of the answer. You will then need to show that you have identified information that the source does not include, but which is needed for a full answer to the question.

If a question begins with '*How fully does Source D …*', it relates to one of the areas of mandatory content.

For a 'How fully' question you will need to come to a judgement about how fully the source explains events or developments from the subject you have studied. Remember, you need to ATQ!

This question is not like the 'Evaluate the usefulness' question because you do *not* need to comment on origin and purpose, *but* in another important way they are very similar.

A source for these sorts of questions can only give us part of the picture so a source is only going to be able to tell us part of the answer.

Underneath each question in the exam paper there is a prompt. It tells you what the examiners are looking for. For the 'How fully ...' question the prompt is as follows:

Use the source and recalled knowledge.

How are answers to this question marked?

The question stem will be as follows: 'How fully does **Source D** explain/ illustrate/show ...'

There will be 10 marks allocated to this question.

- You can get up to 3 marks for the identification of points from the source that supports the judgement you have made. Each point from the source needs to be interpreted rather than simply copied from the source.
- You can get up to 7 marks for the identification of points of significant omission that support your judgement.
- You will only get 2 marks if you fail to make a judgement, so the first sentence of your answer is very important.

The judgement

A judgement needs to be made as to how fully the source explains/ illustrates/shows these causes, characteristics or consequences of an event. Remember advice in previous questions on starting your answer with an evaluation that answers the question. It is exactly the same here, and remember that the presented source will not be enough, so it will not explain a development fully enough or far enough. *Make that judgement!*

Use of source

Up to 4 marks may be gained for interpretation of the parts of the source that are relevant, in terms of the proposed question. For full marks to be given, points need to be explained in terms of the question. Merely selecting relevant information and/or listing can only be considered to be one point.

So, good practice may be to say that:

Source D says ..., which partly explains ... (*what the question is asking*) **as it says ..., which is relevant to ... because ...** (*Do this at least three times.*)

Use of relevant recall

The remaining marks, up to a maximum of 7, are achieved by the application of relevant and developed recall that is provided. This can be either points of extended development from the source content or new, but relevant, information. This has to be developed in terms of the question for full marks to be given.

So, good practice may be to say that:

However, Source D does not explain ..., which is important in ... *(Do this seven times.)*

Checklist

When answering 'How fully ...' questions you should:
- ☞ come to a judgement as to how fully the source explains the causes, characteristics or consequences of an event in terms of the overall question
- ☞ identify the main relevant points made in the presented source and explain these
- ☞ identify areas that are not mentioned in the source, but relate to the question
- ☞ conclude, giving an overall judgement.

4 The 'Explain' question

This question is worth 8 marks. This question will relate to one of the four main key issues identified in each course descriptor, so it will ask about a broad area of the course content. There is no source for this question, so the answer will all be from your recalled knowledge. It is good practice to start with an introductory sentence to your answer that addresses the question. You then need to introduce specific examples that relate to the development or impact identified by the question. Each one of these points will need to be explained for marks to be given. One mark is given for each point and explanation made. This is Higher History, so you will need some specific exemplification to be sure of the mark.

So, if I was asked to explain the differing experiences of immigrant groups in Scotland, a response would look as follows:

Immigrant groups had very different experiences when they arrived and settled in Scotland. Italians experienced little prejudice from the Scots. Italians opened ice-cream shops as well as fish and chip shops, which were welcomed due to the new foods they offered to the Scottish people.

Checklist

When answering the 'Explain' questions you should:
- ☞ start with an overall introductory sentence
- ☞ make individual points
- ☞ explain points with detailed exemplification.

Chapter 2

The assignment

What is the assignment?

The assignment is worth 30 marks. This means that it is worth 27 per cent or just under one-third of the marks that make up the total Higher History mark.

Earlier in this book, you learned how to write an essay-style extended response. This section of the book will build on this skill for the assignment.

There are some important differences between the extended responses you complete in an examination and the assignment:
- You will choose the question or issue that you will answer. (Your teacher or lecturer will provide help if it is needed.)
- You will research the topic.
- You will write a Resource Sheet to help you answer the question.
- You will write up the response in a 1 hour and 30 minutes supervised session.

In other words, you will know the question, unlike when you sit the final examination. Therefore, the assignment is an opportunity for you to show your historical skills. It enables you to plan a response to your chosen question well before the final write-up. This can be your best piece of work because you have the chance to work on it over a period of time. How that time is organised will depend on where you are studying. You will either work at your response over a short, focused period of time, or you will complete it over a number of weeks. Your teacher or lecturer will give you notice of when you will complete this piece of work.

How to choose a question

The question that you choose is very important. You are allowed an open choice of question. In other words, you can choose to complete an assignment on any historical period that you are interested in. However, there are a number of things that you should be aware of when choosing a question.

The assignment should be a piece of work that you enjoy doing. Therefore it is sensible that you choose a subject area that you enjoy. If you enjoy the topic you are going to try harder. However, the topic must also be one that you can reasonably complete in the time you are given. It should be a mainstream topic where there are a lot of resources for you to look at.

Make sure that you are answering a proper question that requires you to assess a development or evaluate the reasons for a development/event. Your question must let you argue a point. It needs to let you debate before drawing an overall conclusion to the question.

Let us look at some examples. A question like: 'Why did Britain become democratic?' is not a good question because the answer will just be a list of the reasons why Britain became more democratic. A better question might be: 'To what extent did Britain become more democratic because of social and economic developments?' This is much better because the question means that you must assess the importance of social and economic developments in the development of Britain as a democracy. This will mean that you will look at other factors such as the role of pressure groups as well. You will have to assess these other reasons before coming to an overall conclusion. *A well-worded question can really help you.*

A good starting point for questions are past exam papers. These give you a good idea as to how questions should be worded. They are also likely to be on mainstream topics that can easily be researched. If you are stuck your teacher or lecturer should be able to help you. You can also create extended responses using topics from the Scottish history exam paper. Although you do not get extended response questions in Section A, the course descriptors can be used to produce questions. So if you are interested in the Scottish Wars of Independence then you can complete your assignment on this topic.

Some good ways to structure a question are as follows.

To what extent … ?

Example: **To what extent was Britain a democracy by 1918?**

This is a good way of structuring an extended response where you are assessing a trend.

How important was … in explaining … ?

Example: **How important was the popularity of Adolf Hitler in explaining the Nazi rise to power by 1933?**

This is a good way of structuring an extended response where there are a number of factors that lead to a historical event/development. You are evaluating a development/event with this sort of question.

' … ' How valid is this view?

Example: **'Public opinion in America was the main reason the Americans lost the war in Vietnam.' How valid is this view?**

This is a variation of how to structure an extended response title. It can either assess a trend or evaluate a development/event.

Checklist

When choosing a question for your assignment you should:

☞ make sure your assignment is on a topic you will enjoy studying. This will often be from a period of history that you are studying in school or college. However, you can also choose another area **if** you have enough knowledge **or** are willing to work very hard and independently

☞ make sure your assignment question is well worded and allows you to argue

☞ make sure your assignment is on a topic that has a range of information on it that is understandable.

Planning your work

Although you will get time at school or college to study for your assignment, the more you manage to work at home the better your assignment response will be. This means that you will have to work independently. Your teacher or lecturer will give you deadlines, but how you achieve the work by that time is up to you. This means that you will need to plan your work.

Firstly, you need to ensure that you have the information to complete the assignment.

Your notes and textbook will give you what you need for an examination extended response but perhaps not all you will need for the assignment. Your textbooks and notes will give you an excellent starting point by outlining areas you are going to include in the assignment response with some detail and argument.

For example, if you are researching an assignment that is answering the question, 'How important were the suffrage movements in women's achievement of the vote in 1918?', then you will probably already know the reasons why women gained the vote in national elections in 1918. An awareness of the role of suffrage movements, the impact of the First World War, the example of other countries and other developments for women before the war are what you might expect to use for the extended response in an examination. They are also an excellent starting point for the topic of your assignment. You already have a basic paragraph plan with this information.

You will now need to add detail and increase the sophistication of your analysis and evaluation. This will help you to directly answer the issue/question that you have chosen.

What is a topic and what is an issue?

For example, 'Why did women get the vote in 1918?' is a *topic*. This is a general area that you might explore.

An issue is: 'To what extent did women get the vote in 1918 due to the actions of the Suffragettes?' This issue is a question that allows you to argue a case and weigh up different factors before coming to a conclusion.

That will mean you need to look at other sources of information. As part of the Higher History course you will weigh up sources of evidence and comment on them. It is worthwhile doing this when looking for more information for your essay. Some material is very useful. Many schools and colleges have small departmental libraries as well as access to the institution library. In many cases, your teacher or lecturer will have chosen relevant textbooks that can help. These can be useful, but can also put you off as some history books are very large. You do not have time to read all of an academic history book, so what do you do? If you have an outline plan and know what is going to be in each paragraph then you can use the index to find out about specific topics. You can also get a real feel for the way a book is going to argue by reading the introduction and the conclusion. This is where authors will outline what they are going to do as well as summarise the arguments they have made. It is also where you can decide if the book is worthwhile looking at in more depth.

They may also have articles from journals, like *History Today*, that can be very beneficial. Articles are useful as they provide snapshots of research and can be straightforward to understand. They also have valuable reading lists. Other sources are less useful. Be very careful if you access the internet when researching your assignment. Some subjects that you may study are still controversial. This can lead to websites where authors have an agenda. Such sites are very biased and should be avoided. On the other hand, some academic websites have articles that can be useful. Do not download essays from any of the numerous sites that sell them. Your teacher will know your style and notice if you do this.

Checklist

When planning your assignment:

☞ use existing textbooks and notes to create an outline topic plan for your essay. Use this information to decide on main topic areas you will need to discuss in your assignment response

☞ gather other relevant information for your assignment from reliable sources such as your History department or institution library

☞ use articles and accessible books written by reputable historians

☞ take care when using the internet. Use reputable websites to gather information

☞ in no circumstances cut and paste material direct from the internet and pass it off as your own work. You may not be aware that you write in a certain style. Sections posted in from the internet will not have that style and markers will spot the change immediately. You may lose marks for doing this.

What do you look for when reading books and articles?

The problems of note taking!

Now you have found more textbooks and articles relevant to your essay, what do you do with them? You need to extract the necessary information for your assignment response.

You are looking for two things when you look at other information.
1 More detail/examples to develop your argument.
2 Views about the event you are studying. Historians have views and like to express them. These views are interpretations. An essay that shows an awareness of these interpretations generally does better than one that does not.

How you organise note taking is up to you, but there are general points you should keep in mind.

Checklist

When making notes you should:

☞ where possible summarise in bullet points under general topic areas that relate to the topic paragraphs you have decided you are going to write about

☞ try to use your own words. Do not write out huge chunks of text from books. This is wasting time and effort. Also, your teacher will know how you write. If you use work that someone else has created you will be caught

☞ look for key examples, arguments and information

☞ if you find a good interpretation of the subject then write out short quotes that illustrate this. Even if you summarise views in your own words they can be used successfully in the assignment

☞ if you do use a historical viewpoint, keep a record of the page where it is in the book or article in your notes. This will save time if you need to check back over the information.

Practice!

Once you have gathered the information you need to do something with it. Having a practice at writing out your historical assignment is a good idea. You can see where you have too much information and where you may need to do some more work. You will also get an idea of how long your assignment will take to write. Remember, you will be writing up the assignment in a 1 hour and 30 minutes supervised session in the school or college where you study so using the time effectively is important. You should be ready to write for the full 90 minutes.

How will I remember all this information?

The History Resource Sheet

As part of writing the assignment you are allowed to take a Resource Sheet into your supervised 1 hour 30 minute write-up. This should fit on one side of an A4 piece of paper. There is no word limit for your Resource

Sheet but be careful. *You are not allowed to copy sections directly from the Resource Sheet to your final assignment.*

The Resource Sheet is intended to guide you when you are writing up your assignment. Therefore, what should go into this Resource Sheet? This very much depends on your style and what suits you, but some general pointers and advice can be given:

- Your Resource Sheet should follow the running order of paragraphs you have decided on for your response.
- Your Resource Sheet should contain key information that you may find difficult to remember. Examples might include figures or dates of events or acts of parliament.
- You may want to help yourself by writing short quotes from historians in your Resource Sheet. This will add to your own assessment or evaluation of events by showing an awareness of historical interpretation and debate.
- If you are writing out a quote from a historian remember to also note the book you got it from. It is important that this is written down so the marker knows you have accessed a reputable source of information.

Your Resource Sheet should be a single A4 sheet of paper and be no longer than 250 words in length.

There are also things that you should not do:

- Do not use symbols that mean something to you, but cannot be understood by a marker.
- Do not cross out words on the Resource Sheet. It should be neat and tidy and easy to read. You can type it and print it out.

> **Hints & tips** ★
>
> *Your Resource Sheet is a way of remembering key information and even arguments. Keep it simple and easy to understand. Use colour if you want to. Make a diagram if it is easier for you.*

How do I gain the most marks possible?

The marker is looking for a number of very specific things from you. Here is a detailed guide with some examples of work that would meet the various levels and descriptions given.

Place the issue in its historical context

This is worth up to 3 marks.

This is the introduction to your assignment. Marks are awarded for context. Context is the background to the issue/question, but for the purposes of this exercise also means giving a line of argument and looking at factors for development.

- One mark is given if the candidate provides at least one point of background to the issue or identifies at least two relevant factors or connects this to the line of argument.
- Two marks are given if the candidate provides at least one point of background to the issue *and* identifies at least two relevant factors *and* connects these to the line of argument.
- Three marks are given if the candidate provides at least two points of background to the issue *and* identifies at least three relevant factors *and* connects these to the line of argument.

Let us use the previous question to help illustrate this.

Example ⚑

Question

To what extent did women gain the vote in 1918 due to the actions of the Suffragettes?

Between the 1860s and 1918 women campaigned for the vote in national elections. (**Background statement.**) Women gained the vote due to the actions of the Suffragettes and the work they did during the First World War. (**Two factors, but no attempt to address the question.**)

This would give you 1 mark.

Between the 1860s and 1918 women campaigned for the vote in national elections. (**Background statement.**) Women gained the vote due to the actions of the Suffragettes to a large extent as they kept the issue of women and the vote in the news. (**Line of argument that addresses the question using the Suffragettes as a factor.**) However, this was not the only reason as the impact of the First World War also needs to be looked at. (**One other factor looked at that is relevant to the question.**)

This would give you 2 marks.

Between the 1860s and 1918 women campaigned for the vote in national elections. This was part of a more general trend that led to increased democracy in Britain. (**Two background statements.**) Women gained the vote due to the actions of the Suffragettes to a large extent as they kept the issue of women and the vote in the news. (**Line of argument that addresses the question using the Suffragettes as a factor.**) However, this was not the only reason as the impact of the First World War also needs to be looked at as do the actions of the non-militant NUWSS. (**Two other factors looked at that are relevant to the question.**)

This would give you 3 marks.

Analyse different factors that contribute to an event or development

This is worth up to 7 marks.

One mark will be awarded for comments which analyse different factors in terms of the issue. This means that when you are looking at a factor, for example the First World War and women, and then relate this to the issue of women and the vote, you get 1 mark.

A maximum of 4 marks will be awarded for comments which analyse aspects within individual factors. The other 3 marks are gained by extending your analysis by showing there is a debate about the factor, such as evidence that the factor is not important. You can also gain these marks by linking between factors, as developed on the next page.

You will need to identify factors that are relevant to your issue/question and clearly show at least one of the following:

- links between different factors
- links between factor(s) and the whole
- links between factor(s) and related concepts
- similarities and consistency
- contradictions and inconsistency.

Examples of relationships between identified factors could include:

Establishing contradictions or inconsistencies within factors

Example 🚩

While old age pensions in 1906 were successful in keeping many of the elderly out of the workhouse, the amount of money it gave was not enough to live on, on its own.

Establishing contradiction or inconsistencies between factors

Example 🚩

While cultural arguments for the growth of German nationalism are important it was only really the middle class who were affected by them. These developments meant little to the working class who were too busy trying to survive.

Establishing similarities and consistencies between factors

Example 🚩

Public opinion in America changed as news of American soldiers behaving badly, such as the My Lai massacre, came out. The same is true of the difficulties the Americans faced fighting. The drawn-out conflict in Vietnam began to have an effect on public opinion as well.

Establishing links between factors

Example 🚩

Without a belief in nationalism that had developed in the nineteenth century, it was unlikely that Bismarck would have been successful in unifying Germany.

Exploring different interpretations of these factors

Example

While some people have viewed the evidence as showing that the war was important in giving women the vote, others have seen it as unimportant as key women war workers, such as the young munitions workers, were denied the vote.

Evaluate factors when you develop an argument

This is worth up to 5 marks.

- One mark is awarded where the candidate makes an isolated evaluative comment on an individual factor that recognises the topic of the issue.
- Two marks are awarded where the candidate makes isolated evaluative comments on different factors that recognise the topic of the issue.
- Three marks are awarded where the candidate connects their evaluative comments to build a line of argument that recognises the topic of the issue.
- Four marks are awarded where the candidate connects their evaluative comments to build a line of argument that recognises the topic of the issue and takes account of counter-arguments or alternative interpretations.
- Five marks are awarded when the candidate connects their evaluative comments to develop a consistent line of argument across all the factors discussed. You are expected to show an awareness of historical debate about the factors and issue you discuss. This could mean looking at counter-arguments or alternative interpretations.

Marks are awarded for developing a line of argument which makes a judgement on the issue in the question. This means you must take a consistent line of argument that develops from the one you develop in your introduction. This argument should be referred to in each of the main factors you develop in the main body of the essay.

Evaluative comments may include:

The extent to which the factor is supported by the evidence

Example

This evidence shows that the National Health Service had a very significant impact on the health of the British people, as it meant people went to see doctors so illness could be diagnosed and treatment was available that was free at the point of access, at least to begin with.

The relative importance of factors

Example

This evidence shows that Soviet intervention in Poland was much more successful than in Hungary because ...

Counter-arguments including possible alternative interpretations

Example

However, more recent research shows that many ordinary people in Nazi Germany actively helped the police do their job and did not simply keep their heads down.

The overall impact/significance of the factors when taken together

Example

While each factor may have had little effect on their own, when we take them together they became hugely important as the Liberal Reform programme of 1906–14 was the first relatively comprehensive set of social reforms.

The importance of factors in relation to the main question

Example

However, Suffragette actions were more successful than the pre-war campaign suggests. This is because the fear of a restarted campaign after the war had an influence on giving women the vote in 1918.

Use information from sources in your response

This information has to be relevant to the issue you have chosen to complete. Make sure the quote is a viewpoint or opinion and not simply knowledge. Also make sure that you quote both the author and book/article you got the quote from as well as the quote itself.

This is worth up to 4 marks.

Up to a maximum of 4 marks, 1 mark will be awarded for each source referred to, in order to support a factor.

'As John Kerr comments in his book ...'

Use knowledge that is relevant to support factors

This is worth up to 8 marks.

One mark will be awarded for each relevant point of knowledge used to support a factor.

For knowledge marks to be awarded, points must be:
- relevant to the topic of the issue
- developed (by providing additional detail, exemplification, reasons or evidence)
- used to respond to the demands of the issue.

Subject	Unlikely to be worth a mark	Example of a K/U point possibly worth a mark
Reign of David I of Scotland	David I developed the royal system of justice.	David I developed the royal system of justice to include the use of juries and sheriffs acting in the name of the king.
Career of William Wallace	Wallace defeated an English army at the Battle of Stirling Bridge.	Wallace won an important victory at the Battle of Stirling Bridge in 1297 where his much smaller army outwitted and defeated a powerful and well-equipped English force commanded by the Earl of Surrey.
Reign of Mary Queen of Scots	Mary faced many problems with the powerful Scottish nobility.	Mary faced many problems with the powerful Scottish nobility who were often very hostile to her. At the start of her reign, she had to deal with a revolt by the powerful Earl of Huntly.
Louis XIV of France	Louis XIV established his royal court at the palace of Versailles.	Louis XIV established his seat of government and his royal court at the palace of Versailles. The structure and organisation of the court was intended to emphasise the power of the king.
The Liberal reforms	The Liberal government introduced the old age pension.	The Liberal government of 1906–14 introduced the Old Age Pension Act which provided pensions for British people when they reached the age of 70.
The Labour government	The Labour government introduced the National Health Service.	The Labour government worked to improve the health of the British people by introducing the National Health Service, which was to be universal, comprehensive and free at the point of treatment.

Reach a conclusion to the question or issue you have chosen to answer

This is worth up to 3 marks.
- One mark is awarded where the candidate makes an overall judgement which directly answers the issue in a summary.
- Two marks are awarded where the candidate makes an overall judgement between the different factors in relation to the issue.
- Three marks are awarded where the candidate makes a relative overall judgement between different factors in relation to the issue and explains how this arises from their evaluation of the presented evidence.

Example ⚑

> Therefore women achieved the vote in 1918 due to the actions of the Suffragettes to an extent. They also achieved the vote due to the non-militant actions of the NUWSS as well as the impact of their work during the First World War. There was also the factor of other countries giving women the vote and the fact that women had made significant advances in society. They could work in the professions and could already vote in local elections.

This is a summary and would gain 1 mark.

> Therefore women achieved the vote in 1918 due to the actions of the Suffragettes to an extent. However, without their work in the First World War it is doubtful that women would have got the vote as quickly as they did. Also, it is important to note the influence of the much more numerous Suffragists. They worked quietly, persuading people of their cause. Of less importance, but still influential, was the fact that women were making economic, political and social progress. The actions of the Suffragettes were important, but so were other factors.

This is linking factors more and would gain 2 marks.

> In conclusion women achieved the vote in 1918 due to the actions of the Suffragettes to an extent. The Suffragettes kept the issue of women and the vote in the eyes of the media. This is more important than the war as although the war allowed women to be seen as deserving of the vote due to their contribution it provided a convenient reason to give women the vote as there was fear of more violence if the vote was not given. The role of the Suffragists was maybe less important than the Suffragettes as despite their persuasion they could be ignored. Therefore, the Suffragettes were responsible for women achieving the vote to a great extent, but it would not have happened in the way it did but for the war.

This is linking factors with evidence and would gain 3 marks.

An evaluation of the reasons why Britain became more democratic, 1851–1928

Part 1 of 'Britain, 1851–1951' asks you to evaluate the reasons why Britain became more democratic, 1851–1928.

In other words, you will be asked why Britain became more democratic between 1851 and 1928 and you will be expected to explain each reason and reach a decision about which of the reasons you think were the most important.

What you should know 👍

To be successful in this section you must be able to:

★ describe how the Reform Acts increased the number of voters in Britain and explain why the Reform Acts happened
★ explain why the Reform Acts and other political changes such as the secret ballot were important in making Britain more democratic
★ explain how the changes created greater democracy in Britain and decide – or evaluate – which were the most important reasons for change and give reasons to support your answer.

Context ❗

In 1851 political power was in the hands of a small group of men who owned land in Britain. They were quite literally the landowners of Britain. Naturally, it was argued that since they owned Britain then they should govern Britain. By 1928 those ideas had completely changed. Britain was by then defined as its people and Members of Parliament represented the people of the country, not its land. Britain had become more democratic and this section is about why the changes happened.

Key words

Conservatives – also known as Tories, the Conservatives were usually against much change.

Electorate – the voters.

Franchise – the right to vote.

Industrialisation – the growing use of machines based in factories which in turn caused a growth in towns and cities. The relevance of industrialisation is that it brought together many people who shared the same poor conditions and these people started to feel a common identity which led to the emergence of the working class.

Labour – a new political party, started in 1900, representing the working class.

Liberals – one of the main political parties.

Pressure groups – groups of people who shared a common aim. They grouped together to apply pressure on the government to make changes.

Urbanisation – the growth of cities and towns.

Key people

Benjamin Disraeli – the leader of the Conservatives in the House of Commons.

William Gladstone – the leader of the Liberals.

Henry Temple, Viscount Palmerston – a famous Prime Minister who was very much against change. When he died in 1865 it made the possibility of change more likely.

The following factors and linked knowledge points are all relevant and could be used in an answer on this issue, but remember to always organise and link your information to the question that you are asked.

The effects of industrialisation and urbanisation

Urbanisation and growing class identity within an industrial workforce and the spread of socialist ideas led to demands for a greater voice for the working classes. Also the growth of the **Labour** Party offered a greater choice.

Demographic change, including rapid urbanisation, sparked demands for redistribution of seats. The growing economic power of middle-class wealth-creators led to pressure for a greater political voice. Basic education, the development of new, cheap, popular newspapers and the spread of railways helped to create an awareness of national issues.

After 1860 the fear of the 'revolutionary mob' had declined. Skilled working men in cities were more educated and respectable. That was an argument for giving more men the right to vote in 1867.

Changing political attitudes

Political reform was no longer seen as a threat. In the USA and in Europe struggles were taking place for liberty and a greater political say for 'the

Hints & tips ★

There are two possible questions you might get which would both use the word 'democracy'. You must be very careful about how you answer the different types of question. Questions on this topic will usually suggest one reason why the changes happened and you will be asked how important that reason was in leading to democracy in Britain. To answer this question you must explain the reason given in the question but also explain fully all the other reasons you know about. Once you have done that you make a decision about the relative importance of each of the reasons.

Hints & tips ★

Remember that there is no one reason that is correct in explaining why Britain became more democratic. The main thing to do is to explain all the reasons and then decide which of those reasons you think was most important. Of course, you must give reasons to support your answer.

people'. Britain tended to support these moves abroad, making it logical for this to happen in Britain too.

The growing influence of the Liberal Party challenged old-fashioned landowning interests. The Liberal Party opposed the power of the old landowning aristocracy. For example, the **Liberals** supported the secret ballot to help working-class voters use their vote to force changes, unafraid of being victimised by their employers or landlords for not voting the way they were told to.

Politicians knew that change was happening and could not be stopped so needed to work out how best to control that change and direct it in the way that would best suit their own interests.

The death of former Prime Minister Palmerston represented the changing tone of politics as the old-fashioned ideas of the early nineteenth century gave way to new ideologies. The House of Lords lost its veto in 1911 and that made the directly elected House of Commons the most important part of the British government.

Party advantage

In 1867 the Conservative Party became the government after twenty years out of power. They rushed to steal the ideas of the Liberal Party and hoped that by giving more men the vote they would be grateful to the **Conservatives** and vote for them in the future.

The Corrupt and Illegal Practices Act of 1883 limited the amount of spending on elections; the Liberals believed the advantage held by wealthier Conservative opponents would be reduced.

By placing the reforms of 1883 and 1884 close to the next election, the Liberals hoped to gain advantage from grateful new voters in towns more fairly represented after the redistribution of seats.

Pressure groups

The 1867 Reform Act was passed after large demonstrations were organised by the Reform League and Reform Union.

Later, but before 1914, the Suffragists and Suffragettes were influential in gaining the **franchise** for women.

Trade unions organised support for change and were important in creating the Labour Party which was originally founded to campaign for better conditions for working-class people.

The effects of the First World War

The war necessitated more political change. Many men still had no vote but were conscripted to fight from 1916. As further reform for males was being considered, fears of a revival of the militant women's campaign, combined with a realisation of the importance of women's war work, led to the Reform Act of 1918 which gave votes to more men and some women.

Hints & tips

The easiest way to tackle this question is to explain why more people gained the vote. This is obvious because your answer can be structured around reasons why the Reform Acts of 1867, 1884 and 1918 happened.

Hints & tips

Be careful! In this question it is relevant to mention that the Suffragettes and Suffragists were important pressure groups in forcing change but this is not a question about votes for women so do not get side tracked into writing lots of information about that. It is an easy trap to fall into so be careful.

The effects of examples of developments abroad

Many countries had a wider franchise (including votes for women) than Britain. These changes had not led to chaos or problems in the countries that introduced the changes so why should political change lead to problems in Britain?

For practice

1 To what extent was the growth of democracy in Britain after 1851 due to the spread of industrialisation and urbanisation? (22 marks)
2 How important was the role of pressure groups in Britain becoming more democratic between 1851 and 1928? (22 marks)

An assessment of how democratic Britain became, 1867–1928

Part 2 of 'Britain, 1851–1951' asks you to assess how democratic Britain became, 1867–1928.

In other words, you must describe the ways that the political system in Britain changed between 1867 and 1928 and reach a decision about how much more democratic these changes made Britain.

What you should know

To be successful in this section you must be able to:

★ describe the main elements that make a country democratic such as choice and the right to vote, and explain why those elements are essential in a democracy
★ describe the events that happened that created the democratic elements, for example, when the Reform Acts happened and how they increased the **electorate** thereby making Britain more democratic
★ judge how far Britain had become democratic by the date in the question and explain what still had to be done to make Britain more fully democratic.

Context

In 1867 the Second Reform Act gave many more men the right to vote but no women. By 1928 all men and women over 21 had the right to vote. But democracy is about more than just the right to vote. What other changes also made Britain more democratic?

Hints & tips

An easy way to tackle this question about how democratic Britain had become by a certain date is to make clear what things are necessary to make any country democratic. By doing that you can use each element of democracy as a separate paragraph. You should explain what happened to create that element of democracy and make the point that the changes did make Britain **more** democratic but did not lead to complete democracy on their own.

Key words

Access to information – this means being able to read as well as being able to get hold of newspapers and see and hear politicians. All these things helped voters make an informed choice.

Ballot Act 1872 – this started secret voting. Ballot means to vote.

Choice – in this question choice refers to the choice voters have between different political parties.

Fairness – everyone's vote counts equally and people can vote without threats, bribery or worry. It also means that each MP represented roughly the same number of people.

Hints & tips

Your question will probably include a date. For example 'To what extent had Britain become a democratic country by 1911?' The date sometimes causes people to worry because they think they cannot include things they know happened after the date. The solution is easy. You should write about the things that happened before the date and explain how these things helped make Britain more democratic. Then state that some things still remained to be done after the date and explain what these things were, why Britain could not be democratic until they happened and also when they eventually did happen.

The following factors and linked knowledge points are all relevant and could be used in an answer on this issue, but remember to always link your information to the question.

The vote

In 1867 most skilled working-class men in towns got the vote. In 1884 many more men in the countryside were given the franchise. In 1918 most men over 21 and some women over 30 joined the electorate. Finally in 1928 all men and women over 21 were given the vote.

Fairness

The **Secret Ballot 1872**, Corrupt and Illegal Practices Act 1883 and the redistribution of seats in 1867, 1885 and 1918 all helped created a fairer system of voting. The effectiveness of these varied; they were less effective in areas where the electorate was small, or where a landowner or employer was powerful and could scare voters, even with a secret ballot.

Choice

Although the working-class electorate increased by the 1880s there was no national party to express their interests. The Liberals and Conservatives promoted middle-, even upper-class values. The spread of socialist ideas and trade unionism led to the creation of the Labour Party by 1900, thereby offering a wider **choice** to the electorate.

Access to information

In the later nineteenth century there was a great increase in literacy and also **access to information** on which to base choice. Railways spread information nationally, cheap newspapers gave people information on which to base their choices and politicians could travel across the country to campaign for the vote.

National party organisation

As the size of the electorate grew, individual political parties had to make sure their 'message' got across to the electorate. The growth of the

National Liberal Federation and the Conservative Central Office are examples of party organisation planning to reach all parts of the country with a unified national policy to attract voters.

Power of Lords reduced

From 1911 Lords could only delay bills from the House of Commons for two years rather than veto them. They had no control over raising money through taxation.

Widening opportunity to become an MP

The property qualification to be an MP was abolished in 1858 and in 1911 MPs were paid, thereby allowing ordinary working men to give up their 'day job' and stand for election. By 1928, parliament was much more fully representative of the British people.

For practice

3 How accurate is it to describe Britain as a fully democratic country by 1918? (22 marks)

4 'Britain was still far from being a democratic country by 1928.' How valid is this view? (22 marks)

An evaluation of the reasons why some women were given the vote in 1918

Part 3 of 'Britain, 1851–1951' asks you to evaluate the reasons why some women were given the vote in 1918.

In other words, describe the reasons why women gained the right to vote and then assess the importance of these reasons.

What you should know

To be successful in this section you must be able to:

★ describe how social attitudes towards women had changed in the later nineteenth century

★ describe the campaign methods of the main women's campaign groups and explain why public opinion was divided over Suffragette tactics

★ explain the importance of the First World War in causing franchise reform for both men and women.

You will also need to 'evaluate', which means you decide which were the most important reasons for change and give reasons to support your answer.

Hints & tips

If a question asks about political equality for women do not be confused. The question is asking about why women gained the right to vote.

Hints & tips

There are several important dates in the story of women gaining the vote but only one date is relevant to the point when women gained political equality. The date is 1928 when women and men gained political equality by having the right to vote at the age of 21.

Context !

British women in 1850 have been described as 'second-class citizens' but during the late nineteenth century social attitudes towards women changed, helped by a series of laws which improved their legal position, such as the Married Women's Property Act. Nevertheless, by 1900 women still could not vote. However, twenty years later, many women over 30 could vote and by 1928 women had gained political equality with men. This section is about why those changes happened.

The following factors and linked knowledge points are all relevant and could be used in an answer on this issue, but remember to always link your information to the question asked

Key words

Cat and Mouse Act – this was the Act which tried to counter the effects of the hunger strikes. Women who were weakened by hunger strike could be released from prison until they had recovered enough to serve the rest of their sentence. It was officially known as the Prisoners (Temporary Discharge for Ill Health) Act 1913.

Militant – a word often used to describe the Suffragettes' methods. It means they were prepared to use violence to put pressure on the government to give women the vote.

NUWSS – the National Union of Women's Suffrage Societies, formed in 1897. They believed in the effectiveness of peaceful, slow persuasion as a means of gaining the vote for women.

WSPU – Women's Social and Political Union, formed in 1903 because of the failure of the NUWSS to cause any change. The WSPU followed direct action and had the motto 'deeds not words'.

The part played by women in the war effort, 1914–18

Britain declared war on Germany on 4 August 1914 and two days later the **WSPU** suspended its political campaigning for the vote.

Undoubtedly the sight of women 'doing their bit' for the war effort gained respect and balanced the negative publicity of the earlier Suffragette campaign. A WSPU pro-war propaganda campaign encouraged men to join the armed forces and women to demand 'the right to serve'.

Women's war work was important to Britain's eventual victory. Over 700,000 women were employed making munitions. The creation of a wartime coalition also opened the door to change.

The traditional explanation for the granting of the vote to some women in 1918 has been that women's valuable work for the war effort radically changed male ideas about their role in society and that the vote in 1918 was almost a 'thank you' for their efforts. But the women who were given the vote were 'respectable' ladies, 30 or over, not the younger women who worked long hours and risked their lives in munitions factories.

Key people

Millicent Fawcett – the leader of the NUWSS.

Herbert Henry Asquith – Prime Minister from 1908 and very much against votes for women. However, Asquith became more willing to support votes for women when he saw the war work that they did.

David Lloyd George – Prime Minister from 1916 who accepted that some women should have the right to vote.

Emmeline Pankhurst – the founder of the WSPU along with her daughters.

Another argument about the 1918 Act is that it only happened because politicians grew anxious to enfranchise more men who had fought in the war but lost their residency qualification to vote and women could be 'added on' to legislation that was happening anyway.

The war acted more as a catalyst but the tide was flowing towards female franchise before it started. The government was afraid that the Suffragette campaign would restart after the war if the government still blocked votes for women.

Women munition workers

The women's suffrage campaigns

The **NUWSS** believed in moderate, 'peaceful' tactics to win the vote such as meetings, pamphlets, petitions and parliamentary bills. Membership remained relatively low at about 6000 until around 1909, but grew to 53,000 by 1914 as women angered by the Suffragettes' campaign found a new home.

The militant Suffragette campaign up to 1914

Emmeline Pankhurst formed the Women's Social and Political Union (WSPU) in 1903. The WSPU adopted the motto 'deeds not words'. The new strategy gained publicity with noisy heckling of politicians. Newspapers immediately took notice. The Suffragettes had achieved their first objective – publicity. Violent protests followed, such as a window smashing campaign and arson attacks aimed to provoke insurance company pressure on the government. The prisons filled with Suffragettes.

Women used starvation as a political weapon to embarrass the government. In response to their hunger strikes, the government introduced the Prisoners (Temporary Discharge for Ill Health) Act – the **Cat and Mouse Act**.

The actions of the Suffragettes mobilised opinion for and against votes for women. It can be argued that were it not for the Suffragette campaign, the Liberal government would not even have discussed women's suffrage before the First World War. But for opponents the **militant** campaign provided an excellent example of why women could not be trusted with the vote.

Changing attitudes to women in society

The campaigns for women's suffrage should also be seen within the context of society's changing attitudes towards women in the late nineteenth and early twentieth centuries. For example, in the words of Martin Pugh, 'their participation in local government made women's exclusion from national elections increasingly untenable'. In other words, giving women the right to vote had to happen fairly soon.

Even before 1900 women could vote in local elections and even become mayors (political leaders) of English cities. Millicent Fawcett, a leader of the NUWSS, had argued that wider social changes were vital factors in the winning of the right to vote.

The example of other countries

Women were able to vote in other countries such as New Zealand and in some American states. So why not in Britain, which liked to think of itself as the mother and leader of democracy?

> **For practice** ◎
>
> 5 'Changing attitudes in British society towards women was the major reason why some women received the vote in 1918.' How valid is this view? (22 marks)
> 6 To what extent can the women's suffrage groups take credit for women gaining political equality by 1928? (22 marks)

An evaluation of the reasons why the Liberals introduced social welfare reforms, 1906–14

Part 4 of 'Britain, 1851–1951' asks you to evaluate the reasons why the Liberals introduced social welfare reforms, 1906–14.

In other words, explain the reasons why the Liberals decided to pass a series of reforms to help the poor and then decide which of those reasons you think were the most important.

What you should know 👍

To be successful in this section you must be able to:

★ explain what was meant by **laissez-faire** and describe what was done to help the poor before 1906

★ describe what Booth and Rowntree did and explain why their reports were so important to the story of the Liberal reforms and the policy of laissez-faire

★ explain why issues of **national efficiency**, **national security**, political advantage and the promotion of younger, more interventionist politicians were important

★ decide which of the pressures for change were the most important in persuading the government to take action.

Context ❗

Before the Liberal reforms of 1906–14 the attitude of government, of politicians and members of the middle and upper classes towards the poor was summed up as 'laissez-faire', a phrase which means to leave alone. If you were poor it was your own fault and it was not the responsibility of the government to help you to look after yourself or your family. This section is about why those attitudes changed and why the Liberal government decided to become involved in helping the poor.

Key people

Henry Campbell Bannerman – Liberal Prime Minister who died in 1908 and opened the door for more interventionist Liberals to be promoted to positions of power.

Herbert Henry Asquith – the new Liberal Prime Minister from 1908 onwards.

Winston Churchill and David Lloyd George – two young Liberal politicians who believed that governments should become involved in helping people who were poor through no fault of their own.

Charles Booth and Seebohm Rowntree – two businessmen who researched into poverty (Booth in London and Rowntree in York), who discovered that about one-third of the population lived in extreme poverty. Their reports, based on hard statistical evidence, were very important in proving that poverty could not be solved by 'self-help'.

The following factors and linked knowledge points are all relevant and could be used in an answer on this issue, but remember to always link your information to the question.

Concerns over poverty – the social surveys of Booth and Rowntree

The reports of Charles Booth and Seebohm Rowntree demonstrated that poverty had causes such as low pay, unemployment, sickness and old age.

Key words

Intervention/ interventionist – the core word here is intervene, which means to get involved in something. An interventionist government gets involved in trying to solve social problems. Interventionism is the opposite of laissez-faire.

Laissez-faire – a government policy which meant that it was not the responsibility of government to try to help the poor and that it was the responsibility of people to help themselves.

National efficiency – the need to ensure a healthy and educated workforce to maintain Britain's position as a top industrial nation.

National security – the need to ensure the health of young men so that if needed they could serve in the army to defend the country.

Self-help – the belief that people should look after themselves and their families by hard work and saving. The reports of Booth and Rowntree proved that self-help was not the answer to poverty.

These were mainly beyond the ability of an individual to '**self-help**' out of the problem.

The extent of poverty revealed in the surveys was also a shock. Booth's initial survey was confined to the East End of London, but his later volumes covering the rest of London revealed that almost one-third of the capital's population lived in poverty. The same proportion of poverty was discovered by Rowntree in York. These studies were statistical analysis and proved that poverty was a vast hidden problem and a nationwide scandal, not only in London.

Municipal socialism

By the end of the century some Liberal-controlled local authorities had become involved in programmes of social welfare. These reforms were paid for by local taxation.

In Birmingham particularly, but also in other large industrial cities, local authorities had taken the lead in providing social welfare schemes. These served as an example for further reforms.

When the Liberal government came to power they realised that what could be done locally in big cities could also be done on a national scale, paid for by national taxation.

Foreign examples

Germany had introduced a system of social security, including old age pensions, twenty years earlier. This raised the question that if Germany could afford to do it then why couldn't Britain do the same?

Fears over national security

The government became alarmed when almost 25 per cent of the volunteers to fight in the Boer War were rejected because they were physically unfit to serve in the armed forces. There was concern whether Britain could survive a war or protect its empire against a far stronger enemy in the future if the nation's 'fighting stock' of young men was so unhealthy.

Fears over national efficiency

Britain was no longer the top industrial nation. Britain was facing competition from the new industrially powerful countries such as Germany and the USA. To compete with those countries Britain needed an educated, trained workforce. How could children be educated to become the efficient workers of the future if they were too hungry and poor to learn?

The rise of the New Liberalism

New, younger Liberal politicians argued that state **intervention** was necessary to help people with social problems over which they had no control.

Hints & tips

Read the question.

This is **not** a question about the Liberal reforms. That is the next part. This is a question asking **why** the reforms happened. Be careful that you answer the exact question that is asked.

Hints & tips

You will find there are about eight main reasons why the reforms happened. Don't worry if you cannot remember them all. As long as you can explain four or five reasons and make the necessary evaluation then you will be okay.

Hints & tips

Most questions include the dates 1906–14 when referring to the Liberal reforms. You can certainly find some reforms that happened that were linked to children in 1906 and 1907 but do not worry about finding reforms after 1911. There are none of any importance after 1911.

New Liberal ideas were not important issues in the general election of 1905. Only when 'old liberal' Prime Minister Campbell Bannerman died in 1908 was the door opened for new '**interventionist**' ideas. A new younger politician called Herbert Asquith became Prime Minister and he promoted new men with new ideas into his government.

Party advantage

Since 1884 many more working-class men had the vote and the Liberals had tended to attract many of those votes. However, after 1900 a new political party called the Labour Party promised social reforms. Many working-class men were tempted to vote for this new party. It can be argued that the Liberal reforms happened for the very selfish reason of keeping working-class votes.

For practice

7 How important were the social surveys of Booth and Rowntree in the Liberal government's decision to introduce social reforms, 1906–14? (22 marks)
8 To what extent did the Liberal government of 1906–14 introduce social reform due to concerns over national security and efficiency? (22 marks)

An assessment of the effectiveness of the Liberal social welfare reforms

Part 5 of 'Britain, 1851–1951' asks you to assess the effectiveness of the Liberal social welfare reforms

In other words, you must describe what the Liberal reforms were and then judge how much they really helped to ease the problem of poverty.

What you should know

To be successful in this section you must be able to:

★ organise your answer into four main categories – the old, young, sick and unemployed and describe what the Liberals did to help those groups in society
★ judge how effective each reform was in helping to ease the problems of poverty linked with each of the four social groups
★ explain what is meant by a transition point and be able to use that idea in connection with judging the success of the Liberal reforms in terms of what the Liberals intended to do.

Hints & tips

The Liberal reforms can be categorised as helping the old, the young, the sick and the unemployed. Organise your revision into these four categories. For each category, note down the reforms that are relevant, what exactly the reforms helped to do and how effective they were.

Context !

Between 1906 and 1914 the Liberal government moved away from the policy of laissez-faire and passed several reforms aimed at helping people who were poor through no fault of their own.

The young could not help being born into poverty while the old could not help becoming too old to work. Meanwhile, people made unemployed or who became ill had to face the loss of wages because of reasons they could do nothing about.

Key words

Borstal – a prison for young offenders.

Contributory – people had to pay something (make a contribution) towards the benefit they got.

Dependants – family members who depend on the wage earner for money, food and shelter. The National Insurance Act (health) did not provide help for the insured person's dependants.

Good character – to qualify for old age pension in 1909, the old person could not have been found guilty of drunkenness, have been in prison over the last ten years or have been guilty of having avoided work in the past.

Half-way house – a point between one thing and another.

Intervention – action by the government to make changes.

Permissive act – this means a law that gives permission for something to happen. In the case of school meals, the Liberal government did not insist that meals were provided for all children nor did the government pay for them. The Liberals allowed (or permitted) local authorities to arrange for school meals in their areas, paid for by a local tax. Many local authorities did not bother to arrange for free school meals for the poor.

Poverty line – the amount of income calculated by Rowntree below which people could not maintain basic human efficiency.

Shillings and pence – the British currency. One shilling was worth five pence today. Of course, money values have changed a lot so it is pointless thinking that old age pensions, for example, were only worth 35 pence a week. You get a better idea of the value of the reforms if you think of a reasonable wage being about £5 per week in 1910.

Transition point – a half-way house between the previous laissez-faire, self-help system (before 1906) and what became known as the welfare state in which the government helped people from 'the cradle to the grave' after 1945.

Welfare state – the state means the government and welfare means health and well-being so 'welfare state' means that the government took responsibility for looking after the health and well-being of all the people of Britain.

Hints & tips ★

Questions about the Liberal reforms tend to ask how successful they were. To judge their success you must establish exactly what the aims were. A useful argument to use is that the Liberal reforms were not meant to 'solve' poverty nor were they meant to create a **welfare state**.

The reforms were the first move away from laissez-faire and marked a **half-way house** or **transition point** between the older self-help ideas and the reforms of the Labour government 30 or so years later that created a fully interventionist welfare state.

Key people

Herbert Henry Asquith – the Prime Minister at the time of the Liberal reforms.

Winston Churchill – a new Liberal who introduced labour exchanges and who made the useful 'drowning man' quote.

The following factors and linked knowledge points are all relevant and could be used in an answer on this issue, but remember to always link your information to the question.

The young

Children were thought to be the victims of poverty and unable to escape through their own efforts. In this way they were seen as 'the deserving poor'. Child neglect and abuse were seen as problems associated with poverty.

The Provision of School Meals Act allowed local authorities to raise money to pay for school meals but the law did not force local authorities to provide them.

Medical inspections after 1907 for children were made compulsory but no treatment of illnesses or infections found was provided until 1911.

The Children's Charter of 1908 banned children under sixteen from smoking, drinking alcohol or begging. New juvenile courts were set up for children accused of committing crimes, as were **borstals** (youth prisons) for those convicted of breaking the law. Probation officers were employed to help former offenders in an attempt to avoid re-offending.

The time taken to enforce all the new laws meant the Children's Charter only helped improve conditions for some children during the period.

The old

Rowntree had identified old age as the time when most people dropped below his **poverty line**. Old age was inescapable and so was clearly associated with the problem of poverty.

The Old Age Pensions Act (1908) gave people over the age of 70 up to five **shillings** a week. Once a person over 70 had income above twelve shillings a week, their entitlement to a pension stopped. Married couples were given seven shillings and six **pence**.

The level of benefits was low. Few of the elderly poor would live until their 70th birthday. Many were excluded from claiming pensions because they failed to meet the qualification rules.

The sick

Illness can be seen as both a cause and result of poverty.

The National Insurance Scheme of 1911 applied to workers earning less than £160 a year. Each insured worker got nine pence a week in benefits but only if they paid their National Insurance contribution of four pence a week – in other words, they got 'nine pence for four pence'.

Only the insured worker got free medical treatment from a doctor. Other family members did not benefit from the scheme. The weekly contribution came out of a worker's low wages, so in reality the contribution was like a wage cut, which might simply have made poverty worse in many families.

The unemployed

Unemployment was certainly a cause of poverty.

The National Insurance Act (Part 2) only covered unemployment for some workers in some industries and, like Part 1 of the Act, required contributions from workers, employers and the government. For most workers, no unemployment insurance scheme existed.

Other reforms which could be argued to have helped address problems associated with poverty

In 1906 a Workman's Compensation Act covered a further 6 million workers, who could now claim compensation for injuries and diseases which were the result of working conditions.

In 1909, the Trade Boards Act tried to protect workers in trades like tailoring and lace making by setting up trade boards to fix minimum wages. The Mines Act and the Shop Act improved conditions.

For practice

9 To what extent did the Liberal reforms of 1906 to 1914 make a significant improvement to the lives of the British people? (22 marks)

10 How successfully did the Liberals' social reforms from 1906 to 1914 deal with the real problems facing the British people? (22 marks)

An assessment of the effectiveness of the Labour reforms, 1945–51

Part 6 of 'Britain, 1851–1951' asks you to assess the effectiveness of the Labour reforms, 1945–51.

In other words, describe what Labour's social reforms were between 1945 and 1951 and judge how good they were at solving the social problems facing Britain at that time.

What you should know

To be successful in this section you must be able to:

★ explain why people hoped for a better Britain at the end of the Second World War and also describe how the Beveridge Report was connected to that hope

★ describe what was done by Labour to tackle the five giants of poverty, ignorance, disease, unemployment and bad housing

★ be able to describe some of the positive and negative points about the reforms and explain why some historians argue the Labour reforms were a big success, while others argue that the Labour government failed to keep its promises.

43

Context !

Between 1939 and 1945 Britain was involved in the Second World War. During the war the public hoped that they would see a better Britain after the war. Those hopes were boosted when the Beveridge Report was published in 1942. The report identified five giant social problems facing Britain. These were ignorance (bad education), idleness (unemployment), disease (bad health), want (poverty) and **squalor** (bad housing). The social reforms of Labour between 1945 and 1951 were aimed at dealing with those problems.

Key people

Clement Attlee – the Prime Minister between 1945 and 1951.
Aneurin Bevan – the Labour politician in charge of setting up the NHS.
William Beveridge – identified the five giant problems facing British society and provided the structure for Labour's social reforms aimed at defeating the giants.

Key words

Cradle to grave – a phrase used to show the range of Labour's social reforms that helped people from birth (cradle) to death (grave).

Intervention – involvement by the government in the everyday lives of the people of Britain.

Nationalise – the government took over industries (nationalised) and managed the economy in the hope that social problems such as unemployment could be removed.

Squalor – bad housing.

Want – another word for poverty.

The following factors and linked knowledge points are all relevant and could be used in an answer on this issue, but remember to always link your information to the question asked.

Want

In 1946 the first step was made – the National Insurance Act. It consisted of comprehensive insurance sickness and unemployment benefits for all. It was said to support people from the '**cradle to the grave**' which was significant as it meant people had protection against falling into poverty throughout their lives.

This was very effective as it meant that if the main wage earner of the family was injured then the family was less likely to fall further into the poverty trap, as was common before. However, this Act can be criticised for its failure to go far enough. Benefits were only granted to those who made 156 weekly contributions.

In 1948 the National Assistance Board was set up in order to cover those for whom insurance did not do enough. This was important as it acted as a safety net to protect these people. This was vital as the problem of people not being aided by the insurance benefits was becoming a severe issue as time passed. Yet some criticised this as many citizens still remained below the poverty level, showing the problem of **want** had not completely been addressed.

Disease

The NHS was the first comprehensive universal system of health in Britain. It offered vaccination and immunisation against disease, almost totally wiping out some of Britain's most deadly illnesses.

Bevan visiting an NHS patient in hospital

It also offered helpful services to Britain's public, such as childcare, the introduction of prescriptions, health visiting and provision for the elderly, providing a safety net across the whole country. The fact that the public did not have to pay for their health care meant that everyone, regardless of their financial situation, was entitled to equal opportunities of health care they had previously not experienced.

The NHS could be regarded as almost too successful. The demand from the public was overwhelming, as the estimated amount of patients treated by it almost doubled. As a result some changes were made for prescriptions, dental treatment and eye tests.

Education

The 1944 Education Act raised the age at which people could leave school to fifteen as part of a policy to create more skilled workers which Britain lacked at the time.

Labour introduced a two-level secondary school system whereby students were split at the age of eleven (twelve in Scotland) depending on their ability. Smarter students who passed the 'eleven plus' exam went to grammar schools and the rest went to secondary moderns. Those who went to grammar schools were expected to stay on past the age of fifteen, take exams and get professional jobs.

The idea was to sort children into an education suited to their ability and in theory meant that children of even poor background could have equal opportunities in life. However, the system actually created a bigger division between the poor and the rich. In many cases, the already existing inequalities between the classes were made worse rather than narrowed. Was it right to decide a child's future at eleven or twelve?

Labour also expanded university education by giving students grants, not loans, so everyone who had the ability could go to university.

> ### Hints & tips ★
>
> Beveridge's five giants provide a very convenient way to structure your essay. After your introduction you should write five paragraphs, each one dealing with each of the five giants, explaining what was done and then analyse the changes by looking at the positive and negative effects.

Housing

The slum clearing programmes of the 1930s had done little to help the problem of bad housing. After the war there was a great shortage of housing as much had been destroyed and damaged. Tackling the housing shortage and amending the disastrous results of the war fell upon Bevan's Ministry of Health.

Labour's target for housing was to build 200,000 new homes a year. 157,000 prefabricated homes were built to a good standard; however, this number was not enough and the target was never met.

Bevan encouraged the building of council houses rather than privately funded construction. The New Towns Act of 1946 aimed to target overcrowding in the increasingly built-up older cities. By 1950, the government had designed twelve new towns.

By the time Labour left government office in 1951 there was still a huge shortage of affordable housing in Britain.

Idleness

After the war unemployment was basically non-existent so the government had little to do to tackle idleness.

The few changes they did make were effective in increasing the likelihood of being able to find work, because they increased direct government funding for the universities which led to a 60 per cent increase in student numbers between 1945 and 1946 and between 1950 and 1951. This helped to meet the manpower requirements of post-war society, provided more skilled workers and allowed people from less advantaged backgrounds to pursue a higher education, aiming to keep unemployment rates down.

The Labour government also **nationalised** 20 per cent of industry – the railways, mines, gas and electricity. This therefore meant that the government was directly involved with people employed in these huge industries which were increasing in size dramatically. This tackled idleness by the government having control – employees were less likely to lose their job through industries going bankrupt and people were working directly to benefit society.

For practice

11 'The social reforms of the Labour government of 1945–51 failed to deal effectively with the needs of the people.' How valid is this view? (22 marks)

12 'The Labour government of 1945 to 1951 met the needs of the people "from the cradle to the grave".' How valid is this view? (22 marks)

Model answers to exam questions

This section will provide you with examples of answers to questions or parts of questions. As you know, in this exam paper you will have to write extended responses, sometimes called essays. Each essay must have parts to them and each section will gain marks.

These sections are:

- introduction* (3 marks)
- use of knowledge – you must include at least six different, relevant and accurate facts that lead into an analysis comment (6 marks)
- analysis* (6 marks)
- evaluation* (4 marks)
- conclusion* (3 marks).

Below you will find an example question with good examples of student answers to each of the four starred sections (*) of the extended response listed above.

The knowledge marks count is simply based on the number of relevant and accurate knowledge points you use in your essay.

The answers may not be on topics you want to revise but the rules are the same for all essays, so find out what things gain marks and why marks are lost!

Hints & tips

You will see that factors to develop are vital in any essay introduction. They list the main headings you will write about in your essay. You can find the factors to develop for every single Higher essay you will ever do in the description of content box in the SQA syllabus for your chosen topic.

Example

Question

How important were the social surveys of Booth and Rowntree in the Liberal government's decision to introduce social reforms, 1906–14? (22 marks)

Introduction

In late nineteenth-century Britain, poverty was seen as a personal failure. It was expected that people should 'self-help' and governments did not think it was their responsibility to help the poor. (context)

The social surveys of Booth and Rowntree were quite important in the Liberal government's decision to introduce social reforms, 1906-14; however, there were several other reasons which also had importance. (line of argument) Other reasons for the introduction of reform include the fact that the government feared for the British Empire due to an unfit workforce and army, as well as the electoral impact of the growing Labour Party on the Liberals and the example of other countries. (factors to develop)

Why is this a good introduction?

This is an effective introduction and gets 3/3 because it has two sentences of context, a clear line of argument that addresses the question posed and has other factors to develop. You need to have all three of these things to gain 3 out of 3.

⇨

Analysis

The rise of the Labour Party after 1900 was an important influence on the Liberal decision to introduce social reforms because the Labour Party was promising to improve living conditions for the poor if they were elected. As a result of Labour's promise, the Liberals feared they would lose votes if they did not do something to help the poor.

Why is this a good example of an analysis comment?

It is good because after the fact it states 'this was important because' and then explains how the fact is important in answering the question.

If you write *three* examples of this sort of comment you will gain 3 analysis marks.

Analysis plus

However, the threat from Labour can be overstated. The Liberals managed the problem of Labour by developing a pact with the Labour Party as early as 1903, so social reform from 1906 was not necessarily a reaction to Labour, as the Liberals were well aware of the problem of Labour before this time.

Why is this a good example of an analysis plus comment?

It is good because this states a limitation on the factor of the Labour Party as a cause of the Liberal Reforms. It explains why this factor may not be as important as thought.

If you write *three* examples of this sort of comment you will gain 3 more analysis marks.

Evaluation

Several factors have a claim to be the main influence on the Liberals.

The Booth/Rowntree reports certainly influenced politicians but six years passed before any action linked to the reports was seen.

National security and efficiency were important goals but they could not be improved without political action.

However, real change could only happen from those who have power and want to use that power for change. After the death of the old PM, new MPs with new ideas entered the cabinet.

Naturally they were influenced by the reports and concern over national security and efficiency and also the challenge for votes from the Labour Party. Therefore it can be argued the most significant reason for the Liberal reforms was the impact of new Liberal politicians with new interventionist ideas.

Is this a good evaluation paragraph?

This is a middle-of-the-road evaluation paragraph because the candidate does not connect their evaluative comments to a line of argument developed through the extended response which is needed for 4 marks to be awarded.

This paragraph is more likely to achieve 2 marks out of 4.

Conclusion

In conclusion, the reports of Booth and Rowntree were quite important in the introduction of the Liberal reforms as they showed that poverty was not the fault of the individual. However, the impact of new Liberal politicians and their new interventionist ideas was the most important factor as it meant that there were people who could actually introduce the laws who believed in state intervention to help others, whereas the reports could not actually change the law. The Labour Party was certainly a threat, but the Liberals managed their challenge with an electoral agreement. The example of local government showed what could be done, but it was not a national development. Therefore, although the reports were undoubtedly important, the fact that new politicians were elected with new ideas for social reform is the most important reason why the Liberals introduced their social reforms.

Why is this a good conclusion?

This conclusion provides a direct answer to the question posed. It provides a relative judgement between factors that addresses the question. This judgement is supported with reasons. Other factors are also mentioned and judgements made on their importance. An overall conclusion is drawn at the end which directly answers the question. A good conclusion needs a judgement in terms of the question; judgement also needs to be made between factors and supported with reasons. All three elements are needed to get 3/3.

Section 2 – European and world history

Chapter 4
Germany, 1815–1939

An evaluation of the reasons for the growth of nationalism in Germany, 1815–50

Part 1 of 'Germany, 1815–1939' asks you to evaluate the reasons for the growth of nationalism in Germany, 1815–50.

In other words, you will be asked why nationalism grew in Germany between 1815 and 1850 and you will be expected to comment on the importance of each of the reasons.

What you should know 👍

To be successful in this section you must be able to:

★ describe how the German states were divided in 1815
★ explain why nationalism and liberalism became popular ideas after 1815
★ describe what is meant by cultural, economic and political nationalism
★ explain why Prussia was becoming such an important German state in and after 1815.

Context ❗

In 1800 'Germany' did not exist. It was a collection of over 300 separate states, each with their own interests and jealousies. Before 1815 Germany had been carved up by Napoleon, the North Sea coast being incorporated into France itself, and the Confederation of the Rhine set up as a puppet state. Divided, the German states could not defend their own territory.

The following factors and linked knowledge points are all relevant and could be used in an answer on this issue, but remember to always link your information to the question asked.

Hints & tips ⭐

Although it is true that a united Germany did not exist until 1871 it is perfectly okay in your answers to refer to the German states as Germany before 1871.

Hints & tips ⭐

This question only asks about the reasons for the growth of nationalism in Germany. Be aware that the first three parts of this section all ask about roughly the same time period so make sure you answer the question that is asked. For example, it is not relevant in this answer to write about how Austria was against nationalism. That is relevant in another section but not this one that only looks for positive reasons why nationalism grew.

> ## Key words
>
> **Burschenschaften –** student unions which were supporters of national and liberal ideas. Student members travelled around German universities spreading nationalist ideas.
>
> **Congress of Vienna –** the meeting of Great Powers in 1815 which redrew the map of Europe and increased the power of Prussia.
>
> **Liberalism –** supporters wanted a new, fairer political system based upon an elected parliament.
>
> **Nationalism/Nationalist –** German nationalism was the desire for an independent, united Germany and nationalists supported that idea.
>
> **Prussia –** the largest German state in the Confederation apart from Austria.
>
> **Zollverein –** a trading and economic union of states with Prussia at its heart.

Economic factors

After 1815 urbanisation and industrialisation of the German states began to grow. Middle-class businessmen called for a more united market to enable them to compete with foreign countries.

Prussian economic expansion was important, especially the drift in power away from Austria and towards **Prussia** as the latter began to build on rich resources such as coal and iron deposits.

Prussia's gain of territory on the River Rhine after 1815 meant it had good reason to reach an agreement with neighbours to ensure relatively free travel of goods and people between its lands in the east and the west.

Businessmen complained that tax burdens were holding back economic development. Prussia created a large free-trade area within Prussia herself which aided the needs of businessmen.

Railway and road development was also important. After the 1830s the development of railways and roads ended the isolation of German states from each other. This enabled the transport and exploitation of German natural resources. Economic co-operation between German states encouraged those seeking a political solution to the issue of German unity.

The Zollverein

The **Zollverein** has been called the 'mighty lever' of German unification by the historian William Carr. By 1836, 25 of the 39 German states had joined this economic free-trade area (Austria was excluded).

Members of the union voluntarily restricted their own independence (even if only in their own selfish interests) to allow for economic gain through joining the Prussian-led customs union. German **nationalists** in the late 1830s saw it as a step towards a wider political union.

Cultural factors

The main unifying force was language – 25 million Germans spoke the same language and shared the same culture and literature.

Writers and thinkers (for example Fichte, Goethe, Brothers Grimm) encouraged the growth of a German consciousness.

After 1815 nationalist feelings were first expressed in universities. Before 1815 there was the growth of a student movement called the **Burschenschaften** dedicated to driving the French from German soil. It continued as a focus for nationalist ideas after 1815 and led to the *Hambacher Fest* and student demonstrations but little was accomplished by the students.

Military weakness

Germany had been used as a recruiting ground by Napoleon: Germans had died to protect France. Even the new enlarged German states after the defeat of Napoleon would be powerless, with the exception of Prussia, to prevent a revived France doing the same again.

Effects of the French Revolution and Napoleonic Wars

Many Germans argued that Napoleon and France had been able to conquer German states before 1815 due to their division as separate, self-governing territories. German princes had stirred national feeling to help raise armies to drive out the French, aiding the sense of a common German identity with common goals.

Meanwhile the ideas of the French Revolution (liberty, equality and fairness) appealed to the middle classes in the German states. In short, the occupation of the French was hated but their ideas began to take root.

Role of the liberals

Many liberals – people who wanted changes in the way that they were governed – were middle class and also receptive to nationalist ideas. The 1848 revolutions in Germany raised consciousness greatly even though they failed.

For practice

1 How important were cultural factors in the growth of national feeling in Germany between 1815 and 1850? (22 marks)
2 How important were economic factors in the growth of nationalism in Germany, 1815–50? (22 marks)

An assessment of the degree of growth of nationalism in Germany, up to 1850

Part 2 of 'Germany, 1815–1939' asks you to assess the degree of growth of **nationalism** in Germany, up to 1850.

In other words, you must judge how much nationalism really grew in Germany between 1815 and 1850.

Key people

The Brothers Grimm – they wrote stories about Germany's past. Although these were described as fairy stories they always had a German theme running through them.

Ludwig van Beethoven – hugely influential German composer in the early nineteenth century. His work was an inspiration for other Germans.

Napoleon I – Emperor of France, he conquered most of Europe before his defeat in 1815.

Johann Fichte – head of Berlin University, he encouraged Germans to think of a united Germany as their fatherland.

What you should know 👍

To be successful in this section you must be able to:

★ describe what had been achieved by nationalists in Germany by 1850 and explain why the political achievements of the nationalists by 1850 were limited and unlikely to last long

★ describe how the Zollverein was called by later historians 'a prototype [early example] of *Kleindeutschland*'

★ explain why the Zollverein – and economic nationalism – was a more successful example of nationalist progress than any attempts at political nationalism

★ describe what Austria did to counter the rise of nationalism

★ explain why Austria was so against any nationalist growth in the German states

★ explain why nationalism seemed 'dead' by 1850.

Key people

Golo Mann – a recent historian who argues that cultural nationalism was not as important as some other historians argue because most Germans 'seldom looked up from the plough'. They were mostly illiterate and more concerned with daily concerns of having enough food to eat without even knowing that composers such as Beethoven existed.

King Frederick William of Prussia – nationalists offered him the crown of a united Germany but Frederick William was more interested in personal survival. At first Frederick William accepted the leadership of the new Germany and wrapped himself in the new German flag, but months later he tried to set up the Erfurt Parliament which would make Prussia the dominant state. When Austria recovered Frederick William was forced to back down at Olmütz.

Klemens von Metternich – Chancellor of Austria who opposed nationalism. He referred to new ideas as 'dark forces'.

Schwarzenberg – after Metternich was forced to flee in the 1848 revolutions, Prince Schwarzenberg became the new Austrian Chancellor.

Context ❗

Historian David Thomson wrote that 'Napoleon brought **liberalism** by design but nationalism by inadvertence'. He meant that Napoleon was happy for new ideas (liberalism) to spread in the states he conquered. That suited Napoleon's plans. What Napoleon did not intend was that the invading French armies became a common enemy that united German states against the invader and so gave the separate states the idea that together they could be a stronger force. The idea of a united Germany in the future was supported by nationalists such as Fichte who wrote about a German fatherland where all the peoples were united by a common language and culture. By 1850 those ideas had not yet found a home in a united Germany. In fact, had any progress been made towards that aim?

Hints & tips ⭐

This is **not** a question about why nationalism grew. That was part 1. This is a question about what happened in Germany between 1815 and 1850 which shows that nationalism was growing. Be careful that you answer the exact question that is asked.

The following factors and linked knowledge points are all relevant and could be used in an answer on this issue, but remember to always link your information to the question.

Signs of growing nationalism

To encourage trade Prussia formed a customs union in 1818 that by the 1830s was called the Zollverein; the Zollverein helped nationalist ideas to spread.

Nationalist ideas were spread by philosophers, historians, poets and dramatists who influenced the literate middle classes and especially students. The *Burschenschaften* movement spread nationalist ideas and meetings/demonstrations in favour of nationalism happened at Wartburg in 1817 and Hamburg in 1832.

Fichte described 'Germany' as the fatherland where all people spoke the same language and sang the same songs and that encouraged Young Germany in 1833 and the Rhine Movement in 1840. German poets and authors, such as the Grimm brothers, and composers such as Beethoven, encouraged feelings of national pride in the German states. In 1830 anti-French feelings were revived by a song called 'The Watch on the Rhine' and festivals such as Hambach in 1832 encouraged nationalist feelings.

In the 1840s trade depression, unemployment and high food prices because of bad harvests led to revolutions throughout Europe. In the **German Confederation** nationalists and liberals saw their chance. The rulers of the small states fled; elections were held for a national convention to meet at Frankfurt to create a united Germany.

Limits to the growth of nationalism

In 1815 the Austrian Chancellor Metternich became worried about the growth of liberal and nationalist student societies.

In 1819 the Carlsbad Decrees banned student societies and censored newspapers.

The following year the power of the **German Diet** was increased so that soldiers could be ordered to stop the spread of new ideas in any of the German states.

Nationalism attracted mainly the educated middle classes and most Germans had little desire to see a united Germany.

The Frankfurt Parliament failed to produce any progress towards nationalism. Nationalists could not agree on the size of a new Germany – should it include Austria and Prussia's Polish possessions? Nor could they agree whether it should it be governed by a king or be a republic – or a mixture of both.

Frederick William, King of Prussia, failed to provide leadership for the new Germany and refused a 'crown from the gutter'. When he tried to increase Prussian power to exclude Austria from the Confederation in the Erfurt Parliament, the new Austrian Chancellor Schwarzenberg said, 'We shall not be forced out of Germany.'

Hints & tips

This question asks you to 'assess the degree of growth of nationalism' so it would be quite appropriate to include in your answer examples of nationalism spreading, but also to balance those positive moves by providing information which shows that the spread of nationalism was limited by various factors.

Key words

German Confederation/ Diet/Assembly – the reorganisation of German states after 1815 which replaced the Confederation of the Rhine.

In 1850 the Treaty of Olmütz signalled the triumph of Austria and humiliation of Prussia. At Olmütz it was agreed to return to the constitution of 1815. German nationalism seemed to be dead.

For practice

3 'By 1850 political nationalism had made little progress in Germany.' How valid is this view? (22 marks)

4 To what extent was there a real growth in German nationalism up to 1850? (22 marks)

An evaluation of the obstacles to German unification, 1815–50

Part 3 of 'Germany, 1815–1939' asks you to evaluate the **obstacles** to German unification, 1815–50.

In other words, describe and then judge how important the various reasons were that made progress towards a united Germany almost impossible between 1815 and 1850.

What you should know

To be successful in this section you must be able to:

★ describe the problems that German nationalism faced before 1850 and explain why those problems were obstacles to nationalism

★ be able to describe the various groups or personalities who were against nationalism and be able to explain the reasons why those groups were against nationalism

★ describe any actions or events which made moves towards nationalism difficult and explain why.

Context

The states within 'Germany' had traditionally been ruled by the Emperor of Austria and after 1815 that continued with Austria being given the chairmanship of the Bund (German Confederation). Austrian Chancellor Metternich's main aim was to oppose liberalism and nationalism. Austrian opposition was a major obstacle on the path towards German nationalism but there were many more, some more serious than others.

The following factors and linked knowledge points are all relevant and could be used in an answer on this issue, but remember to always link your information to the question asked.

Key words

The vocabulary you must know and the names you should know for this section are the same as for part 2 apart from:

Kleindeutschland – literally 'small Germany'. Supporters of this idea wanted a united Germany that did not include Austria.

Grossdeutschland – literally 'big Germany'. Supporters of this idea wanted to include Austria within a new united Germany.

Obstacles – difficulties or problems that stop something happening or delay progress towards something.

Obstacle 1 – nationalists were divided among themselves

Liberal nationalists wanted a united Germany to have a liberal constitution that would guarantee the rights of citizens.

Cultural nationalists believed that unity was more important than individual rights and that what mattered was the preservation of German identity and culture.

Economic nationalists wanted unity to remove the trade barriers between states to allow economic growth and prosperity.

Nationalists were also divided over which territory should be included in any united Germany – **Grossdeutschland** (including Austria) or **Kleindeutschland** (excluding Austria).

Obstacle 2 – the failure of the Frankfurt Parliament

The Frankfurt Parliament revealed a lack of clear aims and it had no power to enforce its decisions. The parliament lacked decisive leadership and there were serious divisions among the 'revolutionaries' regarding aims and objectives.

Nationalists could not agree on whether a new Germany should include Austria and Prussia's Polish possessions. Should it be governed by a king or be a republic or a mixture of both?

Frederick William, King of Prussia, tried to take advantage of the defeat of the 1848 revolution to increase Prussian power to exclude Austria from the Confederation but the Treaty of Olmütz in 1850 signalled the triumph of Austria and humiliation of Prussia. German nationalism seemed to be dead.

Obstacle 3 – Austrian opposition

One-fifth of the population of the Austrian Empire were German. The Austrian Emperor feared nationalism would encourage them to break away and join Germany; this would leave Austria weaker and cause other national groups in the empire to demand their independence.

Austrian Chancellor Metternich's main aim was to oppose liberalism and nationalism. He used diplomacy, threats of force and press censorship. The Carlsbad Decrees and the Six Articles were examples of Austrian repression.

Smaller German states were in fear of the power and position of the Austrian Empire which remained strong until the 1850s.

Obstacle 4 – German princes

The leaders of the German states also obstructed unification. They were protective of their individual power and wanted to maintain the status quo. In other words they wanted no change. Self-interest among German rulers led to opposition to the actions at Frankfurt.

Obstacle 5 – religious differences

Northern German states were mostly Protestant and southern states mainly Catholic, so the north looked to Prussia for help and protection while the south looked to Austria.

Obstacle 6 – economic differences

Even within Prussia there were significant social differences between the industrially advanced territories on the Rhine and the largely agricultural areas in the east, which were dominated by the old-fashioned landowners called *Junkers*. Only in the more industrial areas with an educated middle class did nationalist ideas grow.

Obstacle 7 – the indifference of the masses

Most Germans had little desire to see a united Germany. Nationalism affected mainly the educated/business classes. Golo Mann wrote that most Germans 'seldom looked up from the plough'. He doubted the influence of artists and intellectuals on the majority of the population, whom most Germans knew little or nothing about.

Obstacle 8 – resentment towards Prussia

Smaller states, particularly in the south, were jealous of the economic power of Prussia. The smaller states feared falling under Prussian control and losing their identity and independence. They feared Prussianisation.

Obstacle 9 – attitudes of other foreign states

France had been able to dominate central Europe for centuries due to the lack of unity in the German states. It was not in French interests for Germany to be united, particularly as that would present a barrier to France achieving a frontier on the Rhine.

France and Russia feared that a strong, united Germany would be a political, economic and military rival to them.

Hints & tips

The important thing in answering questions on this topic to realise that the information you have to answer questions from parts 1, 2 and 3 is very similar but what make the difference is how you use your information. Be sure that in the answer to this question you do not waste time explaining why and how support for nationalism grew. This question is entirely about why German nationalism seemed impossible to achieve before 1850.

For practice

5 To what extent was resentment towards Prussia among the German states the main obstacle to German unification by 1850? (22 marks)

6 'The main obstacle to German unification by 1850 was Austria.' How valid is this view? (22 marks)

An evaluation of the reasons why unification was achieved in Germany, by 1871

Part 4 of 'Germany, 1815–1939' asks you to make an evaluation of the reasons why unification was achieved in Germany, by 1871.

In other words, why was Germany united in 1871 and which were the most important reasons?

What you should know 👍

To be successful in this section you must be able to:

★ describe and explain the importance of the factors, including Bismarck, to the story
★ reach a conclusion about the relative importance of the differing factors considering the different views of several historians.

Context ❗

In 1850 German nationalism seemed dead but 21 years later a new German Empire was declared in the **palace of Versailles** near Paris. What had happened to bring the German states together and why was the new German Empire announced in a French palace? Some historians think this turnaround was because of one man – Otto von Bismarck. Others think Bismarck was an opportunist who used other trends moving towards unification to his and Prussia's advantage.

Key words

Crimean War (1854–56) – France and Britain fought against Russia who hoped to get help from Austria. When Austria refused to help, either for or against Russia, Austria was left without friends and this marked an important stage in the decline of Austrian power.

Diplomacy – gaining advantage for oneself or one's country by means of negotiation and treaties.

Ems Telegram – Ems is a place where King Wilhelm I was visiting. A telegram was the fast messaging service used at that time. Bismarck edited the telegram sent by King Wilhelm to Napoleon III to make it deliberately rude so as to provoke Napoleon's anger.

Hohenzollern candidature – Hohenzollern is the family name of the Prussian royal family. In the late 1860s, a member of the Hohenzollern family was the possible next Spanish ruler. He was the candidate for the job. Napoleon III did not want to have Prussian enemies to the north and south of France.

Königgrätz/Sadowa – the battle in 1866 which defeated the Austrian army and ended the war between Austria and Prussia. ⇨

⇨

Palace of Versailles – the place where the new German Empire was declared in 1871. The palace is on the outskirts of Paris and was the glorious residence of earlier kings of France. By declaring the new Germany there and cheering Wilhelm I as the new emperor, Bismarck was rubbing the French noses in their defeat. In 1919, 48 years later, the French did the same thing in the same place to Germany at the end of the First World War.

Realpolitik – doing whatever is realistically possible regardless of ideas of fairness to gain an advantage, sometimes described as 'the end justifies the means'.

Schleswig-Holstein – two small German states that became the excuse for war between Denmark and Prussia/Austria.

Sedan – the battle in 1871 which defeated the French army and ended the war between France and Prussia.

Treaty of Prague 1866 – the treaty that ended the war between Prussia and Austria. Usually a defeated power was punished, lost territory and paid compensation to the victor. Instead, Bismarck made a very sensible peace with Austria that left Austria still on friendly terms with Prussia but no longer a challenger for influence over the German states.

The following factors and linked knowledge points are all relevant and could be used in an answer on this issue, but remember to always link your information to the question.

There were several reasons that led to the creation of a united Germany by 1871. These are outlined below.

Prussian military strength

The military reforms of Moltke and von Roon led to the creation of a modern powerful army which Bismarck used. Without these reforms Bismarck could not have won his wars against Denmark and Austria. At the time military experts expected a long war, but it was over in seven weeks with a total military victory at **Königgrätz (Sadowa)**.

The defeat of France was also due to the powerful Prussian army. The decisive victory at **Sedan** was a triumph of leadership and military skill.

Prussian economic strength

The growth in Prussian economic power (the development of railways and roads, for example) allowed Prussia to exploit its resources in the Rhineland and the Saarland. The industrial development and economic growth allowed the financing and equipping of the Prussian army.

The Zollverein, the Prussian-dominated free-trade area, was significant to German political unification. It was described as the 'mighty lever of German unification' and led to the growing power and influence of Prussia over other states.

The decline of Austria

As Prussian strength increased, Austrian power declined, especially in the 1850s. Austrian economic development was poor and its political and military involvement in Italy was a distraction.

Key people

Helmuth von Moltke/ Albrecht von Roon – Prussian generals who were the 'brains' behind the military reforms that made Prussian victory possible in 'Bismarck's wars'.

Otto von Bismarck – born in 1815. He was almost unknown internationally until he was made Minister President of Prussia in 1860. Eleven years later he was known as the architect of German unification. He used **diplomacy**, ruthless realpolitik and war to achieve his aims, but there is still debate about what exactly his aims were. Were they to unite Germany or Prussianise the German states under the new emperor, the former king of Prussia?

Napoleon III – the nephew of the great Emperor Napoleon who had conquered most of Europe 50 years before. Napoleon III had ambitions to be a 'new Napoleon'. He had limited success building French influence in Europe and in Mexico (!) but was outmanoeuvred by Bismarck and ultimately captured with his defeated army at Sedan.

The role of Bismarck

Bismarck's aim was to increase the power of Prussia by whatever means necessary. He used **realpolitik** in the 'three wars' against Denmark, Austria and France.

Bismarck took the initiative, as opposed to Austria, in the war against Denmark. His 'solution' to the **Schleswig-Holstein** question set the stage for a future war with Austria.

Bismarck's skilful manipulation of events leading up to the war with Austria in 1866, plus his establishment of friendships with potential allies, made victory likely.

Bismarck showed his wisdom in the **Treaty of Prague** in 1866 which removed Austria as a challenger but did not leave it as an enemy.

Bismarck's manipulation of the **Ems Telegram** provoked a war with France in 1870.

Bismarck exploited the weaknesses of European rulers such as Napoleon III and he used his diplomatic skill in isolating his intended targets.

You should be aware of historical debate about the role of Bismarck:

Opinion 1 – Bismarck did not create German unity all by himself. He built on development leading to greater unity such as the Zollverein and the railway network along with other factors such as a strong Prussian army to take Germany more rapidly towards unification under Prussian leadership.

'Bismarck did not fashion German unity alone. He exploited powerful forces which already existed ...' (Williamson)

Opinion 2 – Bismarck was the vital figure and without him German unification may not have happened.

'... it was he [Bismarck] *who created the conditions which rendered possible the creation of a Great Germany.'* (Hitler)

Opinion 3 – Bismarck may not have been as influential as previous historians think and it is always easy to claim the problems in the path of unification were larger than they were so that by overcoming the problems Bismarck seems even more important.

'Bismarck's admirers often exaggerate the extent of the obstacles in his path.' (Medlicott)

The attitude of other states

None of the great powers wanted to see the creation of a strong Germany which might upset the balance of power. Britain, Russia, Austria and France were all happy to see the German states weak and divided. However, attitudes changed after 1850. Britain was increasingly preoccupied with her empire, particularly India. Austria was in decline, Russia was defeated in the **Crimean War** and left without friends and France was defeated by Prussia in 1871.

Bismarck

> **Hints & tips** ⭐
>
> Some teachers and students call this section 'The Bismarck essay'. It is not. Bismarck is part of the story but there are many other reasons why Germany became united in 1871 and it is those reasons you must evaluate or judge alongside the influence of Bismarck.

> **Hints & tips** ⭐
>
> You will have about 40 minutes to write an answer on this topic, so beware that you do not allow yourself to get involved in telling a detailed story of Bismarck's 'three wars'.
>
> Bismarck's wars are an interesting story and they could well be relevant to an answer but not in great narrative detail. His wars are only part of the story of unification by 1871.

The actions of Napoleon III

Napoleon had ambitions to be like his famous uncle. He was tricked by Bismarck's hint that he might make territorial gains in the Low Countries if he stayed neutral in any conflict between Prussia and Austria.

Napoleon over-reacted over the **Hohenzollern candidature**, giving Bismarck the opportunity to edit the Ems Telegram and provoke war.

Napoleon's military leadership in the Franco-Prussian War was poor. He allowed himself to be surrounded and captured at Sedan, effectively ending the war.

For practice

7 How important was the attitude of foreign states in the achievement of German unification by 1871? (22 marks)

8 How important was Bismarck's role in the achievement of German unification by 1871? (22 marks)

An evaluation of the reasons why the Nazis achieved power, in 1933

Part 5 of 'Germany, 1815–1939' asks you to make an evaluation of the reasons why the Nazis achieved power, in 1933.

In other words, what do you think were the main reasons for the Nazis coming to power in 1933 and which do you think were the most important?

What you should know

To be successful in this section you must be able to:

★ describe the problems facing the new Weimar Republic and explain why economic problems and the Treaty of Versailles created such dislike of the new government

★ explain the internal weaknesses of the new Weimar Republic

★ describe the ways that Hitler increased his popularity and political power before 1933

★ explain why the Nazis were seen as a popular alternative to the other political parties in Weimar Germany.

Context

In 1918 Germany lost the First World War and within months the Kaiser had gone and Germany had a new republic based on a new constitution and democratic elections. The new **Weimar** Republic was called 'the world's most perfect democracy' yet by 1933 Hitler and the Nazis had used the political system to destroy itself and democracy was ended. How had that happened?

Key words

Communism – the enemy of Nazism and the biggest political challenge to Hitler during his rise to power.

Hyperinflation – the total collapse in the value of German money following the French invasion of the Ruhr in 1923.

Republic – a form of government that has no royal family and government is by elected representatives who meet in a parliament or assembly. Before the Weimar Republic Germany was a monarchy. After the Weimar Republic Germany was a dictatorship.

SA – the Nazi private army led by Ernst Röhm, who specialised in violence against anyone opposed to the Nazis.

Spartacists – the name for German socialists who wanted change by revolution. They admired the ideas of the Bolshevik revolution in Russia and later became the KPD – The Communist Party of Germany.

Stab in the back – the widely accepted belief in Germany that politicians, communists and Jewish businessmen had betrayed Germany by accepting the armistice which ended the First World War and then signing the Treaty of Versailles.

Weimar – a small town far away from the post-war violence of Berlin where the new Republic Constitution was written in 1919.

Key people

Gustav Stresemann – the most able politician of Weimar Germany. Chancellor Gustav Stresemann guided Germany out of the disaster of the 1923 economic meltdown. He rebuilt Germany's international respectability in the 1920s and there is a strong argument that if he had remained Chancellor then the Nazis would not have gained power. However, he died in 1929 within weeks of the Wall Street Crash which signalled the beginning of the economic depression that hit Germany by 1930.

Kurt von Schleicher – an ex-army officer who was a main 'player' in the struggle to be Chancellor in 1932/33. Schleicher believed he could use Hitler against his rival, von Papen.

Paul Hindenburg – the old and at times confused President of Germany. He had the right and the power to select a Chancellor. He also had the power through Article 48 of the Weimar Constitution to rule Germany as he saw fit during times of crisis.

Franz von Papen – another competitor for the role of Chancellor. When he argued that Hitler should be Deputy Chancellor he famously said, 'In two months we will have pushed Hitler into a corner so tightly that he will be squealing.' Von Papen was wrong.

The following factors and linked knowledge points are all relevant and could be used in an answer on this issue, but remember to always link your information to the question.

Weaknesses of the Weimar Republic

There was a lack of popular support for the new form of government after 1918 and many Germans felt the new politicians were not from the right social class to be part of Germany's government.

There was too much in-fighting between politicians who failed to co-operate for the good of Germany. For example, the socialists were divided between those who wanted parliamentary government and those who wanted revolution. In the later 1920s and early 1930s memories of how the new socialist government used the old imperial army and its officers against the **Spartacists** prevented any future co-operation between the left wing against the Nazis.

The constitution and the so-called 'suicide clause' of Article 48 was arguably too democratic. It was 'the world's most perfect democracy – on paper'. In other words it seemed a good idea but it was not realistic.

Apart from Stresemann, there was a lack of outstanding Weimar politicians who could strengthen the **Republic**. There was only lukewarm support from the German army, the civil service and others who had risen to the top in their careers during the 'good old days' under the Kaiser.

Resentment towards the Treaty of Versailles

Although there was no choice, the new Republic was criticised for accepting the terms of the Treaty of Versailles. The loss of territory and accepting blame for the war was especially hated. The new government was criticised as 'November criminals' who had '**stabbed Germany in the back**'.

Social and economic difficulties

The Ruhr invasion followed by the **hyperinflation** of 1923 devastated the middle classes who had been mostly supporters of the Republic. Despair and worry caused a 'scar that never healed'. Hitler used this feeling to his advantage years later.

The Great Depression of 1929 was the beginning of the end for the Republic. Germany's dependence on American loans showed how fragile the recovery of the late 1920s was. By 1930 millions of Germans were unemployed. Once again Germans faced a desperate future of poverty.

The Depression also polarised politics in Germany. The drift to extremes led to a fear of **communism** among the middle classes and a rise in support for the Nazis.

Hints & tips ⭐

*In any question there is always the topic part and the task part. The topic is what the essay is about and the task is what you must do with your information. When you look at your exam paper for the first time there is a strong temptation to glance over the questions and spot topics you want to answer. Be careful. Check the task. A question on this section may mention the Nazis but the task will really be about the years **before** the Nazis came to power, unlike the next section which will be about the Nazis **in power**. Answer the question you are asked.*

Appeal of the Nazis after 1928

The Nazi Party had attractive qualities for the increasingly disillusioned voting population. They were anti-Versailles, anticommunist and promised to restore German pride and give the people jobs.

The Nazis put their message across well with the skilful use of propaganda under the leadership of Josef Goebbels. Propaganda posters with slogans such as 'Hitler – our only hope' were very effective.

The **SA** were used to break up opponents' meetings and give the appearance of discipline and order in Germany.

The Nazis also used basic psychology in excusing most Germans from any feelings of blame for the bad state of Germany. Instead, Hitler gave the population other groups to blame such as Jews and communists. These 'blame groups' were called 'scapegoats'.

The role of Hitler

Hitler was seen as a young, dynamic leader, who campaigned using modern methods and was a charismatic speaker. He offered attractive policies which gave simple answers and targets for blame, and he used popular prejudices to increase his personal popularity.

Weaknesses and mistakes of others

Divisions within the socialists and communists after the destruction of the Spartacists made joint action against Hitler in the 1930s very unlikely.

Weimar politicians such as von Schleicher and von Papen underestimated Hitler and thought they could invite Hitler to power but use him for their own purposes. They were wrong.

President Hindenburg was old and indecisive. He did not like Hitler but as leader of the largest party in the Reichstag, Hitler was the only choice left as Chancellor after the other candidates proved to be ineffective (mainly because Nazi tactics in the Reichstag made German government unworkable).

Hints & tips

When dealing with the rise of the Nazis it is best to divide your answer into two parts. One part should deal with the weakness of the Weimar Republic and the problems it faced. The other part should deal with the attractions of the Nazis and why people chose to vote for Hitler.

For practice

9 How important were economic factors in the rise to power of the Nazi Party between 1919 and 1933? (22 marks)

10 To what extent were the political weaknesses of the Weimar Republic the major reason for the rise of the Nazi Party between 1919 and 1933? (22 marks)

An evaluation of the reasons why the Nazis were able to stay in power, 1933–39

Part 6 of 'Germany, 1815–1939' asks you to make an evaluation of the reasons why the Nazis were able to stay in power, 1933–39.

In other words, which were the most important reasons in explaining how the Nazis kept their control of Germany between 1933 and 1939?

What you should know 👍

To be successful In this section you must be able to:

★ describe the ways in which the Nazi dictatorship was created
★ describe the positive changes carried out by the Nazis that gained public support
★ describe the methods used to maintain control by means of fear or force
★ explain why many Germans just accepted Nazi control when they were also seeing other Germans being persecuted and punished
★ make a reasoned judgement about what you think were the most important reasons why the Nazis were able to keep control over Germany between 1933 and 1939.

Context ❗

In 1933 Adolf Hitler became Chancellor of Germany. He came to power legally under the Weimar Constitution but very soon established a **totalitarian dictatorship** under his personal rule. Hitler and the Nazis could never have kept control in the face of opposition from the majority of the German population. The truth of the matter was that *some* Germans opposed the Nazis and *some* Germans actively supported the Nazis, but most Germans just 'went with the flow' and as long as Nazi rule did not make their lives harder they were content to 'let sleeping dogs lie'.

Key words

Anti-Semitic/anti-Semitism – hatred/dislike of Jews, which led to Nazi persecution.

Bread and circuses – a phrase (see Hints & tips) which means how political control can be maintained by keeping most of the population fairly content with a political system, even if what is being done to a minority is totally unacceptable.

Enabling Act – the law that enabled (allowed) the Nazis to take on emergency power to deal with the national crisis Hitler claimed was facing Germany in 1934. It started the dictatorship.

Gestapo – secret police used by Nazis.

⇨

Hints & tips ⭐

With a question about how Nazis maintained control, it is a good idea to do an answer with two main parts. One part deals with the use of fear and force. The other part can be summed up as 'bread and circuses'. In Roman times the public were kept content by providing enough basic food and distraction with gladiator contests that were called circuses. So 'bread and circuses' means keeping most people content with the political rulers and the small number who still opposed could then be easily dealt with.

Hints & tips ⭐

Nazi control over Germany lasted until 1945 but remember that this section on Germany only covers the years between 1933 and 1939. Anything about the Second World War or the Holocaust is therefore irrelevant to this question.

⇨
Kristallnacht – in November 1938 a nationwide Nazi-organised attack on Jews and their property. Translated it means night of broken glass, a reference to the smashed windows of Jewish homes, synagogues and shops littering the streets on the morning after.

Night of the Long Knives – 30 June 1934, when Nazi SS were used to murder people who Hitler claimed were a threat to his control over Germany.

Propaganda – deliberate exaggerations and lies to make people believe in the success or rightness of the Nazis and how wicked or un-German groups disliked by the Nazis were.

Strength Through Joy (KdF) – a way of controlling and motivating German workers by rewards of holidays, entertainments and even possibly a private car – but only if they remained loyal Nazis.

Totalitarian dictatorship – all political power totally under control of one political party with one powerful leader.

Key people

Adolf Hitler – leader of Nazi Party, the supreme leader, or Führer, of Germany.

Anschluss – linking Germany with Austria. Banned at Versailles but accepted by Britain as inevitable in March 1938. After *Anschluss*, Czechoslovakia was Hitler's next easy target.

Josef Goebbels – in charge of Nazi propaganda.

Ernst Röhm – head of the SA, a long-time friend of Hitler but who was seen as a political threat when Röhm angered the regular German army and perhaps was plotting against Hitler. He was killed during the Night of the Long Knives.

The following factors and linked knowledge points are all relevant and could be used in an answer on this issue, but remember to always link your information to the question.

Between 1933 and 1939 Hitler and the Nazis maintained control over Germany by a combination of fear and force on one hand and '**bread and circuses**' on the other. Here are the main points to include in an answer:

Success of economic policies

Nazi economic policy attempted to deal with the economic problems affecting Germany, especially unemployment. In 1933 unemployment was near 6 million. By 1939 the Nazis claimed it was almost zero.

- The Nazis began a massive programme of public works.
- Nazi policy towards farming, for example, the Reich Food Estate.
- Göring's policy of 'guns before butter' was popular once foreign policy triumphs appeared to justify it.

Social policies

- The *Volksgemeinschaft* (national community) was created.
- Hitler Youth was made compulsory by 1939.
- Nazi education policy focused all subjects on Nazi aims and ideology.
- Nazi policy towards the Jews was to isolate, then persecute and finally destroy – boycotts, Nuremberg Laws, **Kristallnacht**.
- Nazi family policy – Kinder, Kirche, Küche.
- *Kraft durch Freude* (**Strength Through Joy**) extended Nazi influence into the workplace and also leisure time.
- A Concordat with the Catholic Church was reached.
- A Reichsbishop was appointed as head of the Protestant churches.

The Hitler Youth

Success of foreign policy

- Nazi success in foreign policy attracted support among Germans. Hitler kept his promises to destroy Versailles and restore German pride. By rearming Germany, remilitarising the Rhineland and achieving **Anschluss** with Austria, Hitler was not only restoring German pride but making real his promise to destroy the Treaty of Versailles.

'Much of Hitler's popularity after he came to power rested on his achievements in foreign policy'. (Welch)

Establishment of a totalitarian state

- All political parties apart from the Nazis were banned, as were trade unions.
- Non-Nazi members of the civil service were dismissed.
- The Reichstag Fire gave Hitler the opportunity to claim a national emergency and with Hindenburg's agreement the Nazi dictatorship began. The **Enabling Act** created Nazi dictatorship legally.
- The **Night of the Long Knives** removed the possibility of opposition from within the Nazi Party from the SA.
- The death of Hindenburg was followed by Hitler combining the roles of Chancellor and President. This marked the final death of the Weimar Constitution. Hitler became Führer.
- An 'Oath of Loyalty' from every soldier created loyalty to Hitler personally.
- The speed of the takeover of power and ruthlessness of the regime made opposition largely ineffective.
- Anti-Nazi judges were dismissed and replaced with those favourable to the Nazis.
- Acts Hostile to the National Community (1935) was a wide-reaching law which allowed the Nazis to persecute opponents in a 'legal' way.

Fear and state terrorism

- Fear and terror were used throughout the Nazi police state.
- **Gestapo** (plain-clothed Nazi police) were used which led to the fear of the 'midnight knock on the door'. Although the number of Gestapo members was quite low, the German public believed Gestapo to be everywhere which very quickly silenced any anti-Nazi opinions.
- Concentration camps were set up, at first for political opponents and anyone thought to be against the Nazi State.
- The SS (Hitler's personal bodyguard) were used to control through fear.

Crushing of opposition

- Opponents were liable to severe penalties, as were their families.
- Opponents were never able to establish a single organisation to channel their resistance because of the role of the Gestapo and paid informers.
- Opposition lacked cohesion and a national leader; it also lacked armed supporters.
- There was a lack of co-operation between socialists and communists, the only possible opposition groups who might have challenged the Nazis.

Propaganda

Josef Goebbels was the brain behind Nazi **propaganda**. New technologies such as radio and cinema were used to spread the Nazi message and that message was unchallenged as it entered German homes, ears and brains. Films such as *The Triumph of the Will* promoted the Hitler myth that he was a super saviour of Germany while another film, *The Eternal Jew*, spread indoctrination that Jews were the enemy of Germany. Meanwhile, rallies at Nuremberg developed mass hysteria with shows of military power surrounded with blaring music and chanting people. Everywhere the media projected Nazi ideas to turn them into accepted facts.

For practice

11 To what extent was propaganda the main reason why the Nazis maintained power between 1933 and 1939? (22 marks)

12 'Through their economic policies the Nazis gave the people what they wanted.' How valid is this as a reason for the Nazis maintaining power between 1933 and 1939? (22 marks)

Model answers to exam questions

This section will provide you with examples of answers to questions or parts of questions. As you know, in this exam paper you will have to write extended responses, sometimes called essays. Each essay must have parts to them and each section will gain marks.

These sections are:

- introduction* (3 marks)
- use of knowledge – you must include at least six different, relevant and accurate facts that lead into an analysis comment (6 marks)
- analysis* (6 marks)
- evaluation* (4 marks)
- conclusion* (3 marks).

Below you will find an example question with good examples of student answers to each of the four starred (*) sections of the extended response listed above.

The knowledge marks count is simply based on the number of relevant and accurate knowledge points you use in your essay.

The answers may not be on topics you want to revise but the rules are the same for all essays, so find out what things gain marks and also why marks are lost!

> **Hints & tips** ★
>
> *You will see that factors to develop are vital in any essay introduction. They list the main headings you will write about in your essay. You can find the factors to develop for every single Higher essay you will ever do in the description of content box in the SQA syllabus for your chosen topic.*

Example ⚑

Question

To what extent were the political weaknesses of the Weimar Republic the major reason for the rise of the Nazi Party between 1919 and 1933? (22 marks)

Introduction

In 1918 Germany was defeated by the allied powers and the rule of the Kaiser ended. Although a new democratic Republic was created in the small town of Weimar it only survived sixteen years before its destruction by Hitler and the Nazis. (**context**)

The political weaknesses of the Weimar Republic were a major reason for the rise of the Nazi Party to power. However, there were other factors which were also of importance. (**line of argument**)

Factors such as the economic problems that faced Weimar in 1923 and 1928 were also of great importance, as were the attractions of the Nazi Party. (**factors to develop**)

Why is this a good introduction?

This is an effective introduction and gets 3/3 because it has two sentences of context, a clear line of argument that addresses the question posed and has other factors to develop. You need to have all three of these things to gain 3 out of 3.

Analysis

Hitler's charisma and the Nazi policies were important reasons for attracting Nazi support, because they provided an alternative to the Weimar governments that most Germans thought were weak, confused and unable to take any strong action.

Why is this a good example of an analysis comment?

It is good because after the fact it states 'this was important because' and then explains how the fact is important in answering the question.

⇨

69

→

If you write *three* examples of this sort of comment you will gain 3 analysis marks.

Analysis plus

However, it is important to note that a majority of German voters consistently opposed the Nazis. Even in July 1932 just under 40 per cent of German voters supported the Nazis meaning that 6 in 10 German voters supported other political parties.

Why is this a good example of an analysis plus comment?

It is good because this states a limitation on the factor of Nazi policies as a cause of their rise. It explains why this factor may not be as important as thought.

If you write *three* examples of this sort of comment you will gain 3 more analysis marks.

Evaluation

The political weaknesses of the Weimar Republic were important in explaining the rise of Hitler and the Nazis, but they were not as important as the attractions of the Nazis themselves. The fact that Hitler claimed to be 'the last hope' for Germans and that he promised action to solve Germany's economic problems was hugely attractive compared to the confused policies of the Weimar Republic.

Why is this a good evaluation point?

This is good because here the writer is judging the importance of one main factor against another and reaching a decision that is linked to the main question.

Do this sort of balanced judgement at least *four* times in your essay and you will get 4 evaluation marks, but *only* if your evaluative comments are clearly linked to the line of argument that you outlined in your introduction. One way to do that is to write after your comments: 'This shows that … was more/less/just as important to the rise of the Nazis as Weimar's political weaknesses.'

Conclusion

In conclusion, the political weaknesses of the Weimar Republic were a major reason for the rise of the Nazis because the political system could not cope with problems it faced. However, the most important reason for the rise of the Nazis was the economic crisis of 1929 as it was this crisis that led people to listen to the Nazi message. This message was important, as was the leadership of Hitler, but without the economic crisis Weimar would probably have survived with the Nazis remaining a small and weak political party. Traditional right-wing politicians are also to blame, but again, without the economic crisis their views would not have been listened to by Hindenburg. Therefore, although political weaknesses were a reason, the most important was the economic crisis of 1929.

Why is this a good conclusion?

This conclusion provides a direct answer to the question posed. It provides a relative judgement between factors that addresses the question. This judgement is supported with reasons. Other factors are also mentioned and judgements made on their importance. An overall conclusion is drawn at the end which directly answers the question. A good conclusion needs a judgement in terms of the question; judgement also needs to be made between factors and is supported with reasons. All three elements are needed to get 3/3.

Chapter 5

Russia, 1881–1921

An assessment of the security of the Tsarist State before 1905

Part 1 of 'Russia, 1881–1921' asks you to make an assessment of the security of the Tsarist State before 1905.

In other words, how strong was the Tsar and Tsarism in Russia before 1905? What organisations made it strong and where did opposition come from?

What you should know 👍

To be successful in this section you must be able to:

★ describe the Pillars of Autocracy and explain how they helped to keep the Tsar in power

★ explain why opposition to the Tsar was so weak before 1905.

Context ❗

The Tsar of Russia had total control over the law, police, Church and army. The Church, police and army were also vital to the security of the Tsar because they helped to prevent the growth of opposition.

The following factors and linked knowledge are all relevant and could be used in an answer on this issue, but remember to always link your information to the question asked.

The ways in which the Tsar kept control

The Church

The Church was one of the most loyal supporters of the Tsar. It ensured that the people, particularly the peasants, remained loyal to the Tsar by preaching to the peasants that the Tsar had been appointed by God. Therefore, they should obey the Tsar. The Church made sure the peasants were aware of the Fundamental Laws.

Fundamental Laws

Fundamental Laws means the basic, core laws of the country. They stated: 'God himself commands that the Tsar's supreme power be obeyed out of conscience as well as out of fear.' This statement was the Tsar's justification that all political power should be controlled by him.

The army

Army officers were totally loyal to the Tsar. They controlled the people by conscripting large numbers into the brutal army regime.

In turn, these soldiers ensured that the population and the peasants in particular were loyal to the Tsar. They crushed any rebellions and were used to enforce order in the country and loyalty to the Tsar.

Some groups in the army, like the Cossacks, were given privileges to ensure their loyalty.

The secret police (Okhrana)

The Okhrana was set up to ensure loyalty to the Tsar and search out any opposition to the Tsar. It did this by spying on all people of society, regardless of class. Anyone who opposed the Tsar was imprisoned or sent into exile. Large numbers of political opponents were exiled to camps in Siberia.

Civil service

The civil service ran the organisation of the Tsarist State. The civil service was responsible for enforcing laws on censorship and corruption, as well as about meetings which made it very difficult for the revolutionaries to communicate or even meet with each other.

Censorship

This controlled what people were able to read, write or say. Access to information was restricted and libraries were only allowed to stock 'approved' books.

Russification

This was the policy of restricting the rights of the national minorities in the Russian Empire by insisting that Russian was the main spoken language. As a result, religion, education, law and government were conducted throughout the Russian Empire in the Russian language. This maintained the dominance of the Russian culture over that of the minority nationalities, who were treated as subjects, potential enemies and inferior to Russians.

Zubatov unions

Organised by the police, these were used to divert the attention of the workers away from political change by concentrating on wages and conditions in the factories, thus reducing the chances of the workers being influenced by the revolutionary groups. Unions in 1903 became involved in strikes and so were disbanded due to pressure from employers.

Challenges to the Tsar

Political opposition

Opposition and revolutionary groups were fairly weak. There were various revolutionary groups like the Social Revolutionaries (supported by peasants seeking land reform), Social Democrats (supported by industrial workers) and Liberals (who wanted a British-style parliament). However, these groups on their own were not powerful or popular enough to cause changes. They were divided and disorganised and their leaders were often in prison or in exile.

Discontent among the peasantry

There was a wave of unrest in 1902 and 1903, which had gradually increased by 1905. There were often famines, made worse by the Tsar ordering the export of grain to other countries to earn foreign currency.

Until 1861 Russian peasants were serfs – almost slaves. When they were freed in 1861 they were given land to farm for which they had to pay back the value. These payments were called **redemption payments**. Most peasants were severely behind in their payments. Unrest in the countryside grew as the deadline for meeting the annual payments grew near. There were claims that peasants should boycott paying taxes and redemption payments and refuse to be conscripted to the army.

Political problems

There was discontent among various factions in Russian society. The middle class and some of the gentry were unhappy with the government at the time. They did not like having no participation in government, and were angry at the incompetence of the government during the **war with Japan**. Students rioted and carried out assassinations.

Economic problems

Urban workers' conditions and pay were also dreadful. Economic recession between 1899 and 1903 had also led to growing unemployment throughout the empire.

For practice

1 'The Tsarist State was never seriously threatened in the years before 1905.' How valid is this view? (22 marks)
2 To what extent was the Tsarist State ever threatened in the years before 1905? (22 marks)

Key words

1904–05 war with Japan – this war was caused by the rivalry between Russia and Japan, but the Tsar hoped a successful war would distract the Russian population from problems in Russia. The war was a complete victory for Japan and a disaster for Russia.

Redemption payments – these were the loan payments peasants had to pay in return for receiving land after the 1861 emancipation of the serfs.

Hints & tips

The Tsarist government managed to keep rigid control over Russia for most of the time. However, there were periodic problems or uprisings that showed the problems had simply been buried not resolved.

An evaluation of the causes of the 1905 revolution

Part 2 of 'Russia, 1881–1921' asks you to make an evaluation of the causes of the 1905 revolution.

In other words, you must be able to explain the reasons for the 1905 revolution in Russia and also explain which of the reasons you think were the most important.

What you should know 👍

To be successful in this section you must be able to:

★ explain the long-term reasons for the discontent of various groups in Russian society

★ describe events in 1904–05 which led to protest and revolt breaking out across Russia in 1905

★ decide which of these long-term and short-term causes were the most important in triggering the 1905 revolution.

Context ❗

Nicholas II used the army, Church and Russification policy to maintain control over Russia but discontent among all classes continued to grow. When Russia humiliatingly lost the war against Japan in December 1904, tensions exploded in a series of demonstrations and strikes that rocked the Tsarist government. The most important of the demonstrations were the events of Bloody Sunday in January 1905.

The following factors and linked knowledge are all relevant and could be used in an answer on this issue, but remember to always link your information to the question asked.

Discontent of the working class

The working class's complaints were long hours, low pay, poor conditions, the desire for a constitutional government and an end to the war with Japan.

The year 1904 was a particularly bad one for Russian workers. Prices rose so quickly that the value of wages dropped by 20 per cent. There was a wave of strikes in January 1905 with nearly half a million people on strike. By October there were two and half million people on strike. Many street demonstrations protested against the government. **Soviets** were speaking for the workers and demanding political changes.

Discontent with government policies

There was discontent among various parts of Russian society. The middle class and some of the landowning gentry were unhappy with the government at the time. The gentry had lost power and influence when the serfs were emancipated; they had got compensation but lost political power. The gentry were unable to get the Tsar to make any changes to help them.

Russification

The national minorities were aggrieved at the lack of respect for their culture, language and religion, and the imposition of the Russian language. The national minorities had a great desire for independence or more autonomy and began to assert themselves, as in Georgia, which declared its independence.

Key words

Mutiny – a rebellion against authority.

October Manifesto – issued by Tsar Nicholas II in response to the 1905 revolution. It provided the basis for the constitution which was passed the following year, giving freedoms and rights such as elections to the Russian Duma (parliament).

Repression – the putting down or prevention of any disagreement or rebellion.

Soviets – the soldiers' and workers' councils that were set up by socialists. Members of the Soviets were elected directly by the people, which gave them authority and popularity.

Economic problems

Worsening economic conditions such as famines in 1897, 1898 and 1901 had led to shortage and distress in the countryside. Urban workers' conditions and pay were also dreadful. Economic recession between 1899 and 1903 had also led to growing unemployment throughout the empire.

Discontent among the peasants

The peasants had several grievances such as redemption payments, high taxes, a shortage of good land to farm and poverty.

There was a wave of unrest in 1902 and 1903, which had gradually increased by 1905. There were claims that peasants should stop paying taxes or their redemption payments and refuse to be conscripted to the army.

War with Japan

The Tsar's government hoped the war with Japan would distract the public from problems at home by appealing to their patriotism. However, the incompetence of the government during the war made social unrest worse rather than dampening it.

The war with Japan was a humiliation for the country, which was made worse by the heavy losses suffered by the Russian army. Troops suffered from low morale after the defeat and complained about poor pay and conditions.

In June 1905, there was the *Potemkin* **Mutiny**. The mutiny spread to other military units, and industrial workers all over Russia went on strike.

Although most soldiers remained loyal, it was clear that the Tsarist government could not rely on all its troops without question. This was all the encouragement some workers needed to start protesting.

Bloody Sunday

Father Gapon, a popular Orthodox priest, thought he could settle the growing disputes by making a direct appeal to the Tsar. On 22 January 1905, he tried to lead a peaceful march of workers and their families to the Winter Palace in St Petersburg, to deliver a petition asking the Tsar to improve the conditions of the workers. Marchers were fired on and killed by troops.

Many of the people saw this as a brutal massacre by the Tsar and his troops. They felt rejected by the Tsar. Bloody Sunday greatly damaged the traditional image of the Tsar as the 'little father', the guardian of the Russian people.

Reaction to Bloody Sunday was strong and spread across Russia. There were strikes in urban areas, and terrorism against government officials and landlords, much of which was organised by the Socialist Revolutionaries. The situation was made worse by defeat in the war against Japan in 1905.

Key people

Father Gapon – a priest and leader of a workers' association in St Petersburg in 1905. Gapon tried to co-operate with the police and appeal to the Tsar to achieve his aims.

Role of the Soviets

The Soviets did not plan and lead the 1905 revolution, but they took advantage of the unrest and helped create the crisis in 1905 that led to the Tsar making concessions.

The important Soviets were in St Petersburg and Moscow. By September 1905, over 50 Soviets had been organised in all major cities.

The Soviets had credibility with the Russian people because they had been directly elected by them, unlike the Duma which had a very limited electorate.

The Soviets tried to put pressure on the Tsarist government to deliver on its promises in the **October Manifesto**, but by December 1905 had been **repressed** by the authorities.

For practice

3   To what extent was the 1905 revolution caused by events on Bloody Sunday? (22 marks)
4   How important was discontent among the peasants as a cause of the 1905 revolution? (22 marks)

An assessment of the attempts to strengthen Tsarism, 1905–14

Part 3 of 'Russia, 1881–1921' asks you to make an assessment of the attempts to strengthen Tsarism, 1905–14.

In other words, what was done to make Tsarism stronger after the attempted revolution in 1905? You must also be prepared to make a judgement with reasons, as to how successful the changes were in making Tsarism stronger and more supported.

What you should know

To be successful in this section you must be able to:
★ describe the various political reforms introduced after the 1905 revolution and explain how successful they were
★ describe the various economic reforms introduced and explain how successful they were
★ explain why some Russians did not think the reforms did enough to make Tsarism popular again.

Context

By the end of 1905, the Tsarist government had regained control. They had arrested leaders like Trotsky and smashed the St Petersburg and Moscow Soviets (workers' and soldiers' councils). The granting of the October Manifesto in 1905 seemed to give the Tsarist government the chance to lead reform of Russia and therefore control it.

The following factors and linked knowledge are all relevant and could be used in an answer on this issue, but remember to always link your information to the question asked.

Factors which strengthened the Tsarist government

Political reforms – Dumas

Tsar Nicholas II appointed Stolypin to restore order. He used a 'divide and conquer' policy to deal with each of the threats individually. He secured the loyalty and control of the armed forces by promising overdue pay, improved conditions and training.

The Tsar issued the October Manifesto and the Fundamental Laws which both were crucial in strengthening the Tsarist State. He ruled by divine decree which, along with the support of the Russian Orthodox Church, helped the Tsar use religion to secure his power.

Stolypin aimed to achieve the survival of the Tsarist system. He tried to introduce some political and social reforms which would reduce social bitterness and therefore reduce opposition. Stolypin showed respect for the Duma and tried to work with it rather than against it. Stolypin's work with the Dumas helped to strengthen the Tsarist State as he helped secure the support of the middle class and Liberals for the Tsarist State. However, the majority of Russians still had no political voice in Russia.

Economic reforms

Stolypin's main plan was to use economic reform, particularly land reforms, to prevent revolution. He tried to address some of the economic problems facing Russia like food shortages and rural overpopulation. Stolypin felt that if the peasants and industrial workers were happy then they would be loyal to the Tsar and therefore any revolutions would fail.

Stolypin's land reforms cancelled redemption payments, developed large-scale individual farming (*kulaks*), gave peasants easier credit through the Peasant Loan Bank and made more land available. Meanwhile **Zemstvo** were given the task of carrying out agriculture reforms.

Peasants were encouraged to leave their overcrowded communes and relocate to Siberia or Central Asia. Stolypin also developed agricultural education and spread new methods of land improvement.

Reforms in education were introduced which became compulsory and Stolypin hoped this would allow peasants to get more highly skilled jobs.

He introduced improvements in industrial working conditions and pay and as more factories came under the control of inspectors, there were signs of improving working conditions. These measures had some success as when industrial profits increased, there were signs workers were becoming better off.

Key words

Autocratic rule – rule by the Tsar who had total political and legal power over the Russian people.

Social Democrats – this was a Marxist party that split into two groups after 1903: the Bolsheviks and Mensheviks. The Mensheviks were the larger group and more active before 1914, because many of the Bolshevik leaders, like Lenin, were exiled.

Socialist Revolutionaries – this party was set up in 1902. Its main leader was Victor Chernov. The SRs were not officially Marxist, but shared many of the same ideas. Their plans for land reform made them very popular with the peasantry.

Stolypin's necktie – the execution of radicals as the Tsarist government regained control after October 1905. Known as the 'necktie' because of the rope used to hang people.

Zemstvo – local, regional governments tasked with implementing the agricultural reforms before 1914. Often regional governments exceeded this brief, leading to tension with the peasantry.

In 1912 a workers' sickness and accident insurance scheme was introduced. This strengthened the Tsarist State because it improved life and work for the vast majority of the population.

However, the land reforms did not modernise as much as had been hoped and there was an economic slump, which made life difficult for people and affected their loyalty to the Tsarist State.

Factors which indicated weaknesses in the Tsarist State

Role of the Tsar

Tsar Nicholas II was unsuited to the role of **autocratic ruler** of Russia. He relied on relatives or favourites from the royal court to be his ministers and generals, whether they were up to the job or not. He also undermined loyal minsters like Witte and Stolypin if he thought they were not carrying out his wishes or exceeding their authority.

With ministers uncertain that they had the backing of the Tsar, the personal favourites and friends of the Tsar and his family became more important because they had privileged access. This had two negative effects on the Tsarist State: it led to the rising influence of Rasputin – and unpopularity of the Tsar among some upper classes – and secondly, it undermined the reputation of the Tsarist government, when there were a series of 'flip-flop' decisions depending upon who was in favour or not.

Role of the Tsarina, Alexandra

German-born, the Tsarina was never well-liked by the Russian people. She was reputed to be strong-willed and not very clever.

The Tsar's heir, Alexei, was born in 1904. It was soon discovered he had haemophilia (a blood-clotting disease), inherited from his mother. Alexei had a very serious attack in 1912 that only seemed to be resolved by the holy man Rasputin.

Alexandra became ever more dependent upon Rasputin's advice and opinions, which she made her husband listen to. Unfortunately, Rasputin had a bad reputation for drinking and womanising. The link between the Tsar and Rasputin tarnished the reputation of the Tsarist government and reduced support from some of the middle and upper classes.

Discontent among the middle classes

Although big reforms had been promised in 1905, it was clear that power still rested with the Tsar because he kept supreme authority and ministers were responsible to him, not the Duma. This was far from the sharing of power the middle classes had expected.

Over the course of four Dumas between 1905 and 1914, the Tsar steadily reduced those people who could vote in elections. By 1913, even moderate representatives were alienated from the Tsarist government. Many warned of more political opposition due to the rigid control of the Tsarist government.

Key people

Karl Marx – German writer of the Communist Manifesto, which encouraged workers to unite to seize power from the middle and upper classes by revolution.

Tsarina Alexandra – the wife of Tsar Nicholas Romanov. She was German, which did not make her popular during the war.

Grigory Rasputin – Russian 'holy man'. He appeared to be able to control the haemophilia which affected the Tsar's son, Alexei. The Tsarina believed he had been sent by God to save her son.

Tsar Nicholas II Romanov – came to the throne on the death of his father in 1894. He was unprepared for the job.

Alexandra and Rasputin

Discontent among the working classes

Industrialisation continued to cause new social tension as more peasants flooded to the cities in search of work. New arrivals tended to head for areas and jobs where previous migrants had settled. This ensured experiences and resentments were shared and magnified.

Political strikes rose from 24 in 1911 to 2401 in 1914. In spite of reprisals such as censorship, exile, execution and infiltration by the secret police, support for the **Socialist Revolutionaries** and **Social Democrats**, especially the Mensheviks, remained active.

Discontent among the peasantry

The agricultural reforms bought the loyalty of a growing-richer peasant class (*kulaks*), but did little for poorer peasants. Many of the latter ended up in the towns, doubly resentful of the Tsar.

For practice

5 To what extent was the Tsarist State strengthened in the years between 1905 and 1914? (22 marks)

6 'The Tsarist State did not strengthen in the years between 1905 and 1914.' How valid is this view? (22 marks)

An evaluation of the reasons for the February Revolution, 1917

Part 4 of 'Russia, 1881–1921' asks you to evaluate the reasons for the February 1917 revolution.

In other words, you will have to explain the reasons why the Tsar abdicated from power in February 1917 and then decide which of the reasons were the most important.

What you should know

To be successful in this section you must be able to:

★ describe the problems and difficulties facing Russia in early 1917 which led to revolution starting

★ explain why the reforms carried out after 1905 had not worked to secure the future of Tsarism

★ explain which of the problems that led to revolution were the most important

★ describe how the First World War added to the strains on Russia and how those strains made the end of the Tsarist regime inevitable.

Context !

The promises of reform after the 1905 revolution had only raised expectations from all sections of the Russian people. Unfortunately, the Tsar and his advisers seemed to regard the reforms as short-term changes meant only to defuse the crisis, not solve Russia's problems. By 1914, little had been done to remove the deep discontent that had caused the 1905 revolution. Into this background came the First World War, which was very popular to start with, but did in the end lead to the fall of Tsarism. The war can be seen as a catalyst that simply accelerated processes that already existed in Russian society.

The following factors and linked knowledge points are all relevant and could be used in an answer on this issue, but remember to always link your information to the question asked.

By 1914 Russian society remained a divided society

Political power remained with the well-off in Russian society. The Tsar remained in control. This led the more reform-minded and revolutionary political parties to boycott the Duma.

Despite the growth of a wealthy peasant class, called *kulaks*, the majority of the peasants remained poor. These people went to cities to work or became labourers on the land. Industry grew, but workers remained poorly paid.

Role of Tsar Nicholas II

The Tsar was indecisive, weak and unwilling to reform his autocratic government. He did not want representative government. He was also stubborn and did not listen to warnings from his government about how bad the situation was in Russia. He refused suggestions to create a 'government of public confidence' by allowing the Duma to help him manage the war effort.

In September 1915 the Tsar took personal control of the armed forces, which left him personally responsible for any defeats. By February 1917 the Tsar had lost control of the armed forces, as well as the support and loyalty of the Russian people, which contributed to the February 1917 revolution.

Role of Tsarina Alexandra

The Tsar made the mistake of leaving his wife, Tsarina Alexandra, in charge when he went to the battle front.

She was German and under the influence of the monk Rasputin. Public trust in the monarchy was seriously weakened by the lack of trust in 'Nemka' – the German woman.

Alexandra and Rasputin made a mess of running the country, dismissing able ministers in favour of friends and even on one occasion an alsatian dog was made a minister.

Rasputin had a dreadful reputation as a drinker and womaniser. He was assassinated by right wing aristocrats who feared his influence on the government.

Political problems

Discontent among the bourgeoisie

Frustration grew at the incompetence of the Tsar and his ministers in running the war. The offer of the 'Progressive Bloc' in the Duma to help run the war was rejected, which lost political support among many who, in general, supported the idea of a constitutional monarchy.

Rasputin's influence further alienated this group. When the February Revolution came they did not support the Tsar.

Discontent among the working class

The cold, hard winter of 1916 hit workers and peasants hard. The war caused shortages of food and fuel. A secret police report at the end of 1916 said that the workers in Petrograd were in despair as the cost of living had risen by 300 per cent. The introduction of rationing for bread in February 1917 led to open anti-government action.

Peasant discontent

Peasant discontent over the land issue did not end during the war years. When order began to break down, land seizures by peasants became common.

The war put extra strain on the peasantry with requisitioning of horses and conscription of men. In addition, the horror of Russia's huge casualties was felt most among the peasants who made up the bulk of the army recruits.

Food production fell during the war, making shortages in the towns and cities even worse.

The inherent weaknesses of the autocracy

The Tsar's personality did not help. He was a weak man in charge of a political system that needed strong, effective, decisive leadership. Tsarism under Nicholas II could not survive the stresses and strains of war, incompetent leadership and a failure to reform the system.

The impact of the First World War

Military defeat

The war did not go well for the Russian armed forces and they suffered many defeats. The Battles of Tannenberg and Masurian Lakes are but two examples. Russia also lost control of Poland in 1915, which was a severe blow to Russian pride.

The Russian army lacked vital resources, including adequate medical care, and this led to high fatality and casualty rates. The army suffered from low morale and desertions. The Tsar knew he had lost the loyalty of the army so he abdicated.

Economic problems

The war was costing 17 million rubles a day and Russia had to get loans from Britain and France. Economic problems such as heavy taxes, high inflation and price rises meant that many were living in poverty.

For practice ◎

7   To what extent was the February Revolution caused by the indecisive leadership of Tsar Nicholas II? (22 marks)
8   How important were economic problems in causing the February Revolution of 1917? (22 marks)

An evaluation of the reasons for the success of the October Revolution, 1917

Part 5 of 'Russia, 1881–1921' asks you to evaluate the reasons for the success of the October Revolution, 1917.

In other words, why did the **Bolsheviks** manage to seize power in October 1917 and which of those reasons were the most important?

What you should know 👍

To be successful in this section you must be able to:

★ explain the problems that were faced by the Provisional Government
★ describe what the Bolsheviks did to seize power and explain why the Provisional Government lost power
★ describe the policies and ideas of the Bolsheviks that made them attractive to many people
★ decide which reasons for Bolshevik success in the October Revolution were the most and least important.

Context !

When the Tsar abdicated, politicians from the Russian Duma formed a Provisional Government to lead Russia until a Constituent Assembly could be formed. This Assembly would decide how Russia was to be ruled in the future. The Duma was dominated by Liberals as well as Social Revolutionaries. The Bolsheviks were not represented, though they had power in the developing **Soviets**. At this time of chaos and uncertainty the determined Bolsheviks made their move.

Key words

Bolshevik – a Revolutionary Communist who wanted to overthrow the Tsarist State.
Soviet – a workers' and soldiers' council. These emerged after the February Revolution in many cities across Russia.

The following factors and linked knowledge points are all relevant and could be used in an answer on this issue, but remember to always link your information to the question asked.

The problem of legitimacy and dual control

The Provisional Government was never intended to be a permanent authority.

One of the main problems the Provisional Government had was that it was an unelected government. Many people saw the Petrograd Soviet as having more legitimate authority than the Provisional Government.

Soviet Order Number 1 stated that soldiers should only obey orders that were acceptable to the Petrograd Soviet.

The problem of the First World War

The Provisional Government assured the Allies that Russia would continue to fight in the First World War. Kerensky, as war minister, tried to justify the war as being necessary to save the February Revolution; however, desertion and mutiny continued.

Remaining in the war helped cause the October Revolution and helped destroy the Provisional Government as the misery it caused continued for people in Russia.

The problem of internal revolt

The Provisional Government had to deal with a series of challenges which showed how weak it was.

Some problems were of its own making as it freed many revolutionaries from jail. They actively worked against the government that had released them.

The July Days was a Bolshevik attempt to seize power. It was put down by troops loyal to the Provisional Government, Trotsky was arrested and Lenin fled to Finland.

The Kornilov Revolt saw General Kornilov attempt to remove Kerensky and destroy the revolutionary forces within Russia. Kerensky was forced to turn to the Bolsheviks for help – 25,000 Red Guards were armed. This gave credibility to the Bolsheviks as 'defenders' of the Revolution.

The problem of the countryside

Disturbances in the countryside continued and seizures of land by peasants from the nobles were common. The Provisional Government's failure to recognise these land seizures caused resentment from the peasants. Continuing food shortages added to the political turmoil.

Key people

Alexander Kerensky – a moderate socialist. Deputy leader of the Petrograd Soviet, he was then Justice Minister and then Prime Minister of the Provisional Government.

Lavr Kornilov – Russian General. He made an attempt to seize power in 1917.

Vladimir Lenin – leader of the Revolutionary Communist Bolshevik Party.

Leon Trotsky – leading Bolshevik leader in the October Revolution.

The problem of the economy

The war had caused massive economic problems such as rising inflation and food shortages, which led to hunger for workers in the towns. The Bolshevik message of 'Peace, Bread and Land' appealed increasingly to the mass population.

The appeal of the Bolsheviks

After the July Days, few would have predicted the Bolsheviks' seizure of power. However, the Bolsheviks had a number of advantages:

- 1917 saw a huge increase in the membership of the party.
- Lenin was decisive and committed to the seizure of power. He returned to Russia announcing the April Theses, with slogans such as 'Peace, Land and Bread' and 'All Power to the Soviets', which were persuasive. The Bolsheviks appealed to many sections of society with such slogans.
- Trotsky was an effective organiser.
- After the July Days the Red Guards were armed.
- The Bolsheviks controlled the Petrograd Soviet.
- The Bolsheviks benefited from the revolutionary climate that existed after February. Radical alternatives to the present rule were acceptable to many in such a context.

The seizure of power

The Bolsheviks were well organised, well led and above all knew what they wanted – power. They seized power.

25 October 1917

- Lenin and Trotsky completed plans for the takeover of Petrograd.
- The Red Guards moved to take up key positions in Petrograd.
- The cruiser *Aurora* opened fire. This was a signal for the revolution to start.
- Red Guards stormed and seized the Winter Palace, which was poorly defended.

26 October 1917

- The Provisional Government surrendered.

27 October 1917

- Petrograd was controlled by the Bolsheviks.
- Revolution spread to Moscow and other cities across Russia.

> ## Hints & tips ★
>
> *One way to answer a question about the October Revolution is to divide it into two parts. The first part should deal with the weaknesses of the Provisional Government. The second part should look at the Bolsheviks — they were not the most numerous political party, but they were the best organised, determined and well led.*

> ## For practice ◎
>
> 9 How important was the problem of legitimacy and dual control in the Bolshevik success in the October Revolution of 1917? (22 marks)
>
> 10 'The continuation of the First World War was the main reason why the Bolsheviks were successful in the October Revolution of 1917.' How valid is this view? (22 marks)

An evaluation of the reasons for the victory of the Reds in the Civil War

Part 6 of 'Russia, 1881–1921' asks you to evaluate the reasons for the victory of the Reds in the Civil War.

In other words, why did the Reds win the Civil War and which were the most important reasons for their victory?

What you should know 👍

To be successful in this section you must be able to:

★ describe the strengths of the Bolsheviks and explain why those strengths helped the Bolsheviks to win the Civil War
★ explain why the forces fighting against the Bolsheviks lost the war
★ describe the aims and tactics of the White forces and explain why foreign intervention on the side of the Whites was not a good idea in the Russian Civil War.

Context ❗

The Bolshevik seizure of power in October was the beginning rather than the end of the revolution. Many people predicted that the Bolsheviks would only survive for a number of weeks. In fact, the Bolsheviks survived against the odds and went on to create the world's first communist state.

Key people

Vladimir Lenin – Bolshevik leader. His introduction of War Communism ensured that Red armies were fed, clothed and armed.
Generals Denikin and Wrangel – commanders of southern army of Whites. The army was eventually forced into the Crimea in the south and was evacuated by the British and French.
Admiral Kolchak – head of 140,000 White soldiers in the east. Captured in 1920 by the Reds and shot.
Leon Trotsky – Bolshevik Commissar for War: charismatic and well-organised leader of Red forces.
General Yudenich – his army attacked the Reds from Estonia. Turned back in 1919 by larger Bolshevik forces.

Key words

Cheka or Extraordinary Commission for Combating Counter-Revolution and Sabotage – dedicated Bolsheviks who dealt with any opposition.
War Communism – economic measures introduced by the Bolsheviks to deal with the problems of food and equipment supply.

The following factors and linked knowledge points are all relevant and could be used in an answer on this issue, but remember to always link your information to the question asked.

The apparatus of terror

One Bolshevik strategy to stay in power was to build up its terror apparatus, remove any opposition and make any other groups too frightened to turn against the Bolsheviks.

The **Cheka** was set up by Lenin in December 1917. The role of the Cheka was to remove any opposition to the Reds. To begin with it moved against the Kadets and other political opponents such as the Mensheviks and Social Revolutionaries.

During the years of **War Communism** the Cheka dealt ruthlessly with anyone who questioned Bolshevik policies. Everyone who was suspected of being against the Bolsheviks in any way was threatened. Around 30,000 people are estimated to have been killed by the Cheka.

Role of Trotsky and the organisation of the Red Army

The Red Army had two aims – to survive and to win. Trotsky's energy and organisational abilities enabled the Red Army to achieve its aims.

The Reds won because they were more unified politically and geographically than their enemies. The Whites could not even agree on a unified military strategy.

Trotsky was appointed Commissar for War in 1918 and he reorganised the army and used ex-Tsarist officers to train and command army units. Trotsky restored discipline and professionalism to the Red Army.

Trotsky used fierce discipline to ensure loyalty from his forces. For example, Trotsky ordered the families of officers helping the Reds to be kept as hostages just in case the officers were disloyal.

The Red Army had grown to 5 million by the end of 1920, but it did suffer from desertion and many of its men were not that well equipped.

Disunity among Whites

All of the White armies shared a hatred of communism, but apart from that the Whites lacked unity or organisation.

The Whites were a collection of varied political groups ranging from Liberals, former Tsarists, nationalists and separatists, Socialist Revolutionaries and other moderate socialists.

No White leader of any power or importance emerged to unite and lead the White forces. White leaders emerged in different parts of the country, but they did not trust each other. General Yudenich led forces in the west, Admiral Kolchak in the east and Generals Denikin and Wrangel in the south. None of them could match the leadership and organisation skills of Trotsky and Lenin.

Superior Red resources

The Bolsheviks controlled the central area, including Moscow and Petrograd, in Russia.

Moscow was an important railway hub and this allowed the Reds to transport men and materials to the various battle fronts easily.

Control of the main two cities also meant that the Reds were in command of the main armament factories in Russia. The Reds could, therefore, continue to produce war equipment. They also captured military supplies from the old Tsarist army.

The central area was also the most populous area of Russia, which gave the Reds a greater pool of men to fight in their army.

Control of the central area also meant that Red lines of communication were shorter and more secure than those for the disunited Whites.

The Red Army

Foreign intervention

Originally countries like Britain, France and the USA sent troops in the hope they could keep Russia in the war – otherwise all German forces would be directed against the Western Front, which is exactly what happened when Russia surrendered at Brest-Litovsk.

After the First World War foreign soldiers were unenthusiastic about fighting in Russia and wanted to return home.

Britain provided the Whites with £100 millions' worth of military supplies, which, though welcome, was not really enough to make a decisive difference.

Propaganda

Foreign intervention gave the Reds a propaganda gift. They could claim the Whites were really just the puppets of foreign invaders.

The brutality of the White armies alienated the peasants. The Cossacks in the southern army were especially guilty of this. This drove many peasants to support the Reds.

Early on the Bolsheviks had passed a land decree that gave peasants the right to take over the estates of the aristocracy and allowed them to decide what to do with the land. The Reds kept pointing out that all of the land that the peasants had seized in the 1917 Revolution would be lost if the Whites won. This fear prevented the peasants from supporting the Whites.

Leadership of Lenin

Lenin supported Trotsky's decision to enforce harsh discipline against the wishes of other Bolshevik leaders.

Lenin sought to deal with a collapsing economy and a worsening security situation with the introduction of War Communism:

- Grain was seized from the peasantry to feed the army.
- Professional managers were reintroduced to state-controlled factories and the old workers' committees were replaced.
- Discipline was reintroduced into the factories.
- Rationing was introduced to feed the soldiers and workers while the middle classes were given barely enough to live on.

For practice

11 How important was Red control of superior resources in their victory over the Whites in the Civil War? (22 marks)

12 To what extent can Red victory over the Whites in the Civil War be explained by foreign intervention? (22 marks)

Model answers to exam questions

This section will provide you with examples of answers to questions or parts of questions. As you know, in this exam paper you will have to write extended responses, sometimes called essays. Each essay must have parts to them and each section will gain marks.

These sections are:

- introduction* (3 marks)
- use of knowledge – you must include at least six different, relevant and accurate facts that lead into an analysis comment (6 marks)
- analysis* (6 marks)
- evaluation* (4 marks)
- conclusion* (3 marks).

Below you will find an example question with good examples of student answers to each of the four starred sections (*) of the extended response listed above.

The knowledge marks count is simply based on the number of relevant and accurate knowledge points you use in your essay.

The answers may not be on topics you want to revise but the rules are the same for all essays, so find out what things gain marks and also why marks are lost!

Hints & tips

You will see that factors to develop are vital in any essay introduction. They list the main headings you will write about in your essay. You can find the factors to develop for every single Higher essay you will ever do in the description of content box in the SQA syllabus for your chosen topic.

Example ⚑

Question

To what extent was the 1905 revolution caused by events on Bloody Sunday? (22 marks)

Introduction

Russia in 1905 was ruled by the Tsar. Any protests about the autocratic system of government was crushed by the army and the Okhrana. The power of the Church and the policy of Russification also kept the population of the Russian Empire under control. However, in 1905 a revolution broke out. **(context)**

The events of Bloody Sunday caused the 1905 revolution to an extent; however, there were other important factors that need to be considered. **(line of argument)**

There were long-standing political issues in Russia, such as the lack of political influence of the middle classes. Other factors included long-standing grievances of the peasantry. In the short term, the humiliating defeat in the Russo-Japanese war caused the Tsarist system to be criticised. **(factors to develop)**

Why is this a good introduction?

This is an effective introduction and gets 3/3 because it has three sentences of context, a clear line of argument that addresses the question posed and has other factors to develop. You need to have all three of these things to gain 3 out of 3.

Analysis

The Bloody Sunday protest was an important cause of the 1905 revolution because for the first time the ordinary people started to blame the Tsar personally for their troubles, rather than seeing him as 'the little father'.

Why is this a good example of an analysis comment?

It is good because after the fact it states 'this was important because' and then explains how the fact is important in answering the question.

If you write *three* examples of this sort of comment you will gain 3 analysis marks.

Analysis plus

However, Bloody Sunday was not really a cause of the revolution. The protest was caused by the dreadful hours and conditions in the industrial works of Russia so the protest was a symptom of the problems, not necessarily a cause.

Why is this a good example of an analysis plus comment?

It is good because this states a limitation on the factor of Bloody Sunday as a cause of the 1905 revolution. It explains why this factor may not be as important as thought.

If you write *three* examples of this sort of comment you will gain 3 more analysis marks.

⇨

Evaluation

The events of Bloody Sunday were an important cause of the 1905 revolution, but they were not as important as the increasing discontent with the policies of the Tsarist State which created a situation ripe for revolution. However, that discontent would not have existed had it not been for the harsh, autocratic rule of the Tsar, so it can be argued that the real cause of the 1905 revolution was the Tsar himself since he took total control over all the things that led to the growing discontent.

Why is this a good evaluation point?

This is good because here the writer is judging the importance of one main factor against another and reaching a decision that is linked to the main question.

Do this sort of balanced judgment at least *four* times in your essay and you will get 4 evaluation marks, but *only* if your evaluative comments are clearly linked to the line of argument that you outlined in your introduction.

Conclusion

In conclusion, the events of Bloody Sunday were of importance in causing the 1905 revolution to an extent, as they showed the Tsar to be uncaring and not the little father to his people. However, other factors were of more importance such as the long-standing political and economic problems faced by the mass of Russian people who were politically frustrated and suffered from regular food shortages and poor conditions. Events such as the Russo-Japanese war were also important, but they just confirmed the fact that the Tsarist system was unfit to rule Russia. Therefore, although the events of Bloody Sunday have importance they were really just a result of discontent rather than a cause of revolution, such as the political and economic problems the country faced.

Why is this a good conclusion?

This conclusion provides a direct answer to the question posed. It provides a relative judgement between factors that addresses the question. This judgement is supported with reasons. Other factors are also mentioned and judgements made on their importance. An overall conclusion is drawn at the end which directly answers the question. A good conclusion needs a judgement in terms of the question; judgement also needs to be made between factors and supported with reasons. All three elements are needed to get 3/3.

An evaluation of the reasons for changing attitudes towards immigration in the 1920s

Part 1 of 'USA, 1918–1968' asks you to evaluate the reasons for changing **attitudes** towards immigration in the 1920s.

In other words, you must explain why Americans increasingly disliked **immigrants** in the 1920s and be able to make a judgement about which of the reasons affecting those attitudes were the most important.

What you should know 👍

To be successful in this section you must be able to:

★ explain what is meant by **'old' and 'new' immigrants** and explain why Americans feared and disliked the new-type immigrants
★ make a judgement about what you think the main reasons were for such changes in attitudes.

Context ❗

Around 1890 almost all the population of the USA (apart from Native Americans) were either immigrants from Europe or were the sons and daughters of immigrants. These people were known as **WASPs** – White Anglo-Saxon Protestants. At that time, America had an open door policy which meant that anyone could move to the USA and start a new life. However, after 1890, millions of 'new' immigrants arrived from central and eastern Europe. They had cultures, religions and even political beliefs that were different to the established 'Americans' who now resented the 'new' immigrants. After 1918 attitudes towards immigrants changed quickly and the open door began to close.

Key words

Attitude – how people feel about something.
Emigrants – people who leave their home country to live elsewhere. Emigrants and immigrants are the same people at different stages of their journey.
Eugenics – a false science that claimed Nordics were a master race, superior to all others. Supporters of Eugenics argued that immigrants from inferior countries should be stopped from entering the USA. The USA support for Eugenics influenced Hitler's ideas.
Immigrants – people who arrive in the USA from other countries. ⇨

Hints & tips ⭐

In an essay about immigration to the USA do not write about black Americans. Almost all black Americans were descended from black Africans who had been enslaved and taken to the USA over 100 years earlier. Very few black Americans had chosen to go to the USA.

> **Isolationism** – the desire of many Americans to have nothing to do with Europe.
>
> **New immigration** – from 1900 onwards most immigrants to the USA came from eastern and central Europe. These were new areas so therefore 'new' immigrants.
>
> **Old immigration** – the traditional areas where immigrants to the USA had mostly come from was northern and western Europe, hence 'old' immigrants.
>
> **Red scare** – red was the colour of communist revolution so red scare means a fear of communist revolutionary ideas arriving in America.
>
> **WASP** – the initials stand for White Anglo-Saxon Protestant. Anglo-Saxon means people from Britain and Germany and western Europe. It was the standard description of 'old' immigrant types.

Key people

Madison Grant – the author of the **Eugenics** book *The Passing of the Great Race*.

Mitchell Palmer – the US Attorney General. The top lawyer in the USA who organised attempts to arrest and deport anyone suspected of un-American beliefs.

President Wilson – US president who took the USA into the First World War, but his idea of the League of Nations was rejected by US government.

The following factors and linked knowledge points are all relevant and could be used in an answer on this issue, but remember to always link your information to the question asked.

Isolationism

Attitudes towards immigration had been changing for some time before 1918. A number of measures had been introduced: 1884 Immigration Restriction League, 1882 Federal Immigration Act, Chinese Exclusion Act and the 1913 Alien Land Law.

At the beginning of the First World War American public opinion was firmly on the side of neutrality. They wanted to keep out of foreign problems and concentrate solely on America. That policy was called **isolationism**.

When the war ended, most Americans wanted a return to isolationism. The USA would not join the League of Nations and did not want to be dragged into another European war.

Based on the belief that Europe just caused problems for America, many Americans questioned why so many immigrants should be allowed to come to the USA, bringing Europe's problems with them.

Fear of revolution

The Russian Revolution in 1917 had established the first communist state in the world and it had as its aim to spread revolution and destroy capitalism.

The large numbers of immigrants from eastern Europe and Russia led to the '**red scare**' in 1919 and it looked as if revolution was imminent.

Mitchell Palmer (in charge of law enforcement in the USA) organised Palmer Raids in August 1919, in an attempt to arrest and deport dangerous aliens. His raids were not very successful, but the publicity they got convinced many Americans that immigrants were a threat to the USA.

Hints & tips ★

One way that will help you to answer a question about changing attitudes towards immigrants is to divide those attitudes into two sets of reasons. The first set of reasons is based around how the new immigrants affected people's daily lives, for example, strikebreaking. The second set of reasons is how the new immigrants were affecting the American way of life and were perhaps threatening the whole nation, for example, the fear of revolution and the fear of crime.

Prejudice and racism

The changing nature of immigrants worried 'old' immigrants – **WASPs** mainly from the north and west of Europe. The 'new' immigrants – mainly from southern and eastern Europe – were often Catholic or Jewish and that worried traditional, Protestant WASP America.

- New immigrants were unfamiliar with democracy and were viewed as a threat to the American way of life.
- New immigrants continued to wear traditional dress and looked out of place.
- A new 'science' called Eugenics claimed that the north European 'Nordics' were a superior race of people and new immigrants were inferior and should be kept out of the USA. This idea was made popular by Madison Grant in his book, *The Passing of the Great Race*.
- 'Nativism' ideas saw new immigrants as undermining morality, Protestant religion and the traditional way of life.

Social fears

Immigrants congregated with people from their own culture in ghettos mainly in north-eastern cities, for example, Little Italy, Little Ireland and Little Poland.

Immigrants were blamed for high crime rates in cities – particularly those cities with high levels of immigrants.

There was a major fear of organised crime, for example, the Mafia from Sicily. The Sacco and Vanzetti case fed public fears of Italian-sounding names, crime and political revolutionary ideas.

Crime gangs became big news with the start of **Prohibition**. Gangster Al Capone (the son of immigrants) became famous for supplying illegal alcohol.

> ## Key word
>
> **Prohibition** – the banning of production and selling of alcohol in the USA between 1920 and 1933.

Economic fears

Trade unions believed that anything they did to improve conditions or wages was wrecked by Italian or Polish workers who were prepared to work longer hours for lower wages.

In the 1919 strikes, new immigrants were used as strikebreakers. This caused huge resentment and an increase in the desire to stop immigrants entering the country.

The effects of the First World War

- Many German immigrants supported Germany in the war and society was split when the USA joined the war against Germany.
- Germans were often associated with making beer so when Prohibition started their activities were seen as unpatriotic.
- Irish Americans were suspected of being anti-British.
- Many citizens felt hostile to anything foreign.

For practice

1 To what extent was fear of crime the main reason for changing attitudes towards immigration in the USA after 1918? (22 marks)
2 'Fear of revolution was the main reason why attitudes changed towards immigrants after 1918.' How valid is this view? (22 marks)

An evaluation of the obstacles to the achievement of civil rights for black people, up to 1941

Part 2 of 'USA, 1918–1968' asks you to evaluate the obstacles to the achievement of civil rights for black people, up to 1941.

In other words, why was it so difficult to gain civil rights for black Americans before 1941 and which were the most important reasons?

What you should know

To be successful in this section you must be able to:

★ describe how the '**Jim Crow**' laws segregated and discriminated against black Americans and explain how the 'Jim Crow' laws were big obstacles to the achievement of civil rights for black Americans before 1941
★ describe the activities of the **Ku Klux Klan** and why they were so determined to stop black Americans achieving civil rights
★ explain the importance to black Americans and civil rights of the 1896 'separate but equal' decision of the Supreme Court
★ describe the ideas of the UNIA and NAACP and explain why those organisations achieved so little in the 1920s and 1930s
★ describe **the Great Migration** and explain why it might have delayed progress to civil rights before 1941.

Hints & tips

A question on this topic may ask about the lack of progress towards civil rights up to 1941, but there is nothing special about 1941 except that it is a convenient break point in the campaigns for civil rights. In 1941 the USA entered the Second World War which ended in 1945. After 1945 a whole new series of civil rights campaigns started, but that is not relevant to this essay.

Context

By the end of the American Civil War in 1865, slavery had been abolished and black Americans were technically free. However, over 50 years later black Americans were far from free. By 1918 black Americans faced prejudice, discrimination, segregation and difficulties finding well-paid jobs or good housing. Black Americans, especially in '**the South**' had their lives restricted by laws and fear of violence against them. In 1918 the possibility of gaining civil rights was a long way off.

Key words

The Great Migration – the move of thousands of black Americans from the South to the northern cities during and after the First World War. They migrated north to the 'promised land' looking for better jobs, higher wages and a better life.

Jim Crow – the name given to many 'home-made laws' created in the 1870s and 1880s that prevented black Americans in the South from gaining civil rights.

Ku Klux Klan – an organisation created in the 1860s to terrify newly freed slaves and to stop them claiming their rights as Americans citizens. By the 1920s it was called the greatest social organisation ever for WASP Americans and had the slogan '100 per cent Americanism'.

Lynching – the murder or torture of black Americans by a mob who were seldom punished since there was no law against lynching until the 1950s.

Separate but equal – in 1896 the Supreme Court was asked to judge if the 'Jim Crow' laws took away the constitutional rights of black Americans. The Supreme Court decided that the 'Jim Crow' laws were legal as long as the segregated black community had the same facilities as the white community, but were kept separate and equal.

The South – the southern states of the USA where the vast majority of the black American population lived.

Supreme Court – the highest law court in the USA whose job is to decide if new laws damage any American's constitutional rights.

Hints & tips ★

Be careful that you answer the question that is asked. You might get questions about progress to civil rights before 1941, after 1945 or there might be no questions at all. Answer the question you are asked and check especially the date boundaries of the question.

The following factors and linked knowledge points are all relevant and could be used in an answer on this issue, but remember to always link your information to the question asked.

Activities of the Ku Klux Klan (KKK)

The KKK was a racist organisation formed in the 1860s to prevent former slaves achieving equal rights. Their methods were horrific and included beatings, torture and **lynching**. Activities took place at night and members wore white robes and carried guns, torches and burning crosses.

After 1915 there was a revival of the KKK. The 'second' Klan grew most rapidly in cities which had high growth rates of black population migrating north from the South between 1910 and 1930.

President Roosevelt refused to support a federal bill to outlaw lynching in his New Deal in the 1930s, because he feared loss of Democrat support in the South.

The Klan was important in preventing progress towards civil rights because they used fear to prevent the organisation of protest campaign groups and also because they had influence in local and even national political groups.

Key people

President Roosevelt – by the 1930s President Roosevelt needed his Democrat Party to support him in his economic reforms to get America out of the Depression. Much of Roosevelt's support came from the South and that support would vanish if Roosevelt did anything to help black Americans.

The KKK

Legal impediments

The 'Jim Crow' laws which said that there should be separate education, transport and toilets for white and black people, for example, were passed in the southern states after the Civil War to maintain white superiority.

The '**separate but equal**' **Supreme Court** decision of 1896 was the result of a test case about the legality of the 'Jim Crow' laws. The 1896 decision in favour of Jim Crow made segregation and discrimination legal and respectable across the whole of the USA and especially the South. That decision blocked any progress to civil rights until 1954 when the decision was partly overturned.

Another impediment was the attitudes of presidents who did not consider civil rights an important issue or, more importantly, a vote-winning issue. For example, President Wilson said, 'Segregation is not humiliating and is a benefit for you black gentlemen.'

Lack of political influence

By the 1890s the states in the South had found ways to prevent black men from voting even though they had been given the right to vote after the Civil War. For example, the 1898 case of Mississippi v Williams ruled that voters must understand the American Constitution but that rule was not applied to white voters!

Of course any new law that tried to restrict voting on the basis of property owning or literacy would also take away the rights of poor,

> ## Hints & tips ★
>
> *You will never get a question that requires you to combine details of the time **before 1941** and the campaigns for civil rights **after 1945**. If you find yourself writing about both time periods then something has gone wrong with your reading of the question.*

illiterate white voters who had no land and could not read or write. That problem was avoided by ruling that that those whose ancestors (for example, grandfathers) had the right to vote before the Civil War could still vote. So poor white men could still vote but black men could not.

Most black people in the South were sharecroppers and they did not own land and some states identified ownership of property as a voting qualification.

Therefore black people could not vote, particularly in the South, and could not elect anyone who would oppose the 'Jim Crow' laws.

White politicians did not try to pass civil rights laws because it would gain them no votes from the black community, it would lose them votes from white voters and possibly endanger their lives.

Divisions in the black community

Booker T Washington and his Tuskegee Institute argued that civil rights had to be earned and only an educated minority of black Americans should gain the vote.

In contrast WEB De Bois founded the NAACP (National Association for the Advancement of Colored People) – a national organisation whose main aim was to oppose discrimination through legal action. In 1919 he launched a campaign against lynching, but it failed to attract most black people, who did not even know it existed.

Marcus Garvey promoted 'black pride' and founded the UNIA (Universal Negro Improvement Association) which aimed to get black people to 'take Africa, organise it, develop it, arm it, and make it the defender of Negroes the world over'.

These three organisations represented totally different ideas on how to achieve progress towards civil rights so little of national importance was achieved before 1941.

Popular prejudice

For white people brought up with slavery and for whom it was the normal way of life, it was very difficult to see the black Americans as free and equal. The image of the black slave as property was hard to remove from popular ideas especially in the southern states. After the institution of slavery the status of Africans was stigmatised, and this stigma was the basis for the anti-African racism that persisted.

The relocation of millions of African Americans from their roots in the southern states to the industrial centres of the north after the First World War increased racial tensions, particularly in cities such as Boston, Chicago, and New York (Harlem). The most violent clashes occurred during the Chicago race riots of 1919 and in Tulsa, Oklahoma, in 1925.

Mob-directed hangings, known as 'lynchings', which were usually racially motivated, increased dramatically in the 1920s.

Hints & tips ⭐

*Questions on this topic have **nothing** to do with Martin Luther King, Rosa Parks or anything else that happened in the 1950s or 1960s.*

For practice

3 To what extent was the 'separate but equal' decision of the Supreme Court the main obstacle facing black Americans in achieving civil rights before 1941? (22 marks)

4 'The activities of the Ku Klux Klan was the most important obstacle to the achievement of civil rights for black people up to 1941.' How valid is this view? (22 marks)

An evaluation of the reasons for the economic crisis of 1929–33

Part 3 of 'USA, 1918–1968' asks you to evaluate the reasons for the economic crisis of 1929–33.

In other words, why did America face such economic problems between 1929 and 1933 and which were the most important reasons for the 'Depression'?

What you should know

To be successful in this section you must be able to:

★ describe the main features of the US economy in the 1920s, concentrating on the underlying weaknesses

★ explain how **laissez-faire** policies, weak banks and overproduction led to problems in the economy.

Hints & tips

Although the dates within the topic are 1929–33 that is a reference to the Great Depression in America. Questions asked will therefore be about why that Depression happened, so the bulk of your answer should deal with the events and economic situation of the 1920s.

Context

In the 1920s, US President Coolidge said: 'The business of America is business.' The USA was the richest country in the world and for many Americans the boom years of the 1920s were set to last forever. Nevertheless, the image of a prosperous young country in which poverty did not exist hid uncomfortable realities. When the economy collapsed in 1929 it was seen just how fragile the boom had been.

Key words

Laissez-faire – the leave alone policy of the Republican government which meant there was no government control over banks or the economy.

Protectionism – raising tariffs (or taxes) on foreign goods coming into the USA in order to raise their prices so people bought the cheaper home-produced goods.

⇨

> ⇨
> **Saturated market –** once everyone who wants a product has got the
>   product no more of the product can be sold.
> **Wall Street Crash –** Wall Street, New York, is the centre of the USA financial
>   world where stocks and shares are bought and sold. Over a few days in
>   October 1929 the stock market crashed.

The following factors and linked knowledge points are all relevant and
could be used in an answer on this issue, but remember to always link
your information to the question asked.

Republican government policies in the 1920s

- The Republican administration's policy of laissez-faire meant that the
  economy grew unrestricted by government intervention but also
  when hard times came the government did very little to help.
- The government failed to help farmers, who did not benefit from the
  1920s boom.
- Low capital gains tax encouraged share speculation which resulted in
  the Wall Street Crash.
- The Depression was also due to the actions – or inactions – of
  President Hoover.

Overproduction of goods

New mass-production methods and mechanisation meant that
production of consumer goods had expanded enormously.

Cars, radios and other electrical goods had flooded the market and more
were being made than people could buy.

By 1929 those who could afford consumer goods had already bought
them so the market became **saturated**.

Underconsumption – the saturation of the US market

Throughout the 1920s business had benefited from low tax policies. The
result of this was that the bottom 40 per cent of the population received
only 12.5 per cent of the nation's wealth. In contrast, the top 5 per cent
owned 33 per cent of the nation's wealth. Therefore, domestic demand
never kept up with production.

Weaknesses of the US banking system

A major problem was the lack of regulation. The banking system was
made up of hundreds of small, state-based banks. When one bank
collapsed it often led to a 'run' on other banks, resulting in a banking
collapse and national financial crisis.

International economic problems

The First World War had a big impact on the European economies. All European states, except Britain, placed tariffs, or taxes, on imported goods. This is called **protectionism**.

When the USA tried to protect US businesses from foreign competition by putting tariffs on imported goods, foreign countries simply placed tariffs on American exports so there was no benefit from protectionism.

The Wall Street Crash

In October 1929 there was an atmosphere of uncertainty and shareholders began to sell their stocks. 'Black Thursday' was the name given to 24 October 1929 and 'Black Tuesday' was the following week on 29 October 1929. Share collapse caused panic.

The stock market crash did play a role in the Depression but its significance was as a trigger leading to the collapse of credit and confidence. The **Wall Street Crash** was the symptom of economic illness, not the disease itself.

For practice

5 'The weakness of the US banking system was the main reason for the Great Depression of the 1930s.' How valid is that view?
(22 marks)

6 To what extent were the policies of Republican governments in the 1920s responsible for the economic crisis of 1929–33?
(22 marks)

An assessment of the effectiveness of the New Deal

Part 4 of 'USA, 1918–1968' asks you to assess the effectiveness of the New Deal.

In other words, what was the New Deal, what was it meant to achieve and did it achieve its aims?

What you should know

To be successful in this section you must be able to:

★ describe the main stages and reforms of the New Deal and explain why some groups were against the New Deal

★ explain how the New Deal was intended to help the US economy recover

★ describe some of the New Deal's successes and failures

★ reach a decision about how effective the New Deal was in solving the economic problems of the USA in the 1930s.

Context !

The economic depression that struck America in 1929 lasted well into the 1930s. The Republican government seemed unable to find any answers and in fact their laissez-faire attitude suggested that it was not their responsibility to find answers or to help directly the millions of people reduced to desperate poverty. In 1933 new hope arrived with the election of a new Democrat President, Franklin Delano Roosevelt, who promised, 'Action, and Action now!' and 'a New Deal for the American people'.

Key words

Alphabet Agencies – the nickname of the federal agencies set up to tackle the Depression. They were known by their initials hence Alphabet Agencies.

Federal – word used of the US government that has influence across the whole USA rather than just the governments of individual states.

Interventionism – the belief that governments should play a role in managing the economy. It is the opposite belief to laissez-faire.

Key people

FD Roosevelt – US President who won the 1932 election.

The following factors and linked knowledge points are all relevant and could be used in an answer on this issue, but remember to always link your information to the question asked.

The New Deal: aims

The New Deal is associated with Roosevelt and the Democrats who took a more **interventionist** approach to deal with the economy than the Republicans. The New Deal aimed to provide relief for the unemployed, aid recovery of the economy and reform to create a fairer society.

Confidence building

A number of confidence-building measures were introduced.

Banking was vital to the economy as banks used savers' money to invest in businesses and help them expand. The Emergency Banking Act in 1933 allowed the closing and checking of banks to ensure they were well run and credit worthy. Only 'sound' banks were allowed to reopen.

By end of 1933 many small banks had closed or were merged. Most depositors regained much of their money.

Roosevelt also began his 'fireside chats' – there were over 30 from March 1933. He declared that 'the only thing we have to fear is fear itself' and his 'fireside chats' on the radio did a great deal to help restore the nation's confidence.

The First New Deal, 1933–34

The main aims of New Deal were:
- Relief – short-term immediate help for those suffering in the Depression.

- Recovery – a longer-term plan to help the economy to recover from the Depression.
- Reform – to ensure such an economic disaster, resulting in such damage to the American people, did not happen again.

The First New Deal launched the '**Alphabet Agencies**' giving relief and recovery in the first 100 days of Roosevelt's presidency. The Federal Emergency Relief Administration (FERA), Tennessee Valley Authority (TVA) and Public Works Administration (PWA) provided relief and work.

The Economy Act sought to balance the budget and economic prudence was shown by cutting wages of state employees by 15 per cent and spending the savings on relief programmes.

The unpopular Prohibition was also ended to raise revenue, boost grain production (to make alcohol) and cheer people up!

The Second New Deal, 1935–37

The Second New Deal introduced reforms to improve living and working conditions for many Americans through Acts such as:

- National Labour Relations Act ('Wagner Act') (1935) – protected the rights of workers to collectively bargain with employers.
- Banking Act (1935) – established the Federal Bank Deposit Insurance Corporation that insured deposits up to $5000 and, later, $10,000.
- WPA (Works Progress Administration) (1935) – launched a programme of public works across America. By 1938 it provided employment for 3 million men and some women.
- Rural Electrification Act (1936) – provided loans to provide electricity to rural areas of America.
- Social Security Act (1935) – provided a state pension scheme for the old and for widows, as well as help for the disabled and poor children.

Power of the federal government

The New Deal increased the role of the **federal** government in American society and in particular the economy.

The government also played a role in strengthening the power of organised labour, and the government's role as regulator between business, labour and agriculture was confirmed by its increased intervention.

However, there were challenges to this in the Supreme Court and opposition from state governments, especially in the South. Employers' groups who formed the Liberty League opposed the New Deal.

Economic effects

There is a debate on the economic effects in terms of relief and recovery. They certainly helped in providing basic relief.

Roosevelt's first term in office saw one of the fastest periods of GDP growth in US history. However, a downturn in 1937–38 raised questions about just how successful the policies were.

Hints & tips

Don't get bogged down trying to remember all of the Alphabet Agencies and then describing what each one did. The question does not ask you to do that. What you should do is select some of the main Alphabet Agencies and, after describing what they did briefly, make sure to gain analysis marks by judging their effectiveness.

Hints & tips

In any question where you are asked to assess or judge how effective something was, you should always start by making clear what the aims were. In this case, identify what the aims of the New Deal were and then describe what the New Deal did. Then judge, or assess, if the actions were a success or not.

Although it never reached the heights of before the Depression, the New Deal did see a couple of positive results economically. Between 1933 and 1939 GDP increased by 60 per cent from $55 billion to $85 billion. The amount of consumer products bought rose by 40 per cent while private investment in industry increased by five times in just six years.

However, unemployment continued to be a problem, never running at less than 14 per cent of the working population.

The importance of rearmament in reducing unemployment and revitalising the American economy was considerable, particularly after the mini-slump of 1937.

For practice

7 How effective was the New Deal in solving America's problems in the 1930s? (22 marks)
8 To what extent did the New Deal solve the economic problems facing the USA in the 1930s? (22 marks)

An evaluation of the reasons for the development of the civil rights campaign, after 1945

Part 5 of 'USA, 1918–1968' asks you to evaluate the reasons for the development of the civil rights campaign, after 1945.

In other words, why did the civil rights movement grow after 1945 and in what ways did the campaigns attract new leaders and adopt new methods?

What you should know

To be successful in this section you must be able to:

★ explain why soldiers returning from the war were motivated to campaign for greater civil rights and describe how prejudice and discrimination continued in the years following the Second World War
★ describe events such as the Supreme Court decision of 1954, the **bus boycott** of 1955 and the murder of Emmet Till, and explain why those events inspired and motivated people to campaign for civil rights
★ describe how new organisations and new leaders emerged to continue the struggle for civil rights.

Hints & tips

Questions on this topic are not only about the triggers that existed in 1945 for a civil rights movement. The word 'development' means not only how and why it started but also how it grew and evolved into different campaigning methods with different targets and different leaders.

Context !

In 1945 the Second World War ended. Black American soldiers who had been fighting against racism and persecution overseas returned home to find those same problems facing them in their everyday lives. The end of the Second World War was a trigger for many black Americans who wanted 'no more Jim Crow' and the achievement of full civil rights.

Key words

Bus boycott – the black population of Montgomery, Alabama, refused to use buses for over a year. The bus company was forced to desegregate its buses. This event showed the economic power of the black population if they stuck together.

Double V campaign – returning soldiers from the Second World War wanted victory over the Nazis alongside victory over racism in the USA.

Key people

Elizabeth Eckford – the black girl who went to an all-white school in Little Rock, Arkansas, in 1957 and sparked off a major test for civil rights.

Martin Luther King – a young Baptist minister on his first job in Montgomery in 1955 found himself at the centre of the civil rights protest. King rapidly became the public face of the civil rights movement.

Rosa Parks – a member of NAACP who became famous when she refused to give up her seat on a bus and so sparked the Montgomery bus boycott.

W Philip Randolph – a civil rights leader during the Second World War who forced Roosevelt to improve conditions for black federal workers.

The following factors and linked knowledge points are all relevant and could be used in an answer on this issue, but remember to always link your information to the question asked.

Influence of Second World War

Black soldiers talked about 'the **double V campaign**' – victory in the war and victory for civil rights at home.

Several black airmen reported how much better they were treated in the German prisoner of war camps than they were back home in the USA. The irony of fighting against Nazi racism and discrimination was not lost on black Americans when they returned home.

Philip Randolph is credited with highlighting the problems faced by black Americans during the Second World War. He planned a march on Washington in 1941 to protest against racial discrimination.

Roosevelt's response was to issue the Executive Order 8802. It was signed by the President in June 1941 and banned racial discrimination in the national defence industry. It was the first time that the federal

Hints & tips ★

Be aware that a lot of the information you learn for this section is also useful for the next issue about the successes of the civil rights movement.

government tried to treat black and white workers equally and to prevent employment discrimination. Roosevelt also established the Fair Employment Practices Committee to investigate incidents of discrimination.

In 1942 the Congress of Racial Equality (CORE) was created. This marked the beginning of a mass movement for civil rights.

Inspirational and motivational events

The experience of war emphasised freedom, democracy and human rights, yet in the USA, the Jim Crow laws still existed and lynching went unpunished.

There were a number of inspirational and motivational events that convinced many people that the prejudice and discrimination faced by black Americans could not continue and that things had to change, including:

- the Emmet Till murder trial and its publicity
- Brown v Board of Education of Topeka in 1954
- the events at Little Rock Central High School 1957
- Rosa Parks and the Montgomery bus boycott in 1955.

The emergence of effective black leaders

Martin Luther King became an inspirational figure. He was linked to the SCLC (see below) and advocated peaceful, non-violent methods. He made effective use of the media, for example, when he gave his famous 'I have a dream' speech.

Malcolm X was also inspirational, but he was much more confrontational. He provided a voice for the Nation of Islam.

Stokely Carmichael preached 'black power' and rejected King's non-violent approach. He was a direct ideas descendant of Marcus Garvey.

All the leaders attracted media coverage, large followings and divided opinion across the USA.

Martin Luther King

The Black Panthers (see page 105) attracted attention but lost support by their confrontational tactics. Other leaders and organisations were largely eclipsed by the media focus on the main personalities.

Effective black organisations formed

In 1957 Martin Luther King and other black clergy formed the Southern Christian Leadership Conference (SCLC) to co-ordinate the work of civil rights groups. King urged African Americans to use peaceful methods.

In 1960 a group of black and white college students organised the Student Nonviolent Coordinating Committee (SNCC) to help the civil rights movement. They joined with young people from the SCLC, CORE and NAACP in staging sit-ins, boycotts, marches and freedom rides.

The combined efforts of the civil rights groups ended discrimination in many public places including restaurants, hotels and theatres.

> ### Hints & tips ⭐
> *In its simplest form this question is about why the civil rights movement really got going after 1945. The next section is about how successful the civil rights movement was.*

For practice ◎

9 How important was the emergence of effective organisations to the development of the civil rights campaigns after 1945? (22 marks)

10 To what extent was the emergence of effective black leaders important to the development of the civil rights campaign between 1945 and 1968? (22 marks)

An assessment of the effectiveness of the civil rights movement in meeting the needs of black Americans, up to 1968

Part 6 of 'USA, 1918–1968' asks you to assess the effectiveness of the civil rights movement in meeting the needs of black Americans, up to 1968.

In other words, what problems did black Americans face in 1968 and had the civil rights campaign done anything to make those problems any less serious?

What you should know 👍

To be successful in this section you must be able to:

★ describe and explain the methods and tactics of civil rights groups such as NAACP, SCLC, CORE and any others you find out about which are relevant for the civil rights struggle

★ describe the gains of the civil rights movement up until 1965

★ explain why black society, especially in the northern cities, felt that the civil rights movement had been almost irrelevant to their needs

★ describe the black radical movements and explain why those movements increased in popularity before 1968.

Context ❗

By 1965 it seemed to many white Americans that civil rights for black Americans had been achieved. An effective Civil Rights Act had been followed by the Voting Rights Act. Nevertheless, in 1964 and in the long hot summers that followed over the next four years, US cities erupted in race violence. The protests of the civil rights movement had been successful in removing discrimination and segregation in the South but how far had life really improved for all black Americans, especially in the northern cities, by 1968?

Key words

Black Panthers – an organisation set up in Oakland, California, which deliberately challenged the white media by carrying weapons and posing aggressively. On the other hand, the organisation set up breakfast clubs for black children and claimed to be defending black communities against white police bullies.

Black power – a protest movement that evolved through the 1960s which encouraged pride in being black and often rejected the idea of co-operation with white America.

Ghetto – an area of slum housing in a city populated by poor black Americans.

Kerner Commission – issued an important report in 1968 after the urban riots, which said, among other things, that US society was split into two: one black and one white.

The following factors and linked knowledge points are all relevant and could be used in an answer on this issue, but remember to always link your information to the question asked.

The aims of the civil rights movement

The aims were mainly pacifist and intended to bring civil rights and equality in law to all non-white Americans. The Black Radical Movement had more radical, segregationist aims.

Role of the NAACP

The NAACP were involved in Brown v Board of Education of Topeka in 1954 and in the Montgomery bus boycott in 1955.

Role of the Congress of Racial Equality (CORE)

CORE organised sit-ins during 1961 and the freedom rides. It helped organise a march on Washington and was instrumental in setting up Freedom Schools in Mississippi.

Role of SCLC and Martin Luther King

In 1955 Martin Luther King was in his first post as a Baptist minister in Montgomery, Alabama, when the bus boycott started. He was a natural speaker and leader and from there grew the Southern Christian Leadership Conference.

The method of protest the SCLC used was non-violent civil disobedience. Examples of such tactics are sit-ins, freedom rides and the marches, such as at Birmingham, Alabama, in 1963 and the Selma to Montgomery march in 1965. King was an inspirational speaker (for example, his 'I have a dream' speech in 1964). The use of the media by smart young black protestors made complex issues easily understandable to sympathetic northern audiences when they saw the violent reaction of southern policemen and politicians on TV.

Key people

Stokely Carmichael – a supporter of 'black power'. He used phrases such as 'black is beautiful' and inspired radical groups who did not want to be given civil rights. As American citizens, black radical leaders demanded that they should *take* their rights, with violence if necessary.

Malcolm X – a charismatic member of the Black Muslims, Malcom X supported separation of races and is famous for calling white people 'devils'. He later softened his approach to co-operation and some say he was assassinated for his change of heart.

Changes in federal policy

Between 1945 and 1965 US presidents became personally involved in the civil rights issue – not necessarily because they believed in the justice of the struggle but because of the damage the civil rights campaign was doing to America's image abroad. Truman used Executive Orders to make black appointments and order equality of treatment in the armed services. Kennedy signed the 1962 Executive Order which outlawed racial discrimination in public housing.

Eisenhower sent in army troops and National Guardsmen to protect nine African-American students enrolled in a Central High School. Kennedy sent troops to Oxford, Mississippi, to protect black student James Meredith.

Johnson's presidency saw the passing of the 1964 Civil Rights Act which banned racial discrimination in any public place and the 1965 Voting Rights Act, which helped over 250,000 black people to register to vote for the first time.

Social, economic and political changes

The Voting Rights Act made it easier for black Americans to register to vote, especially in the South. As a result more black politicians were elected. Black congressmen were not new. In black communities in the northern cities black politicians had been elected for some time, but the big change in the 1960s came in the South where black communities could now make their voices heard.

However, the Civil Rights Act and the Voting Rights Act were mostly irrelevant in the north. Segregation and discrimination had never been the main problem in the north. There, the main problems were unemployment, poor-quality housing and poverty. The problems faced in urban **ghettos** exploded into violent riots in Watts, Los Angeles, in 1964. When Martin Luther King headed north to try to help, he found his tactics of peaceful demonstration just would not work. King's methods and manners were seen as increasingly irrelevant.

Rise of black radical movements

By the mid-1960s another leader – Stokely Carmichael – was calling for **'black power'**. He urged black Americans to reject white society and take pride in their own culture and black identity. Meanwhile Malcolm X and the Nation of Islam also rejected co-operation with white society.

By 1968 young black Americans in the urban centres were increasingly attracted to the **Black Panthers**. Although they were involved in self-help projects in cities and they called themselves an organisation for the defence of black communities, the Black Panthers gained a reputation for violence and gun fights with police.

In 1968 President Johnston set up an investigation into urban riots called the **Kerner Commission**. The report from the commission caused shock waves across the USA. It reported that US society was divided into one white society and one black society – one rich and one poor. The commission also went on to say that the poverty and difficulties of the black community were accepted and even caused by the white community.

Hints & tips

When dealing with black radical groups such as the Black Panthers it might be helpful to remember the wording of the syllabus which uses the phrase 'resultant rise of black radical movements'. In other words, the point is that the radical groups only rose up because of the failure of the earlier civil rights movement to really improve lives in the cities.

Hints & tips

In 1968 the Kerner Commission issued its report. What it said about black and white society in 1968 is a gift to you to use in answering the question. The Kerner report said many things, but the most important was that black and white societies were separate and unequal. Those words could be used as your main argument in an essay.

For practice

11 How successful was the civil rights movement in meeting the needs of black Americans, up to 1968? (22 marks)
12 To what extent did the civil rights campaigns of the 1950s and 1960s result in significant improvements in the lives of black Americans? (22 marks)

Model answers to exam questions

This section will provide you with examples of answers to questions or parts of questions. As you know, in this exam paper you will have to write extended responses, sometimes called essays. Each essay must have parts to them and each section will gain marks.

These sections are:
- introduction* (3 marks)
- use of knowledge – you must include at least six different, relevant and accurate facts that lead into an analysis comment (6 marks)
- analysis* (6 marks)
- evaluation* (4 marks)
- conclusion* (3 marks).

Below you will find an example question with good examples of student answers to each of the four starred (*) sections of the extended response listed above.

The knowledge marks count is simply based on the number of relevant and accurate knowledge points you use in your essay.

The answers may not be on topics you want to revise but the rules are the same for all essays, so find out what things gain marks and also why marks are lost!

Hints & tips

You will see that factors to develop are vital in any essay introduction. They list the main headings you will write about in your essay. You can find the factors to develop for every single Higher essay you will ever do in the description of content box in the SQA syllabus for your chosen topic.

Example

Question

To what extent was fear of crime the main reason for changing attitudes towards immigration in the USA after 1918? (22 marks)

Introduction

Before the 1890s, America had an open-door policy which meant anyone could enter the country. Old immigrants, known as WASPs, came from northern and western Europe. But by the end of the nineteenth century new immigrants from poorer areas of Europe had arrived in the USA looking for a better life. **(context)**

Fear of crime was the main reason for changing attitudes towards immigration in the USA after 1918 to an extent, but there were other factors that need to be considered. **(line of argument)**

⇨

Other important factors include the changing attitudes that white Americans had towards immigrant groups, especially from southern Europe, as well as the impact of the First World War on American politics, the development of isolationism, fear of revolution, racism and economic fears. **(factors to develop)**

Why is this a good introduction?

This is an effective introduction and gets 3/3 because it has three sentences of context, a clear line of argument that addresses the question posed and has other factors to develop. You need to have all three of these things to gain 3 out of 3.

Analysis

Fear of crime was an important reason for changing attitudes towards immigrants because organised crime groups such as the Mafia had their roots in Sicily and most of the gang members were either immigrants themselves or the sons of immigrants. It seemed obvious that one way to stop the Mafia would be to stop Italian immigrants arriving in America.

Why is this a good example of an analysis comment?

It is good because after the fact it states 'this was important because' and then explains how the fact is important in answering the question.

If you write *three* examples of this sort of comment you will gain 3 analysis marks.

Analysis plus

However, this view of immigrants was a myth as the real causes of crime were the poor conditions and poverty many immigrants faced. Most of the crimes that immigrants were arrested for, such as drunkenness, vagrancy or petty theft, were crimes of poverty. However, the view that crime was caused by immigrants did not go away easily.

Why is this a good example of an analysis plus comment?

It is good because this states a limitation on the factor of fear of crime as a reason of changing attitudes towards immigration in the USA after 1918. It explains why this factor can be challenged.

If you write *three* examples of this sort of comment you will gain 3 more analysis marks.

Evaluation

Fear of crime was important in changing attitudes towards immigrants but it was not as important as fears about housing and jobs, as more and more immigrants arrived and threatened the homes and jobs of Americans living in the big cities.

Why is this a good evaluation point?

This is good because here the writer is judging the importance of one main factor against another and reaching a decision that is linked to the main question.

Do this sort of balanced judgement at least *four* times in your essay and you will get 4 evaluation marks, but *only* if your evaluative comments are clearly linked to the line of argument that you outlined in your introduction.

⇨
Conclusion

In conclusion, fear of crime was a reason for changing attitudes towards immigration in America as many Americans believed immigrants were behind criminal activity. However, it was not the main reason for changing attitudes. Economic fears were more important as they had an impact on Americans' jobs, which had serious consequences as people feared losing their jobs and homes. Other factors are also of great importance, such as the fear of revolution which led to the red scares. Overall, fear of crime was a reason for changing attitudes towards immigrants, but economic reasons and fear of revolution were more important as they affected people directly and fed their worries about the future.

Why is this a good conclusion?

This conclusion provides a direct answer to the question posed. It provides a relative judgement between factors that addresses the question. This judgement is supported with reasons. Other factors are also mentioned and judgements made on their importance. An overall conclusion is drawn at the end which directly answers the question. A good conclusion needs a judgement in terms of the question; judgement also needs to be made between factors and supported with reasons. All three elements are needed to get 3/3.

Chapter 7

Appeasement and the road to war, to 1939

An evaluation of the reasons for the aggressive nature of the foreign policies of Germany and Italy in the 1930s

Part 1 of 'Appeasement and the road to war, to 1939' asks you to evaluate the reasons for the **aggressive nature** of the foreign policies of Germany and Italy in the 1930s.

In other words, you will be asked why Germany and Italy were so warlike and prepared to use force against other countries in the 1930s.

What you should know 👍

To be successful in this section you must be able to:

★ explain what is meant by 'foreign policies' and describe what foreign policy aims Germany and Italy wanted to achieve by using aggression

★ explain how the basic beliefs of **Fascist** Italy and Nazi Germany were bound to lead to conflict with their neighbours and describe examples of aggressive acts by Germany and Italy

★ give reasons to explain why Germany and Italy were so warlike and then decide which of those reasons were the most important in explaining their actions.

Context ❗

Fascist belief was founded on the idea of national unity and in the cases of Italy and Germany it was also **expansionist** in outlook. Mussolini looked to create a new Roman Empire while Hitler sought living space for the 'excess' German population. A number of factors led to this. British appeasement to an extent encouraged both Germany and Italy to increase their demands and to use force or the threat of force in getting what they wanted.

The following factors and linked knowledge points are all relevant and could be used in an answer on this issue, but remember to always link your information to the question being asked.

Key words

Aggressive nature – in this case a country that is prepared to use war to get what it wants.

Expansionist – both Germany and Italy wanted to take over land that was not theirs to take. They wanted to expand, or spread, their power over other countries.

Fascism – a political ideology that grew up in the 1920s and 1930s. Fascist states were usually dictatorships with total control in the hands of one leader. Fascist states wanted to expand their territory and that led to conflict. Mussolini looked to create a new Roman Empire while Hitler sought living space for the 'excess' German population.

Foreign policy – how one country decides it will behave in relation to its neighbours.

Lebensraum – Germany used this phrase to mean territory they wanted in eastern Europe and Russia. Literally it means 'living space'.

Economic difficulties after 1929

The impact of the world economic crisis 1929–32 on the German and Italian economies made those countries look abroad for resources and markets. This led to aggressive, expansionist foreign policies, for example, Italy in Abyssinia, Germany and **Lebensraum** (living space).

The Peace Settlement of 1919

Both Germany and Italy were determined to revise or overturn the Paris Peace Settlement. Germany resented war guilt, reparations, disarmament and lost territory and also wanted revenge for defeat in the First World War. Italy resented the failure to gain promised territory from the old Austro-Hungarian Empire.

Fascist ideology

Fascist states hated both communism and democracy. They were also militaristic and glorified war.

In the cases of Germany and Italy, their foreign policies were also driven by Hitler's and Mussolini's own beliefs, personalities and charismatic leadership.

Mussolini had 'Roman' ambitions in the Mediterranean – he wanted to rebuild a new Roman Empire. Hitler's ambitions lay in eastern Europe and Russia. The living space that Hitler wanted was new land for Germans, along with the resources, such as Russia's cereal crops and oil. To achieve this, Hitler's **foreign policy** revived the idea of 'Drang nach Osten', meaning the 'move to the east', which was a very old German ambition stretching back to the Middle Ages.

Weakness of the League of Nations

There was very little done to stop fascist expansionism.

The failure of the League over Japanese aggression in Manchuria in 1931, the divided response of other powers (for example, British appeasement, US isolationism and the relative weakness of new countries in eastern Europe) all encouraged Germany and Italy to 'push their luck'.

The British policy of appeasement

British attempts to appease Mussolini over Abyssinia resulted in the Hoare-Laval Plan which produced a popular outcry when the terms were leaked. The plan never happened, but Mussolini saw that Britain and France were not opposed in principle to gains for Italy in East Africa and he was able to defy League pressure and keep Abyssinia.

Hitler knew of British reservations about some terms of the Versailles Treaty and was able to play on these, increasingly realising that he would not be stopped. British acceptance of rearmament, the reoccupation of the Rhineland and then *Anschluss* (the takeover of Austria) convinced Hitler that he had nothing to fear from Britain.

Key people

Adolf Hitler – leader of the Nazi Party and dictator of Germany from 1933.

Benito Mussolini – leader of the Fascist Party and dictator of Italy from 1925.

Joseph Stalin – the leader of Communist Russia.

Haile Selassie – the leader of Abyssinia.

Sir Samuel Hoare – British Foreign Secretary responsible for part of the Hoare-Laval Plan.

Pierre Laval – French Foreign Minister also involved in the Hoare-Laval Plan to appease Mussolini and abandon Abyssinia and its leader Haile Selassie.

Hints & tips

In questions on the most important reason for aggression, there is not one answer that is correct and all the others are wrong. What you must do in your answer is include the different reasons for being aggressive and then prioritise them, giving reasons to support your decision about which were the most important and which were less so.

For practice

1 To what extent does disappointment over the terms of the Peace Settlement of 1919 explain the aggressive nature of fascist foreign policies in the 1930s? (22 marks)
2 'The weakness of the League of Nations was directly responsible for encouraging the aggressive foreign policies of Germany and Italy in the 1930s.' How valid is this view? (22 marks)

Hints & tips

If a question asks about Germany and Italy be sure that you give examples for each country. You will lose marks if your answer only mentions Germany.

An evaluation of the methods used by Germany and Italy to pursue their foreign policies from 1933

Part 2 of 'Appeasement and the road to war, to 1939' asks you to assess the methods used by Germany and Italy to pursue their foreign policies from 1933.

In other words, what did Germany and Italy do after 1933 to make sure they got what they wanted from other countries? You will then be expected to make a judgement about how successful these methods were.

What you should know

To be successful in this section you must be able to:

★ describe examples of peaceful diplomatic tactics used by Germany and Italy to achieve their foreign policy aims after 1933 and explain what benefits Germany and Italy got from the different methods they used

★ describe examples of Germany and Italy using military threats or more direct examples of bullying. Two examples could be German pressure on Austria in early 1938 and Italian aggression in Abyssinia

★ make a decision supported by reasons about which of the methods used by Germany and Italy were most successful.

Context

Hitler's and Mussolini's foreign policies were expansionist in nature. However, the methods used to fulfil their aims varied owing to the circumstances faced by the fascist powers. At times diplomacy and agreements were used; at other times the fascist powers preferred to use military threats, bluffs and force to achieve their targets.

Key words

Alliance – a promise to support another country if a conflict broke out.

Anglo – in treaties this word means British.

Anti-Comintern Pact – an anticommunist agreement between Germany, Italy and Japan.

Condor Legion – the name of the German airforce sent to fight in Spain during the Civil War.

Diplomacy – countries trying to gain advantages over other countries peacefully by using discussions and agreements.

Disarmament – reducing the number of weapons owned by a country. Disarmament was a hope of the League of Nations because if countries were disarmed then war would be less likely.

Mare Nostrum – an Italian phrase for the Mediterranean Sea. Literally it means 'our sea'.

Non-aggression pact – a promise between countries not to fight each other.

Pact – an agreement or promise of help between countries.

Rearmament – building new weapons and recruiting more soldiers.

The following factors and linked knowledge points are all relevant and could be used in an answer on this issue, but remember to always link your information to the question being asked.

Fascist strategies: use of military threat and force

For example:

- Italy's naval ambitions in the Mediterranean – '**Mare Nostrum**'.
- Italian invasion of Abyssinia – provocation, methods, and relatively poor performance against very poorly equipped enemy.
- German remilitarisation of Rhineland – Hitler's gamble and timing, his generals' opposition, lack of Allied resistance.
- Spanish Civil War – aid to the Nationalists, testing weapons and tactics, bombing of Guernica by **Condor Legion** (German airforce).
- *Anschluss* – attempted takeover in 1934, but in 1938 the takeover of Austria was popular with most Austrians.
- The extent to which it was the threat of military force which was used, rather than the force itself, and the extent to which military force itself was more of a bluff, such as in 1936 in the Rhineland.

German rearmament

German **rearmament** from 1935 was openly publicised and exaggerated. The speed and scale of rearmament, including conscription, worried Britain. The emphasis was on air power and the growing threat from the sky.

By 1939, Hitler had an army of nearly 1 million men, over 8000 aircraft and 95 warships.

Hints & tips ★

Remember to include both Germany and Italy in your answer, and another way of making sure you answer the question properly is to split your answer on methods into peaceful and non-peaceful. By doing that you are meeting the demands of the question.

Germany's military strength may have had an effect on other countries. Britain, for example, feared air bombing especially after the destruction of Guernica, Spain, by the German Condor Legion.

The bombing of Guernica

Military agreements, pacts and alliances

- The German–Polish **Non-Aggression Pact** between Nazi Germany and Poland signed on 26 January 1934 promised peace for ten years. Germany gained respectability and it calmed international fears.
- The Rome–Berlin Axis was a treaty of friendship signed between Italy and Germany on 25 October 1936.
- The **Anti-Comintern Pact** between Nazi Germany and Japan on 25 November 1936 was directed against the Communist International (Comintern) but was specifically directed against the Soviet Union. In 1937 Italy joined the **pact**.
- Negotiations at the Munich Agreement led to Hitler gaining Sudetenland and weakening Czechoslovakia.
- Both Hitler and Stalin bought time for themselves with the Nazi–Soviet Non-Aggression Pact in August 1939. For Hitler it seemed war in Europe over Poland was unlikely – Poland was doomed. Britain had lost the possibility of an **alliance** with Russia.

Fascist diplomacy as a means of achieving aims

- Fascist aims can be generally accepted as the destruction of the Versailles Treaty, the weakening of democracies, the expansion of fascist powers and countering communism.
- **Diplomacy** and the use of excuses and justifications such as 'peaceful' intentions and 'reasonable' demands always made Britain think twice before taking any action against Hitler.
- Fascist powers appealed to a sense of international equality and fairness and the righting of past wrongs, for example, Versailles.
- Withdrawal from League and **Disarmament** Conference.
- The **Anglo-**German Naval Agreement (1935) allowed Germany to expand its navy. Versailles was ignored and it was a gain for Germany.
- Prior to the remilitarisation of Rhineland, Hitler made an offer of a 25-year peace promise. Diplomacy was used to distract and delay reaction to Nazi action.

Fascist strategies: economic

Aid supplied to Franco (Spain) was tactically important to Hitler, not only for testing weapons, but also for access to Spanish minerals.

For practice

3 To what extent did fascist governments use military threat and force in pursuing their foreign policies from 1933? (22 marks)
4 To what extent did fascist powers use diplomacy to achieve their aims? (22 marks)

An evaluation of the reasons for the British policy of appeasement, 1936–38

Part 3 of 'Appeasement and the road to war, to 1939' asks you to evaluate the reasons for the British policy of appeasement, 1936–38.

In other words, why did Britain appease Germany between 1936 and 1938, and which of those reasons were most important?

What you should know

To be successful in this section you must be able to:

★ explain what appeasement meant and describe what events in the early and mid-1930s caused Britain to see appeasement as a good option
★ describe events between 1936 and 1938 which show Britain appeasing Germany
★ describe the different reasons for supporting appeasement and decide which of those reasons were more important than the others. Give reasons to support your decision.

Context

In the 1920s the British public felt that there would never be another world war because the First World War was 'the war to end all wars'. The public was reassured that Germany was weakened, all countries would be peace-loving democracies and the League of Nations would prevent any aggression.

By the mid-1930s those assumptions had been proven wrong. Germany was rearming, the League had failed and fascism was spreading. As fears of conflict and instability increased, it looked as if appeasement was the only means of securing British interests and avoiding conflict.

The following factors and linked knowledge points are all relevant and could be used in an answer on this issue, but remember to always link your information to the question being asked.

Economic difficulties

The 1929–32 economic crisis and depression led to economic difficulties.

Britain was unwilling to damage chances of international trade and commerce by taking action against Italy or Germany.

Britain was financially very weak after the First World War and even by the 1930s Britain could not afford any large-scale rearmament.

Attitudes to the Paris Peace Settlement

By the 1930s the Treaty of Versailles was seen as too harsh on Germany and there was sympathy for what were seen as Germany's genuine grievances. As a result, Britain was reluctant to enforce the exact terms of the treaty and preferred making revisions or changes to the treaty.

Public opinion and pacifism

- There was a public anti-war feeling and a fear of a repeat of the First World War. There was also the worry that a future war would result in gas bombing of British cities.
- There were isolationist feelings, summed up in Chamberlain's pre-Munich speech – why should we risk war for 'a faraway people about whom we know nothing'?
- In 1936 a movie called *Things To Come* was released which predicted a war in 1940 that would destroy the world.
- At Oxford University a debate ended in victory for those against fighting for 'King and Country'.
- In 1936, 11 million people signed a petition against war organised by the Peace Pledge Union. This showed that **pacifism** was strong in Britain. Any government that spoke about rearming and preparing for war risked losing votes.
- In Fulham, London, a by-election showed the strength of anti-war feeling when the appeasement supporting candidate won.

Concern over the Empire

The **Empire** was thought to be crucial to British economic well-being and to her status as a great power.

Heads of the British army and navy believed Britain could not defend the Empire against a 'three front war' in northern Europe, the Mediterranean and the Far East.

In 1937 South Africa told the UK that if Britain got involved in a European war then South Africa would not help. The British government was worried about the Empire breaking up which would leave Britain without the resources of the Empire which had been vital for survival in the First World War.

Key words

Communism – the ideology that had led to the Russian Revolution. In the 1930s Russia was communist and Britain and France were terrified of communism spreading across Europe.

Empire – in the 1930s the British Empire was huge and was the main reason why Britain was a superpower. The need to protect the Empire was Britain's top priority.

Isolationism – the policy of the USA was to avoid any involvement with European problems. Isolationism was the name of USA foreign policy until Japan attacked Pearl Harbor in December 1941.

Pacifism – a refusal to go to war for any reason. Millions of Britons were pacifists in the 1930s.

Lack of reliable allies

- Failure of the League in Manchuria and Abyssinia.
- France was politically divided and unlikely to take strong action.
- US **isolationism** – as Prime Minister Chamberlain wrote in a letter to his sister, 'We can expect nothing but words from America.'
- Italy was drifting towards friendship with Germany by 1936.

Military weakness

Following the First World War the British armed forces were in a run-down state. In 1919 the UK had 120,000 military aircraft – by 1920 it had been reduced to 120.

Conscription to the army ended after the First World War when the army was scaled right down in size.

The navy was not reduced but it was not fully maintained. There were many obsolete ships.

There was a lack of adequate air defences and fear of aerial bombing.

There were multiple threats from other countries – Japan in the east, Italy in the Mediterranean and North Africa, and Germany in central Europe.

There were also exaggerated assessments of German military strength.

Fear of spread of communism

The British government was very suspicious of Soviet Russia. Nazi Germany was seen as a block against communist expansion and there was a common phrase at the time, 'Better Hitlerism than **communism**.'

Beliefs of Chamberlain

Chamberlain took personal control of foreign policy. He believed that problems could be solved rationally, by negotiation.

Chamberlain was also a realist. He understood that Hitler could not be 'wished away' so the best deal possible for Britain would have to be made.

Czechoslovakia, and in fact most of central Europe, was not a vital British interest. Why get involved in a conflict that was not British?

Hints & tips

A question in this section might include the phrase, 'British foreign policy'. All you need to know is that another word for British foreign policy at this time was appeasement.

Hints & tips

In this section and most of the sections that follow, you do not need to worry about including Italy as Italy does not feature again in the story of appeasement, apart from a small part of section 4. You only need to write about Germany and Italy when you are directly asked about the fascist powers – and that is only likely in parts 1 and 2 and a bit of part 4.

For practice

5 To what extent does British public opinion explain the policy of appeasement between 1936 and 1938? (22 marks)

6 'Britain was scared of communism and too weak to fight. Appeasement was the only choice.' How valid is this view? (22 marks)

An assessment of the success of British foreign policy in containing fascist aggression, 1935 to March 1938

Part 4 of 'Appeasement and the road to war, to 1939' asks you to make an assessment of the success of British foreign policy in containing fascist aggression, 1935 to March 1938.

In other words, what did the fascist powers do between 1935 and March 1938 and how successful was the British policy of appeasement in preventing the actions of the fascist powers leading to a serious European war?

What you should know 👍

To be successful in this section you must be able to:

★ describe the aggressive actions of Germany and Italy between 1935 and March 1938 and explain why these incidents could have led to a major European war
★ describe what Britain did to contain the aggression of Germany and Italy and to maintain peace
★ reach a judgement on whether or not British policy was successful. To do that you must be clear what the aim of the appeasement policy was.

Context ❗

In the 1930s Britain was not prepared for war. The main aim of British foreign policy was keeping the peace in Europe and avoiding any situation that might drag Britain into a war in Europe. Between 1935 and March 1938 Britain achieved its aim. Conflicts that did occur (Abyssinia, Spain) were on the edge of Europe/the Mediterranean and could be presented to the public as 'not a British interest'.

The following factors and linked knowledge points are all relevant and could be used in an answer on this issue, but remember to always link your information to the question being asked.

Relations with Italy

Mussolini's plans for a new Roman Empire in the Mediterranean Sea and Abyssinia worried the British government who hoped to turn Mussolini into an ally.

The secret **Hoare-Laval Plan** sickened the public who had hoped for clear support for League principles of justice from Britain. The huge public outcry against the secret British–French plotting to reward Italy and betray Abyssinia led to Hoare's resignation as British Foreign Secretary.

Key words

Anschluss – linking Germany with Austria. Banned at Versailles but accepted by Britain as inevitable in March 1938. After *Anschluss*, Czechoslovakia was Hitler's next easy target.

Hoare-Laval Plan – the name of a secret plan by Britain and France to appease Italy by allowing it to take much of Abyssinia in exchange for ending the war.

Non-intervention – the policy agreed by most European powers not to get involved in helping either side in the Spanish Civil War. The agreement was broken by Germany, Italy and Russia.

Hints & tips ⭐

*This issue asks about 'containing' fascism. That means you will be asked about Britain's attempts to limit the spread of fascism – it does **not** mean to stop fascism or defeat it.*

Limited sanctions were imposed on Italy which alienated Mussolini, thereby driving him closer to Hitler, yet failed to save Abyssinia.

Relations with Germany

Hitler was successful in rearming and reintroducing conscription. The growth of the Luftwaffe (the German airforce) was a serious worry for Britain.

The Anglo-German Naval Agreement in 1935 successfully limited German naval strength to 35 per cent of British strength. Britain believed this contained German military expansion.

Hitler was successful in remilitarising the Rhineland. This was more as a result of bluff, clever timing and French/British weakness than German military strength.

In 1938 Austria was successfully annexed (**Anschluss**). This was another fait accompli (a done deal) and Britain could have done little to prevent it.

The Spanish Civil War

Britain's main aim was to prevent the civil war within Spain from becoming an international war.

Britain supported a policy of **non-intervention**. The non-intervention agreement was openly broken by Germany and Italy, and to a lesser extent the Soviet Union.

The Spanish Civil War did not spread and Britain remained on good terms with the fascists despite clear evidence of German bombers destroying the Spanish town of Guernica. This was a demonstration of the power of bombers and what they could do in a future war.

Anschluss

In 1934 *Anschluss* had failed because of Italian opposition. By 1938 British policy over Abyssinia and in Spain had driven Mussolini into the arms of Hitler. As a result *Anschluss* was achieved easily in March 1938.

Although Austria was invaded by German troops, there was no resistance in Austria, and Austrians mainly welcomed *Anschluss*. Britain was powerless to act and *Anschluss* gave Hitler a huge strategic advantage in eastern Europe.

For practice

7 'British foreign policy was a complete failure in containing the spread of fascist aggression up to March 1938.' How valid is this view? (22 marks)

8 To what extent was public opinion the reason why Britain adopted the policy of appeasement in the 1930s? (22 marks)

Hints & tips

In any question that asks you to judge the success of something you must be clear what the actions were meant to do and how success would be judged.

Your main argument should be that if the aim of appeasement was to protect countries against German or Italian attack then it was a failure. However, if the aim of appeasement was to prevent local wars becoming big wars and if it meant supporting British interests and not getting involved in conflicts, then it was certainly a success.

Hints & tips

In answering questions on fascism always use examples from Germany **and** Italy. The Italian example to use is the attack on Abyssinia and you should use the Hoare-Laval Plan as evidence of British and French self-interest in an attempt to contain the Abyssinian War and keep Mussolini as a friend rather than an enemy.

Hints & tips

Do **not** go on to write about Czechoslovakia. This part of the course only goes up to March 1938, before the Czechoslovakian crisis.

Hints & tips ⭐

Abyssinia, German rearmament, the Anglo-German naval treaty, the remilitarisation of the Rhineland, intervention in the Spanish Civil War and Anschluss are all part of this section. Be prepared to include all of these in your answer.

An assessment of the Munich agreement

The signing of the Munich Agreement

Part 5 of 'Appeasement and the road to war, to 1939' asks you to make an assessment of the Munich agreement.

In other words, do you think that the agreement reached at Munich about the future of **Czechoslovakia** was good or bad? Also, what do you think of the private agreement between Hitler and Chamberlain?

What you should know 👍

To be successful in this section you must be able to:

★ describe how the Sudetenland became the centre of a crisis in September 1938

★ describe the reasons and outcome of the three visits of Chamberlain to Hitler at **Bad Godesberg and Berchtesgaden** in September 1938

★ explain why Britain was on the brink of war when Chamberlain flew to meet Hitler at Munich and describe what was agreed at the Munich meeting in late September 1938

★ give several reasons in favour of the Munich Agreement and several why the Munich Agreement is criticised as a disgraceful betrayal of Czechoslovakia.

Context ❗

Hitler's long-term aim was *Lebensraum* in Russia, but before he could achieve that he had to complete his control of several 'stepping stone' countries between Germany and Russia. After *Anschluss*, it was obvious that Hitler's next target was Czechoslovakia. Hitler's excuse for pressurising Czechoslovakia was the Sudetenland – territory on the borderlands within Czechoslovakia that was home to 3 million German-speakers. The Munich Agreement was controversial because those who supported appeasement believed the agreement prevented a war from breaking out and those who were against appeasement believed that Britain betrayed Czechoslovakia.

The following factors and linked knowledge points are all relevant and could be used in an answer on this issue, but always remember to link your information to the question being asked.

Key words

Berchtesgaden and Bad Godesberg – the two places where Chamberlain met Hitler in the fortnight before the third meeting at Munich.

Czechoslovakia – a country created in 1919 by the Paris Peace Treaties out of parts of the Austro-Hungarian Empire. It did *not* contain any ex-German territory.

Sudetenland – an area of Czechoslovakia containing 3 million German-speaking people.

Arguments in favour of the Munich Agreement

To argue that the Munich Agreement was reasonable under the circumstances you could use the following information:

- Czechoslovakian defences were effectively outflanked anyway following *Anschluss*.
- Britain and France were not in a position to prevent a German attack on Czechoslovakia in terms of the difficulties of getting assistance to Czechoslovakia.
- British public opinion was reluctant to risk war over mainly German-speaking **Sudetenland**.
- Britain was not prepared for war, especially its air defences.
- Munich bought another year for rearmament which Britain put to good use.
- There was a lack of an alternative, unified international response to Hitler's threats:
  - Failure of the League of Nations in earlier crises.
  - The French had an alliance with Czechoslovakia. The treaty had been signed in the mid-1920s when the French expected the Czechs to help protect France. Now the French were uneasy about doing anything to help Czechoslovakia.
  - US isolationism.
  - British suspicion of Soviet Russia.
  - It was quite possible that countries in the British Empire would not support Britain in a war over Czechoslovakia.
  - Poland and Hungary were quite happy with cutting up of Czechoslovakia as they would gain some land for themselves.

Arguments against the Munich Agreement

To argue that the Munich Agreement was not fair or reasonable you could use the following information:

- It was a humiliating surrender to Hitler's threats.
- It was another breach in the post First World War settlement.
- It was a betrayal of Czechoslovakia and democracy.
- It left Czechoslovakia wide open to further German aggression as happened in March 1939.
- It allowed Hitler to gain more resources and more manpower from the population absorbed into the Reich.
- The deal further increased Hitler's influence and ambitions in eastern Europe.
- Poland was left even more under threat.
- A British–French–Soviet agreement could have been a more effective alternative but those hopes were destroyed by the Munich Agreement. The Soviet Union (Russia) became even more suspicious of Britain and would be very unlikely to help Britain in any action against Germany.

Key people

Neville Chamberlain – the British Prime Minister who flew to meet Hitler three times inside two weeks.
Joseph Stalin – the leader of Russia, not invited to the Munich meeting.
Edvard Beneš – the Czech leader, not invited to the Munich meeting.

Hints & tips

Beware that you do not claim that people in the Sudetenland were German. They were not. They were German-speakers but the Sudetenland had never been part of Germany. In 1919 Czechoslovakia, including the Sudetenland, was created from land taken from Austria–Hungary.

Hints & tips

This question will **always** ask you to consider both sides of the Munich Agreement so be prepared to provide detailed reasons to support the conflicting opinions about the settlement.

9 'Munich was a triumph for British foreign policy.' How valid is this view? (22 marks)

10 To what extent was the Munich Agreement of 1938 a success for British foreign policy? (22 marks)

An evaluation of the reasons for the outbreak of war in 1939

Part 6 of 'Appeasement and the road to war, to 1939' asks you to evaluate the reasons for the outbreak of war in 1939.

In other words, why did war break out in September 1939?

What you should know 👍

To be successful in this section you must be able to:

★ give several reasons why appeasement was abandoned and make a decision about which reasons you think were the most important

★ describe the events of March 1939 that led Britain to change its policy and promise to support Poland and Rumania

★ describe the events that led to Britain declaring war on Germany in September 1939 and explain the importance of the **Nazi–Soviet Pact**

★ judge (or evaluate) which were the most important reasons in causing Britain to declare war on Germany.

Context ❗

In March 1939 Hitler broke the Munich Agreement and Czechoslovakia collapsed as an independent country. The eastern parts of Czechoslovakia, called **Bohemia and Moravia**, were occupied by Nazi forces, while **Slovakia**, the western part, remained self-governing but under Nazi influence. The British government and public accepted that all attempts to maintain peace had been exhausted. Prime Minister Chamberlain felt betrayed by the Nazi seizure of Czechoslovakia, realised his policy of appeasement towards Hitler had failed, and began to take a much harder line against the Nazis. Britain promised support to Hitler's next two likely targets – Poland and Rumania.

Key words

Bohemia and Moravia – the western part of Czechoslovakia left after the Sudetenland was taken away. These two areas were occupied by Nazi soldiers in March 1939.

Maginot Line – in the 1920s France built a huge line of fortifications along the French–German border. It was called the Maginot Line.

Nazi–Soviet Pact – of August 1939 is sometimes called the Molotov/Ribbentrop Agreement after the Russian and Nazi foreign ministers who signed the deal.

Polish Corridor – a strip of land that divided East Prussia from the rest of Germany. At the Versailles Treaty the land had been given to Poland to allow that country access to a sea port, Danzig.

Slovakia – the eastern part of Czechoslovakia left as a self-governing area under Nazi influence after March 1939.

The following factors and linked knowledge points are all relevant and could be used in an answer on this issue, but remember to always link your information to the question.

Changing British attitudes towards appeasement

Even during the Munich crisis there was evidence of growing opposition to appeasement with demonstrations against the policy in places such as London. Anti-appeasers like Churchill were joined by the leader of the Labour Party, Clement Attlee, in criticism of the agreement and policy of appeasement.

Occupation of Bohemia and the collapse of Czechoslovakia

The Germans occupied the Slav Czech province of Bohemia and Moravia in March 1939. The previous German justification for expansion, that they were saving fellow Germans, was shown to be a lie. The inhabitants of Bohemia and Moravia were not ethnic Germans.

British diplomacy and relations with the Soviet Union

Stalin knew that Hitler's ultimate aim was to attack Russia. Lord Halifax, the British Foreign Secretary, was invited by Stalin to go to Russia to discuss an alliance against Germany. Britain refused as they feared Russian communism, and they believed that the Russian army was too weak to be of any use against Hitler.

In August 1939, with war in Poland looming, the British and French eventually sent a military mission to discuss an alliance with Russia. Owing to travel difficulties it took five days to reach Leningrad.

The Russians asked if they could send troops into Poland if Hitler invaded. The British refused, knowing that the Poles would not want this. The talks broke down. Britain had hoped they could eventually do a deal with Russia to protect Poland but Britain was unwilling to make friends with communist Russia so the chance of an anti-Nazi alliance slipped away.

This merely confirmed Stalin's suspicions regarding the British. He felt they could not be trusted, especially after the Munich Agreement, and they would leave Russia to fight Germany alone. This led directly to opening talks with the Nazis who seemed to be taking the Russians seriously by sending the Foreign Minister von Ribbentrop and offering peace and land.

Importance of the Nazi–Soviet Pact

In August 1939 the world was shocked by the Nazi–Soviet Pact. It was an example of realpolitik – neither side liked the other but an agreement was useful to both for the immediate short term.

Key people

Vyacheslav Molotov – the Russian foreign minister who arranged the non-aggression treaty with Germany. Later, his name was given to a petrol bomb – the Molotov Cocktail.

Hitler was freed from the threat of Soviet intervention when Germany invaded Poland.

Hitler still had his long-term aim for the destruction of the Soviet state and conquest of Russian resources, *Lebensraum*.

Hitler believed that the British and French were 'worms' who would not turn from their previous policy of appeasement and avoidance of war at all costs. Hitler had no reason to believe that Britain and France would go to war over Poland without Russian assistance.

The position of France

Hitler could all but guarantee that in 1938 the French would do nothing as their foreign policy was closely tied to the British.

French military planning was locked in a **Maginot** mentality of hiding in their fortified defences and they were unable to take rapid action where necessary in eastern Europe.

The French military, and particularly their airforce, were allowed to decline in the years after 1919.

Developing crisis over Poland

Hitler's long-term aims for the destruction of Versailles, including the regaining of Danzig and the **Polish Corridor**, reached a peak in 1939. The British and French decision to stick to their guarantees to Poland made war inevitable.

Invasion of Poland

On 1 September 1939, Hitler and the Nazis faked a Polish attack on a minor German radio station in order to justify a German invasion of Poland. An hour later Hitler declared war on Poland.

France and Britain had a defensive pact with Poland. This forced France and Britain to declare war on Germany, which they did on 3 September 1939.

For practice ◉

11 To what extent was the outbreak of war in September 1939 brought about by the failure of British diplomacy and relations with the Soviet Union? (22 marks)
12 'The Nazi–Soviet Pact of August 1939 made the Second World War inevitable.' How valid is this view? (22 marks)

Model answers to exam questions

This section will provide you with examples of answers to questions or parts of questions. As you know, in this exam paper you will have to write extended responses, sometimes called essays. Each essay must have parts to them and each section will gain marks.

These sections are:

- introduction* (3 marks)
- use of knowledge – you must include at least six different, relevant and accurate facts that lead into an analysis comment (6 marks)
- analysis* (6 marks)
- evaluation* (4 marks)
- conclusion* (3 marks).

Below you will find an example question with good examples of student answers to each of the four starred (*) sections of the extended response listed above.

The knowledge marks count is simply based on the number of relevant and accurate knowledge points you use in your essay.

The answers may not be on topics you want to revise but the rules are the same for all essays, so find out what things gain marks and also why marks are lost!

Hints & tips

You will see that factors to develop are vital in any essay introduction. They list the main headings you will write about in your essay. You can find the factors to develop for every single Higher essay you will ever do in the description of content box in the SQA syllabus for your chosen topic.

Example

Question

How important was changing public opinion as a reason for Britain adopting the policy of appeasement in the 1930s? (22 marks)

Introduction

The First World War was meant to be the war to end all wars. However, by the mid-1930s the League of Nations had failed and the fascist powers of Germany and Italy were rearming and acting aggressively. (**context**)

Public opinion was certainly an important reason for the adoption of appeasement by the British government, but there were many other factors. (**line of argument**)

Other factors that need to be considered include the fact that Britain had disarmed and was militarily unprepared for war, the lack of support from key allies in the Empire and the feeling that communism was more of a threat to world peace than fascism. (**factors to develop**)

Why is this a good introduction?

This is an effective introduction and gets 3/3 because it has two sentences of context, a clear line of argument that addresses the question posed and has other factors to develop. You need to have all three of these things to gain 3 out of 3.

Analysis

A main reason for supporting appeasement was the fear that enemy bombers could destroy cities and kill women and children. This was an important reason for adopting appeasement because a future war would put civilians in British cities at risk of bombing attack for the first time ever.

$\Rightarrow$

⇨
Why is this a good example of an analysis comment?

It is good because after the fact it states 'this was important because' and then explains how the fact is relevant to answering the question.

If you write *three* examples of this sort of comment you will gain 3 analysis marks.

Analysis plus

However, this risk was overstated and based on concentrated bombing of targets such as Guernica in the Spanish Civil War. Britain was developing radar detection systems from 1935 and advanced fighter aircraft such as the Spitfire to deal with bombing. However, this was a real, if exaggerated, fear.

Why is this a good example of an analysis plus comment?

It is good because this states a limitation on the factor of fear of bombing as a reason for the development of the policy of appeasement in the 1930s. It explains why this factor can be challenged.

If you write *three* examples of this sort of comment you will gain 3 more analysis marks.

Evaluation

There were many reasons why the British government supported appeasement in the late 1930s. Fear and self-interest were important as was the genuine desire to remove any legitimate grievances that Germany had, but perhaps the most important reason was the impossibility of taking a different course of action. Lack of money, the weak economy and the possibility of losing Empire support gave the British government no option but to appease in the hope of avoiding war.

Why is this a good evaluation point?

This is good because here the writer is judging the importance of one main factor against another and reaching a decision that is linked to the main question.

Do this sort of balanced judgement at least *four* times in your essay and you will get 4 evaluation marks but *only* if your evaluation comments are clearly linked to the line of argument that you outlined in your introduction.

Conclusion

In conclusion, public opinion was the most important reason for the British decision to appease the fascist powers, as Britain was a democracy and public opinion mattered, as anti-appeaser politicians found out. People feared war; however, politicians also feared that Britain would fight a future war alone as France was politically unstable and the Empire was not supportive of war, though this was less important than public opinion and it merely reinforced British attitudes. Also, Britain was militarily weak, though this can be linked to public opinion as a large military was not popular in the early 1930s.

Therefore, overall public opinion was the most important reason as it influenced how many of Britain's politicians acted in the inter-war years.

Why is this a good conclusion?

This conclusion provides a direct answer to the question posed. It provides a relative judgement between factors that addresses the question. This judgement is supported with reasons. Other factors are also mentioned and judgements made on their importance. An overall conclusion is drawn at the end which directly answers the question. A good conclusion needs a judgement in terms of the question; judgement also needs to be made between factors and supported with reasons. All three elements are needed to get 3/3.

Chapter 8

The Cold War, 1945–1989

An evaluation of the reasons for the emergence of the Cold War, up to 1955

Part 1 of 'The Cold War, 1945–1989' asks you to evaluate the reasons for the emergence of the Cold War, up to 1955.

In other words, this means you have to explain why the Cold War broke out between the USA and its allies on one side and Russia (USSR) and its allies on the other. You will need to use detailed information about events between 1945 and 1955.

What you should know 👍

To be successful in this section you must be able to:

★ explain why the ideologies of capitalism and communism opposed each other
★ describe how the Soviet Union protected itself with buffer states
★ describe the effects of the use of the atom bomb on relations between the Soviet Union and the USA
★ describe what the USA did as part of the policy of **containment**
★ explain what the Truman Doctrine was and why it had a big effect on Europe.

Context ❗

When Nazi Germany was defeated in 1945 the tensions that had existed between the USA and USSR before the war emerged once again. The USSR and America began a Cold War which meant the two main enemies never actually fought a real war. Instead they fought the war through an arms race, the spread of their **ideology**, spies and through conflicts in other countries.

Key people

Joseph Stalin – leader of the Soviet Union from the mid-1920s until his death in 1953. He oversaw the defeat of Nazism as well as the development of the Cold War.

Harry S Truman – 33rd president of the USA between 1945 and 1953. He succeeded to the presidency on the death of Franklin D Roosevelt in 1945. He approved the use of the atom bomb against Japan. He also encouraged American policies to contain communism and give massive aid to the economies of Europe with the Marshall Plan.

Key words

Collectivisation – where individual farms are joined together into collective units.

Containment – a US policy to prevent the spread of communism. The USA gave financial and even military help to stop communism spreading.

Ideology – a system of ideas and ideals that form a political and/or economic belief.

Marshall Plan – American economic support to Europe and Asia to help rebuild European economies after the Second World War and help to contain communism.

Satellite state – a country that is technically independent, but in reality is under heavy political and economic influence by another country.

Soviet Union – a soviet is a workers' and soldiers' committee. For our purposes Soviet Union, Russia and the USSR all mean the same thing.

Superpower – a very powerful country. This term referred to the USA and the Soviet Union in the Cold War period.

The following factors and linked knowledge points are all relevant and could be used in an answer on this issue, but remember to always link your information to the question asked.

Differences in ideology

The Russian Revolution of October 1917 had created the world's first communist state. Communist Russia was also known as the Union of Soviet Socialist Republics (USSR) or **Soviet Union** from 1923.

Communist beliefs were a direct challenge to the beliefs held by countries such as America and Great Britain. These countries believed in capitalism.

The beliefs of the USA

The USA believed in:

- Free elections, with a choice of parties for voters to choose from.
- Democratic rights such as freedom of speech.
- Independent newspapers, radio and television, not run by the state.
- Free enterprise – businesses run to make a profit and not controlled by the government.

The beliefs of the Soviet Union

The Soviet Union believed in:

- A one-party **totalitarian** state, with the Communist Party being the only permitted political party.
- An emphasis on equality at all levels of society.
- Strict control of the mass media with extensive censorship.
- State control of industry and agriculture.
- Suppression of all opposition – with strict enforcement by a political police, or 'secret' police.

Tensions within the wartime alliance

Suspicion and hostility between the Western democracies and Soviet Russia had a history. The Bolshevik revolution of 1917 meant that Russia withdrew from the First World War, making a separate peace with Germany in 1918, called the Treaty of Brest-Litovsk. Britain and America then intervened in the Russian civil war on the side of those opposed to the communist revolution, called the Whites. When the communists won the civil war, this suspicion meant that America did not even recognise the new government of Russia until 1933. In the years before 1939 the Soviet Union did not trust the democracies. Stalin saw them appeasing Hitler. In return the Allies saw Stalin do a deal with Hitler's Germany in 1939.

The US decision to use the atom bomb

Stalin's distrust of the Americans increased with the dropping of the atomic bomb on the Japanese cities of Hiroshima and Nagasaki in August 1945. Although the bomb was used to bring the war to an end, it also gave President Truman increased confidence when dealing with Stalin.

Key word

Totalitarian – where the state holds absolute power over all aspects of life.

Hints & tips

*The ideological rivalry between the **superpowers** is central to an understanding of the Cold War. Each side had its own distinct ideology, a body of beliefs and values, which influenced all its policies and initiatives, as the Cold War developed. In many ways the ideological struggle between the two countries underpinned the other reasons for the Cold War breaking out, although the Soviets' practical concerns for protecting their country after the devastation of the Second World War are also a factor.*

The arms race

On 29 August 1949 the USSR exploded its own atomic bomb, effectively cancelling out the early lead of the Americans. The USA then developed the hydrogen bomb. This bomb had a vast destructive capacity, one thousand times greater than the atomic bomb. Nine months later in 1953 the Soviets tested their own super bomb. The Soviet bomb could also be carried on a conventional bomber.

Why is the arms race important?

Apart from the ability of each side to totally destroy the other the conflict took on a symbolic meaning as each side used it to show the strengths of capitalism and communism.

The Americans also saw the race as necessary to counteract the numerical superiority of the large Red Army.

Their allies in Europe saw American nuclear strength as providing a shield over them to deter the Soviet Union from attacking.

Disagreements over the future of Germany and the post-war world

The Western powers had very different views to the Soviets about what would happen to countries freed from Nazi rule.

The Western powers wanted to hold democratic elections in countries. They wanted trade between the states of the world to be free and open.

The Soviet Union saw the world very differently. Protection of Russia was the key for Stalin. Eastern Europe had to be dominated by the Soviet Union and Germany kept weak.

During the war Soviet forces moved into countries like Poland, Czechoslovakia and eastern Germany. In reality these were communist countries that were **satellite states** led by pro-communist rulers who were sympathetic to the Soviet Union.

This move was opposed by the USA and Britain. They wanted countries to be free to choose their own governments after the war.

This disagreement was especially fierce over Germany. At the end of the war Germany had been divided up into four zones, each zone controlled by Britain, France, America or Russia. Berlin, the capital of Germany, was divided up in the same way.

The Soviet-controlled parts of Germany became communist, while the British, French and American sectors became a democracy.

The Truman Doctrine

America was very concerned by the spread of communism in Eastern Europe. In 1947 President Truman gave a famous speech in which he offered help to those who opposed communism. Communism was to be contained.

American aid was pumped into the economies of Europe with the **Marshall Plan**. America did not want countries in Europe becoming communist.

The crisis over Korea

Between 1950 and 1953 a war was fought in Korea between the communist North Korea and capitalist South Korea.

North Korea was supported by communist China and Russia, while South Korea was supported by United Nations backed forces that included American and British troops.

The war eventually fizzled out across what is known as 'the 49th parallel'.

For practice

1 How important was the arms race in causing the Cold War in the years up to 1955? (22 marks)
2 'The Cold War was caused by ideological differences between the two sides.' How valid is this view? (22 marks)

An assessment of the effectiveness of the Soviet policy in controlling Eastern Europe, up to 1961

Part 2 of 'The Cold War, 1945–1989' asks you to assess the effectiveness of Soviet policy in controlling Eastern Europe, up to 1961.

In other words, how did Soviet Russia control their Eastern European satellite states and how effectively did Russia deal with demands for political freedom in these areas?

What you should know

To be successful in this section you must be able to:
* describe the effect of Khrushchev's secret speech criticising Stalin
* describe Russia's methods of taking over and keeping control of its Eastern European satellite states
* explain why the Soviets did not intervene in Poland but did use violence against Hungary
* describe the events leading up to the building of the Berlin Wall and explain its purpose.

Context !

After Stalin died in 1953 there was a power struggle in the USSR. It was eventually won by Nikita Khrushchev. In 1956 Khrushchev made a speech which attacked Stalin. He criticised Stalin's use of violence to maintain authority and suggested that the route towards communism followed by Russia was not the only one. This was a shock to the satellite states. They had suffered harsh rule by pro-Stalinist leaders. Food shortages were common. Khrushchev now seemed to offer the possibility of greater freedom and change.

Key people

Wladyslaw Gomulka – Polish communist leader between 1956 and 1970. He introduced a number of reforms to communism in Poland. However, reform was limited and he was always loyal to the **Warsaw Pact** and communism.

Nikita Khrushchev – First Secretary of the Communist Party of the Soviet Union between 1953 and 1964. He criticised his predecessor Stalin and said that there were many paths to **socialism**. This arguably opened the way to demands for reform in Poland and Hungary. He was removed from office in 1964 and replaced by Leonid Brezhnev.

Imre Nagy – Hungarian communist politician. He was reformist and when appointed Chairman of the Council of Ministers in Hungary in 1956, he moved towards introducing a multi-party democracy. His announcement that Hungary was leaving the Warsaw Pact led to Soviet intervention. He was hanged in 1958 by the Soviets.

Mátyás Rákosi – a Hungarian politician, a hardline communist who supported Stalin and Russia's control over Eastern Europe.

Walter Ulbricht – German communist leader in East Germany from 1950 until his replacement in 1971. He oversaw the building of the Berlin Wall.

Key words

North Atlantic Treaty Organisation (NATO) – military alliance formed in 1949 between the USA and her Western Allies, including Britain. An attack on one member would be considered to be an attack against all members.

Propaganda – biased or one-sided information that is used to promote a particular political view.

Socialism – after the ending of capitalism, socialism is when states take control of their economies.

Warsaw Pact – military alliance between the Soviet Union and its satellite states.

The following factors and linked knowledge points are all relevant and could be used in an answer on this issue, but remember to always link your information to the question asked.

The Soviet reaction to events in Poland in 1956

In June 1956 there were riots in the city of Poznań in central Poland over shortages of food as well as bad housing and a decline in income.

Poland still had a Stalinist government and it cracked down on the rioters with security forces killing many and calling the rioters 'counter-revolutionaries and imperialist agents'.

However, the Polish government soon recognised that the rioters did not want to change the government. Therefore the rioters became 'honest workers' who had reasonable demands. Wages were raised by 50 per cent and limited economic and political change was promised.

A new leader called Wladyslaw Gomulka was invited to become leader of the Polish Communist Party. Gomulka was interested in genuine reform. He insisted on the removal of the Soviet Marshal Rokossovsky from the Polish government as he had ordered troops to move against the workers in Poznań. These moves worried the Soviet leadership but Gomulka was allowed to pass his reforms but only the Communist Party was allowed.

Soviet actions over Polish demands for reform can be seen successful. Socialism was allowed to reform, but within strict limits. Polish membership of the Warsaw Pact continued and only communism was allowed as a political system in the country. However, the Polish reforms only increased demand for change from other satellite states. Also, the limited Polish reforms only kept a lid on problems within Poland. Economic stagnation and a lack of political rights would lead to further Polish demands for change in the 1980s.

The Soviet reaction to events in Hungary in 1956

The situation in Hungary looked similar to Poland in that the Hungarians were fed up with the harsh rule of Mátyás Rákosi and declining standards of living.

Even before Khrushchev's speech in 1956, there had been signs of resistance to communism from writers and literary organisations. The Petofi Circle is perhaps the most famous of these organisations.

Protests in Hungary increased with large demonstrations in the capital, Budapest. Demands were made by nationalist students for freedom of expression and the removal of Soviet troops from Hungarian land. Troops were sent to break up crowds of demonstrators but they sided with the protestors. The Hungarian Communist Party lost control of events.

A new government was formed, led by János Kádár as First Secretary and Imre Nagy as Prime Minister. Nagy appealed for an end to violence and promised political reform such as a return to the old multi-party system of government and free elections.

Nagy managed to get Soviet military forces to withdraw from Budapest but he pushed his luck. On 1 November 1956, Nagy demanded the withdrawal of Russian troops from Hungary. He also wanted Hungary to withdraw from the Warsaw Pact. These demands were totally unacceptable to the Soviet leadership. Soviet troops moved into Budapest on 4 November 1956 and Hungary's resistance was brutally crushed. Nagy and 2000 others were later executed.

Even though Soviet actions were violent they were successful in the sense that Hungary remained part of the Warsaw Pact and had a communist government. However, it was a dreadful advert for the 'success' of communism and led to lasting resentment in Hungary.

The Soviet reaction to events in Berlin in 1961

At the end of the Second World War Germany was divided into areas of occupation. The area controlled by France, Britain and the USA eventually formed the democratic, economically prosperous Federal Republic of Germany or West Germany.

Hints & tips

*When answering questions on this issue you should think carefully about what is meant by the word 'effectively'. After each event communism survived in the Eastern Bloc and the buffer zone of sympathetic regimes that shielded Russia from the West remained. However, such a situation came at a cost. There was resentment over Russian actions in many East European states and their actions were a **propaganda** gift for the West which wanted to show communism as harsh and lacking support from the people. So was Soviet policy really 'effective'?*

The Soviet sector became a pro-communist German Democratic Republic or East Germany.

Berlin was also split into four parts. However, Berlin was deep inside pro-communist East Germany. The 'free' sectors controlled by France, Britain and America were an embarrassment to Russia since they offered the promise of freedom and prosperity of West Germany. As a result West Berlin became a focal point for East Germans who wanted to leave the East. Between 1950 and 1961 it is estimated that 3 million East Germans made the journey to the West.

For the communist government in the East this was not good. It looked like communism was failing and the loss of people was threatening the ability of East Germany to survive. Walter Ulbricht, the East German leader, and Khrushchev could not allow this to continue. Western powers feared that West Berlin might be invaded. This could cause a war as West Berlin was part of **NATO**.

In fact, on the morning of 13 August 1961 East German soldiers and police sealed the border with barbed wire. A few days later a more substantial wall of concrete blocks began to take shape. This was reinforced by watchtowers with armed guards. Within a short time Berlin became a divided city.

Soviet action was successful in that it dealt with the problem of population loss. It also lessened the threat of a possible misunderstanding between Western and Soviet armed forces escalating. However, it allowed Western leaders to point to the economic stagnation and lack of political rights in the East.

The construction of the Berlin Wall

For practice

3 To what extent did the Soviet Union control the Eastern satellite states in the years before 1961? (22 marks)

4 'Soviet control of Eastern Europe was effective and fair.' How valid is this view? (22 marks)

Key words

Blockade – to seal Cuba off in order to prevent people or nuclear weapons from entering.

Quarantine – to place in isolation.

An evaluation of the reasons for the Cuban Missile Crisis of 1962

Part 3 of 'The Cold War, 1945–1989' asks you to evaluate the reasons for the Cuban Missile Crisis of 1962.

In other words, you must be able to describe why there was a crisis over Cuba in 1962 and then explain which of the reasons you think was most important.

What you should know 👍

To be successful in this section you must be able to:

★ describe how Cuba was almost totally controlled by the USA before Castro's revolution
★ explain why the Americans did not like Castro and why he felt threatened by the Americans
★ describe how the Russians offered help to Castro and explain why
★ explain why Khrushchev sent nuclear missiles to Cuba and describe the reaction of the USA.

Context ❗

Between 16 and 28 October 1962, the world came close to a nuclear war between the Soviet Union and the USA. As Russian ships containing nuclear weapons moved towards the island of Cuba the Americans set up a **quarantine** zone around the island. If Russian ships breached the quarantine zone then the Americans would act. The world held its breath until the Russians decided to return to port. The reasons why nuclear missiles were making their way to Cuba is what this part of the course is all about.

Key people

Fidel Castro – revolutionary and then communist leader of Cuba between 1956 and 2008.

John F Kennedy (JFK)– 35th president of the USA. Served between 1961 and his assassination in 1963.

Bobby Kennedy – brother and adviser to his brother JFK. He was senator for New York between 1965 and 1968, when he was also assassinated. He was US Attorney General between 1961 and 1964.

Nikita Khrushchev – First Secretary of the Communist Party of the Soviet Union between 1953 and 1964.

The following factors and linked knowledge points are all relevant and could be used in an answer on this issue, but remember to always link your information to the question asked.

Castro's victory in Cuba

Cuba is a Caribbean island 90 miles from the American state of Florida. Until 1959 it was ruled by a military dictatorship led by General Batista.

The vast majority of Cubans were poor. American businesses invested a lot of money in Cuba, especially in sugar growing.

Between 1956 and 1959 a guerrilla war was waged by Fidel Castro against the Batista regime. At the beginning of 1959 Castro won the war.

Castro was not a communist to begin with, but he wanted to make life better for ordinary Cubans. He wanted to improve standards of health and education. Hospitals and schools were built and living standards for ordinary Cubans began to improve. Castro also seized the large American-owned sugar plantations and redistributed the land to peasant farmers.

America tried to force Castro to stop his reforms so Castro looked to the Soviet Union for help. In response the Americans refused to buy the Cuban sugar crop. The Soviet Union stepped in and bought the crop instead.

Why was Castro's victory important?

Cuba became a communist country. The Soviet Union faced American forces directly on their border with Turkey so the fact that Cuba was now a communist country so close to the American mainland provided an opportunity for the Russians.

US foreign policy

The USA did not like seeing a communist country so close to them in the Caribbean. The US Central Intelligence Agency began to plot the overthrow of Castro's government.

When new President John F Kennedy came to power he famously said that America would, 'oppose any foe, in order to assure the survival and the success of liberty'. Cuba was clearly an enemy of liberty according to Kennedy.

Why was the Bay of Pigs important?

The Bay of Pigs disaster was an attempt by the USA to invade Cuba and overthrow Castro. It failed.

Castro believed that American leaders would soon attempt another attack against him so he looked to the Soviet Union for help. Russian advisers and engineers were sent to Cuba and a Russian military base was built on the island.

Kennedy had promised to be tough on communism when he was elected as president. Now he looked weak and was criticised within the USA.

Khrushchev's domestic position

Within the Soviet Union Khrushchev had problems. He was being criticised by other important communist leaders within the Soviet Union.

To make matters worse, the other major communist power, China, was showing signs of independence and moving away from the Soviet Union. Khrushchev feared that Cuba would turn towards China rather than the Soviet Union.

One way of protecting Cuba and helping Khrushchev's domestic positon would be to place nuclear weapons on Cuba.

Khrushchev's view of Kennedy

Khrushchev took entirely the wrong lessons from the Bay of Pigs. He felt that Kennedy was weak. His views seemed to be confirmed by events over Berlin. The Russians wanted the Western powers to withdraw from Berlin and in August the building of the Berlin Wall began. Kennedy did nothing.

Khrushchev thought that if the Americans took military action over Cuba then the Russians could justify seizing Berlin.

The arms race

The communist takeover of Cuba also offered the Soviet Union a way of reducing the 'missile gap' between American and Soviet forces.

Despite Khrushchev's claims that the Soviet Union was producing long-range intercontinental ballistic missiles (ICBMs) 'like sausages', the Americans had a significant superiority in numbers. American spy satellites confirmed this.

However, the Soviets did have a lot of medium-range ballistic missiles (MRBMs). If they could place some of these on Cuba then American cities would be in range of Soviet missiles.

Why did nuclear war not break out?

American U2 spy planes identified missile bases being built on Cuba in October 1962. Some US military leaders wanted America to invade Cuba but Kennedy was persuaded to quarantine or **blockade** Cuba. The quarantine would give time for negotiations, but would also signal America's determination to oppose the Russians.

In the meantime, the USA began to build up its military forces and announced the problem to the world. Many thought a Third World War was only one step away.

High-level negotiations took place and eventually an agreement was thrashed out. The Soviet Union would remove any missiles on Cuba and its ships would turn back. In return America promised not to invade Cuba and removed its Jupiter missiles from Turkey.

War had been avoided. Kennedy won the following public relations battle and was considered a hero in America. Khrushchev was removed from office in 1964 and replaced by Leonid Brezhnev.

For practice

5 How important was Castro's victory in Cuba in causing the Cuban Missile Crisis of 1962? (22 marks)
6 'The Cuban Missile Crisis of 1962 was caused by Khrushchev's miscalculation of Kennedy.' How valid is this view? (22 marks)

An evaluation of the reasons why the US lost the war in Vietnam

Part 4 of 'The Cold War, 1945–1989' asks you to evaluate the reasons why the USA lost the war in Vietnam.

Hints & tips

There is no one reason why Khrushchev decided to place nuclear missiles on Cuba. Rather it is a complex combination of several. It is probably best to think about this subject as a series of chronological events that cumulatively added up to the attempt by the Soviets to put nuclear missiles on the island of Cuba.

Key words

My Lai massacre – the mass killing of unarmed civilians in South Vietnam on 16 March, 1968. Victims included men, women, children, and infants. Twenty-six soldiers were charged with criminal offences, but only one was convicted.

The massacre was later called 'the most shocking episode of the Vietnam War' and it caused global outrage when it became public knowledge in November 1969. The My Lai massacre increased domestic opposition to US involvement in the Vietnam War.

NVA – North Vietnamese Army.

Vietcong – communist guerrilla fighters.

In other words, you need to know why the USA lost the war in Vietnam and make a decision about which of the various reasons for defeat you think was the most important.

What you should know 👍

To be successful in this section you must be able to:

★ explain why the Americans intervened in Vietnam
★ describe how the Vietcong fought the USA superpower
★ explain why America lost the war
★ describe how the international isolation of the USA contributed to America's decision to withdraw from Vietnam.

Context ❗

In the 1950s Vietnam was divided between the communist North and anticommunist South. The South was ruled by Ngo Dinh Diem. He was unpopular. Civil war broke out in the South between Diem's forces and those of the National Liberation Front or **Vietcong**. The Vietcong looked to the communist North for help.

America was concerned to stop the spread of communism so supported Diem's government. The Americans believed that if South Vietnam became communist then other neighbouring countries would fall to communism like dominos knocking each other down. By 1968 the USA had 550,000 troops and 'advisers' in Vietnam. However, military victory proved difficult. By the early 1970s the US began withdrawing its forces and transferring responsibility and direction of the war effort to the government of South Vietnam. This policy was called **Vietnamisation** but it failed. South Vietnam was conquered by the North and America lost the war.

The following factors and linked knowledge points are all relevant and could be used in an answer on this issue, but remember to always link your information to the question asked.

Difficulties faced by US military

Despite being a superpower American military forces found that there were difficulties when fighting in Vietnam.

South Vietnam is hilly and is covered in dense jungle. It is a wet country with a tropical climate. American troops found this terrain difficult to fight in and it effectively cancelled out US technological superiority over the Vietcong.

The Vietcong used the terrain well. They were masters of hit and run tactics as well as booby traps. They hid in cleverly concealed complexes of bunkers that were difficult to destroy.

American forces expected to win. However, they found it difficult to locate the enemy as the Vietcong did not wear military uniforms and would blend in with local villagers.

Key word

Vietnamisation – the US policy of withdrawing its troops and transferring the responsibility and direction of the war effort to the government of South Vietnam.

Key people

Ngo Diem – first president of South Vietnam. Widely considered corrupt. He was assassinated in a CIA-backed coup in 1963.

Lyndon B Johnson – 36th president of the USA. He increased American involvement in Vietnam. He was succeeded by Richard Nixon.

Ho Chi Minh – Vietnamese communist revolutionary leader. Prime Minister of North Vietnam between 1945 and 1955 and president between 1945 and 1969.

Americans relied on heavy air bombardment and used chemical agents, such as Agent Orange, to strip all leaves from trees. Such indiscriminate weapons killed many locals and therefore alienated the local population. It also had minimal effect on the Vietcong and did not look good on television back home in the USA.

American troops were drafted in to fight. Frequently this meant only a year serving in Vietnam. Therefore they did not build up a body of experienced soldiers who knew how to deal with the Vietcong.

When faced with the hit and run guerrilla tactics of the Vietcong, the morale of many American troops dropped. There was a massive increase in drug use. American soldiers were supposed to go on 'search and destroy missions', but many joked that they went on 'search and avoid' missions instead.

Frustrated American troops committed acts of atrocity: one example is the **My Lai massacre** in March 1968. In contrast the Vietcong were under strict orders not to steal food and to treat the local peasants with respect.

The Vietnam War

What was the difference between North and South Vietnam?

North Vietnam was led by Ho Chi Minh who was an inspirational leader. In contrast the South Vietnamese were poorly led by unpopular leaders.

The South Vietnamese army was militarily poor despite being equipped by the Americans. It was poorly led and was effectively a collection of competing war lords.

Defending a corrupt government proved to be difficult back home in America.

Changing public opinion in the USA

Despite initial enthusiasm for the war, opinion began to change from 1966 onwards. President Lyndon B Johnson, who led America for much of the Vietnam War and escalated troop numbers, became increasingly unpopular. Young men who did not want to fight burnt their draft cards.

Americans who felt that they were on the side of good were uneasy when stories of American atrocities began to emerge. Vietnam was a media war and daily news of American deaths in a war that did not seem to be ending did not go down well at home.

The key event was the Tet Offensive of 1968. The American commander, General Westmorland, had been giving regular news briefings about how America was winning the war. Then the North Vietnamese Army (**NVA**) invaded the South. The American public were treated to images of the Vietcong attacking the American Embassy in Saigon, the capital of South Vietnam. This did not look like a victory to Americans.

Protests in America grew in size and developed on the campuses of the universities. The fact was that America was a democracy and public opinion counted. America was spending vast amounts of money to fight the war when there was a need for money at home.

International isolation of the USA

America was a key part of the NATO military alliance. It did not get active support from its NATO allies such as Britain. However, it did get support from allies in Asia, such as South Korea as well as Australia. America suffered a large amount of negative publicity as a result of its intervention in Vietnam.

> **Hints & tips** ⭐
>
> *When considering this topic it is important to realise that perceptions mattered. In 1968 the Vietcong and North Vietnamese launched the Tet Offensive against the South and their American allies. Militarily it was a disaster for the North and the Vietcong, but perceptions in America were that the war was unwinnable. This is the important point about the domestic context for the Americans. They were part of a democracy where public opinion mattered. The North Vietnamese were in a dictatorship.*

> **For practice** ◎
>
> 7 To what extent were the military tactics of the Vietcong the main reason why the Americans lost the Vietnam War? (22 marks)
> 8 'American public opinion was the reason why the Americans lost the Vietnam War.' How valid is this view? (22 marks)

An evaluation of the reasons why the superpowers attempted to manage the Cold War, 1962–79

Part 5 of 'The Cold War, 1945–1989' asks you to evaluate the reasons why the superpowers attempted to manage the Cold War, 1962–79.

In other words, why did the USA and the USSR try to control and manage the events of the Cold War between 1962 and 1979? You then need to decide which of those reasons was the most important.

What you should know 👍

To be successful in this section you must be able to:

★ explain why the Cuban Missile Crisis led to improved contact between the two sides
★ describe what MAD was and explain why it made the world a very dangerous place
★ describe the arms limitations arrangements that happened
★ explain the policy of détente and Ostpolitik and describe examples of the policies in action.

Context ❗

By the early 1960s it was obvious that the arms race could lead eventually to the destruction of the world. Both the USA and the USSR realised it was in their interests to negotiate with each other through a series of treaties and events. As confidence and the technological ability to check each side was keeping their arms limits promises increased, the superpowers moved towards further attempts to reduce the threat of nuclear confrontation.

Key people

Leonid Brezhnev – General Secretary of the Communist Party of the Soviet Union between 1964 and 1982. He pushed for détente with the Western powers, but was harsh to dissent in the Warsaw Pact.

Willy Brandt – West German politician. He was mayor of West Berlin between 1957 and 1966 and Chancellor of West Germany 1969–74. He sought to improve relations with East Germany, Poland and Russia.

Mikhail Gorbachev – General Secretary of the Communist Party of the Soviet Union between 1985 and 1991. He sought to improve relations with the West and improve the life of ordinary Russians. However, his reforms helped bring an end to communism.

Richard Nixon – president of the USA between 1969 and 1974. He encouraged a thaw in relations with the Soviet Union as well as ending American involvement in Vietnam. He resigned from office following the Watergate scandal.

Ronald Reagan – president of the USA between 1981 and 1989. His policies would increase tension with the Soviet Union by challenging them. He had considerable personal charm. His role in the end of communism is debated.

The following factors and linked knowledge points are all relevant and could be used in an answer on this issue, but remember to always link your information to the question asked.

Key words

Détente – the name given to a period of improved relations between the United States and the Soviet Union that began tentatively in 1971.

ICBM – intercontinental ballistic missile.

MAD – mutually assured destruction.

MIRV – multiple independently targetable reentry vehicle is a collection of nuclear weapons carried on a single intercontinental ballistic missile (ICBM) or a submarine-launched ballistic missile (SLBM).

Ostpolitik – (German for 'new eastern policy') refers to the improvement in relations between West Germany (BRD – German: Bundesrepublik Deutschland; English: Federal Republic of Germany) and Eastern Europe, especially East Germany (DDR), which started in 1969.

SLBM – submarine launched ballistic missile.

Star Wars – nickname for the Strategic Defence Initiative pursued by the Americans. It aimed to place an antiballistic missile in outer space. It was nicknamed after the popular film from 1977!

The arms race

Russia and USA spent huge amounts of money on military growth and by the 1960s both sides had vast nuclear arsenals that were capable of destroying the world many times over.

Khrushchev's desire for better relations between the superpowers in the 1950s and 1960s was, in part, about freeing up resources for economic development in the USSR. Even in the 1960s Russia was having difficulties finding the resources to maintain its arms and space race with the USA. Developments in technology raised the costs of the arms race in the 1960s and 1970s even more.

Limiting the Cold War

The development of antiballistic missile technology and the cost of war led to the Strategic Arms Limitation Talks in 1972. The SALT Agreement froze the number of missile launchers both sides could have.

Limiting the **MIRV** and intermediate missile technology led to the Strategic Arms Limitation Talks II in 1975. SALT II limited strategic launchers and the number of nuclear warheads that could be deployed on an **ICBM** or SLBM.

SALT II was never ratified by the US senate, but both sides did follow it, until Soviet invasion of Afghanistan in 1979.

Mutually assured destruction

After 1945 the development of vast stocks of nuclear weapons by both superpowers meant that a military attack by one side would result in horrific retaliation from the other. This led to a stalemate known as **MAD**. The arms race was built on fear.

Dangers of military conflict as seen through Cuban Missile Crisis

The Cuban Missile Crisis showed that there was a lack of formal contact between the superpowers to defuse potential conflicts. This led to the introduction of a 'hot-line' between the Kremlin and White House in order to improve communication between the superpowers. Khrushchev and Kennedy also signed the Limited Nuclear Test Ban Treaty, the first international agreement on nuclear weapons.

Hints & tips

At the end of the day, both the leaders of the Soviet Union and America were rational people. The Cuban Missile Crisis and arms race served to concentrate the minds of the leaders as to the consequences of a nuclear war.

Technology – the importance of verification

American development of surveillance technology, through U2 spy aircraft and satellites, meant that both sides could check that the other side was keeping its arms agreement promises.

Some historians think arms control would never have taken root, but for the ability of the sides to verify, or check, what the other was doing.

Co-existence and détente

Policies of co-existence and **détente**, or the easing of tension, developed at the time of President Nixon's presidency in the early 1970s. The meetings between the two sides led to the SALT treaties, for example.

Other Western politicians like Willy Brandt, Chancellor in West Germany, helped by defusing tension through their policies of **Ostpolitik**. This policy normalised relations between East and West Germany.

For practice

9 How important was the arms race as a reason for the superpowers' attempts to limit the Cold War between 1962 and 1979? (22 marks)

10 'Surveillance technology was the reason why the superpowers tried to limit the Cold War between 1962 and 1979.' How valid is this view? (22 marks)

An evaluation of the reasons for the end of the Cold War

Part 6 of 'The Cold War, 1945–1989' asks you to evaluate the reasons for the end of the Cold War.

In other words, why did the Cold War end and which of those reasons was most important?

What you should know

To be successful in this section you must be able to:

★ explain the importance of the war in Afghanistan for the Soviet Union

★ describe the attitude of Ronald Reagan towards the Soviet Union and explain why he believed that the Cold War could be won

★ describe the policies of **glasnost** and **perestroika** introduced by Gorbachev and explain the effect of those changes

★ explain why communism collapsed so quickly.

Context !

By 1990 the communist governments in the satellite states had all collapsed and Soviet Russia was the only communist state left in Europe. Events before 1989 showed that the foundations on which the Soviet Union was built were fragile. Western economic strength and technological superiority meant that any attempts to reform communism and 'catch up' with the West were doomed to failure. The Communist Party in Russia was declared illegal in August 1991 and the USSR was dissolved in December 1991. The Cold War had ended.

Key people

Mikhail Gorbachev – General Secretary of the Communist Party of the Soviet Union between 1985 and 1991. He sought to improve relations with the West and improve the life of ordinary Russians. However, his reforms helped bring an end to communism.

General Jaruzelski – Poland's last communist leader. He imposed martial law in 1981 in an attempt to control the pro-democracy groups, including Solidarity, in Poland.

Pope John Paul II – pope of the Catholic Church between 1978 and 2005. He was Polish and is credited with helping end communism, by giving Poles the confidence to fight for their rights.

Ronald Reagan – president of the USA between 1981 and 1989. His policies would increase tension with the Soviet Union by challenging them. He had considerable personal charm. His role in the end of communism is debated.

Lech Walesa – trade union activist. He co-founded 'Solidarity', the first independent trade union in the communist East. He won the Nobel Peace Prize in 1983 and was president of Poland from 1990 to 1995.

Boris Yeltsin – Russian politician. The Russian Federation's first post-communist president between 1991 and 1999.

Key words

Glasnost – Russian for 'openness'. Russians were encouraged to speak freely and discuss and debate issues with their government.

Perestroika – Russian for 'reconstruction'.

Star Wars – nickname for the Strategic Defence Initiative pursued by the Americans. It aimed to place an antiballistic missile in outer space. It was nicknamed after the popular film from 1977!

The following factors and linked knowledge points are all relevant and could be used in an answer on this issue, but remember to always link your information to the question asked.

The Soviet Union and Afghanistan

By 1979 the USSR was concerned about the growth of Muslim opposition groups in Afghanistan which might have a destabilising effect on the Muslim population in the southern republics of the Soviet Union.

The Muslim opposition groups were known as the Mujaheddin. They were expert guerrilla fighters who used the mountainous terrain of Afghanistan well.

The Soviets installed a pro-Russian government in the Afghan capital Kabul. The Red Army was sent to fight the Mujaheddin. The Red Army could not cope with the guerrilla tactics of the Mujaheddin. Over 20,000 Soviet soldiers died.

The war led to a slump in living standards for ordinary Russians. They began to question the actions of their own government.

Gorbachev withdrew Russian troops from Afghanistan in 1988. The war led to a massive deterioration in relations with the USA.

Role of President Ronald Reagan

Ronald Reagan became president of the USA in January 1981.

He was a passionate anticommunist and in 1983 he described the Soviet Union as an 'evil empire'. He believed that détente had been a mistake and had led to Soviet intervention in Afghanistan because America was not strong enough to stop it.

Reagan started a policy of improving US armed forces, including nuclear weapons. He proposed a **Star Wars** missile shield (called the Strategic Defence Initiative, SDI) in 1983 to challenge the belief in MAD. If the Americans could build a defensive system that would protect them from incoming nuclear missiles, then a nuclear war could, theoretically, be won.

Western economic strength

The Western powers were richer and more economically successful than the USSR. This economic wealth allowed America to embark on the Star Wars weapons programme.

The fact that the Western powers were richer with a wide range of consumer goods undermined communist claims of the superiority of their economic system.

Role of President Mikhail Gorbachev

Mikhail Gorbachev became leader of the Soviet Union in 1985. He saw that the USSR could not afford a new arms race. The Soviet economy was at breaking point.

Gorbachev implemented policies of perestroika and glasnost which aimed to reform the Soviet economy and free up its political system.

Gorbachev worked to improve relations with the USA. Gorbachev also took the decision to remove Soviet troops from Afghanistan.

Gorbachev told leaders of the satellite East European states in March 1989 that the Soviet army would no longer help them to stay in power.

Crisis in Poland and the collapse of communism in Eastern Europe

Poland was the largest of the satellite states with a population of 30 million people. It had a strong sense of its own identity and also had a history of hostility with Russia.

By the 1970s, Poland was in an economic slump. Protests grew in the city of Gdansk in 1980. Industrial workers went on strike based around a new trade union called Solidarity led by Lech Walesa. The Polish leader, General Jaruzelski, tried to break up Solidarity.

In March 1989, Gorbachev announced that the Soviet Union would no longer help the satellite communist parties stay in power. When Soviet troops left Poland there were elections which resulted in a massive victory for Solidarity.

In Czechoslovakia political prisoners were released in November 1989 and by the end of the month, the communist government had gone.

With the dismantling of the Berlin Wall in November 1989, the division of Germany finally came to an end.

For practice

11 How important was the crisis in Poland as a reason for the end of the Cold War? (22 marks)

12 'The role of Mikhail Gorbachev was the most important reason for the end of the Cold War.' How valid is this view? (22 marks)

Hints & tips ⭐

It is important to work out why the Cold War ended. There is tension between people who think that there were long-term economic processes that meant communism was bound to fail. Other people look at the role of individuals like Ronald Reagan and Mikhail Gorbachev. As with most historical events it is a mixture of the two.

Model answers to exam questions

This section will provide you with examples of answers to questions or parts of questions. As you know, in this exam paper you will have to write extended responses, sometimes called essays. Each essay must have parts to them and each section will gain marks.

These sections are:
- introduction* (3 marks)
- use of knowledge – you must include at least six different, relevant and accurate facts that lead into an analysis comment (6 marks)
- analysis* (6 marks)
- evaluation* (4 marks)
- conclusion* (3 marks).

Below you will find an example question with good examples of student answers to each of the four starred (*) sections of the extended response listed above.

The knowledge marks count is simply based on the number of relevant and accurate knowledge points you use in your essay.

The answers may not be on topics you want to revise but the rules are the same for all essays, so find out what things gain marks and also why marks are lost!

Hints & tips ⭐

You will see that factors to develop are vital in any essay introduction. They list the main headings you will write about in your essay. You can find the factors to develop for every single Higher essay you will ever do in the description of content box in the SQA syllabus for your chosen topic.

Example ⚑

Question

'American public opinion was the most important reason why America lost the Vietnam War.' How valid is this view? (22 marks)

Introduction

By the early 1960s the USA was afraid of the spread of communism across the world as it felt countries would fall like dominoes as it spread. As a result the USA was determined that South Vietnam would not fall to communism which led to large-scale military intervention. (context)

The view that the American public was the most important reason why America lost the Vietnam war is a very valid statement. However, there are other factors which need to be considered. (line of argument)

Other factors to be considered include the difficulties faced by the American military in fighting the war as well as the strengths of North Vietnam, the weaknesses of South Vietnam and the international isolation of the USA. (factors to develop)

Why is this a good introduction?

This is an effective introduction and gets 3/3 because it has two sentences of context, a clear line of argument that addresses the question posed and has other factors to develop. You need to have all three of these things to gain 3 out of 3.

Analysis

Television reporting was important in turning public opinion against the war because the watching American public was horrified and shocked by scenes showing atrocities committed by American soldiers in the name of 'freedom'. The public began to question why the USA was fighting in Vietnam.

Why is this a good example of an analysis comment?

It is good because after the fact it states 'this was important because' and then explains how the fact is relevant to answering the question.

If you write *three* examples of this sort of comment you will gain 3 analysis marks.

Analysis plus

However, significant support remained for the Vietnam War from groups in American society, such as construction workers and the so-called hawks in the American government. Even those who were against the war did not want to leave the South in the lurch when asked. This directly led to the policy of Vietnamisation.

Why is this a good example of an analysis plus comment?

It is good because this states a limitation on the factor of public opinion as a reason why America lost the Vietnam War. It explains why this factor can be challenged.

If you write *three* examples of this sort of comment you will gain 3 more analysis marks. ⇨

⇨
Evaluation

Changing public opinion was one important reason why the Americans lost the war in Vietnam but perhaps it was not the most important. The tactics of the Vietcong were well adapted to fighting the technological superiority of the USA and this is an important reason. Even more importantly the Vietcong were fighting for their country and their beliefs. The idea that public opinion in America lost the war reinforces the idea that the USA could have won the war had public opinion not changed but the facts are that the US military could not cope with the North Vietnamese tactics or forces.

Why is this a good evaluation point?

This is good because here the writer is judging the importance of one main factor against another and reaching a decision that is linked to the main question.

Do this sort of balanced judgement at least *four* times in your essay and you will get 4 evaluation marks, but only if your evaluative comments are clearly linked to the line of argument that you outlined in your introduction.

Conclusion.

In conclusion, changing American public opinion can be argued to be the most important reason for the American loss of the Vietnam War, because changing public opinion had an impact on the political will to fight the war as well as the morale of troops who were fighting in Vietnam. However, other factors were also important as they link to public opinion. The military difficulties faced by the Americans meant the war was not a quick victory as expected by the American public and the rising number of casualties helped change their opinion of the war. Of lesser importance was international isolation. This was irritating, but as a superpower America could ignore the lack of support from her NATO allies. Therefore, American public opinion was the most important reason for the American loss in Vietnam as this undermined the American war effort and ultimately led to their Vietnamisation of the conflict and eventual withdrawal.

Why is this a good conclusion?

This conclusion provides a direct answer to the question posed. It provides a relative judgement between factors that addresses the question. This judgement is supported with reasons. Other factors are also mentioned and judgements made on their importance. An overall conclusion is drawn at the end which directly answers the question. A good conclusion needs a judgement in terms of the question; judgement also needs to be made between factors and supported with reasons. All three elements are needed to get 3/3.

Section 3 – Scottish history

Chapter 9
The Wars of Independence, 1249–1328

Alexander III and the succession problem 1286–92

What you should know 👍

To be successful in this section you must be able to evaluate, identify interpretation and judge sources based on:
* ★ why the death of King Alexander III caused such problems for Scotland
* ★ why Edward of England become involved in the future of Scotland
* ★ what the Great Cause was.

Context ❗

Alexander III reigned Scotland between 1249 and 1286. He was a successful ruler and relations with England were largely good in this period. All of this was to change with the death of Alexander in an accident.

Key words

Faction – a small group within a larger whole that disagrees with the rest of the larger group.

Feudalism – a set of customs in medieval Europe where land was exchanged for loyalty and service.

Guardians – people chosen to look after Scotland's interests until Scotland once again had a strong ruler.

Homage – public acknowledgement of loyalty to a lord or king.

Overlordship – where one lord or ruler is superior over another.

What problems were caused by King Alexander III's death?

King Alexander III's 36-year reign of Scotland ended in March 1286, when he fell off his horse and died on a stormy night while attempting to return to his young bride, Yolande. This led to a problem about who would rule Scotland next. Alexander's children had all died before him. The main Scottish noble families could not agree on a successor to Alexander.

Two powerful rival noble families (the Bruces from south-west Scotland and the Comyns/Balliols) saw this as a possible opportunity to gain more power. Both were descended from David I of Scotland and had a claim to the throne.

The Scots eventually decided to offer the crown to Margaret, Maid of Norway. She was Alexander's only surviving grandchild. The Scots elected six **Guardians** to run affairs in Scotland until the young queen arrived in Scotland. Important Scottish lords swore **homage** to the Maid of Norway at the Scone agreement of 1284.

What was the Treaty of Birgham?

This Treaty was signed in 1290 and it arranged a marriage between Margaret, Maid of Norway, and Edward I's son, also called Edward. An alliance with the powerful English king would cool the threat of civil war in Scotland as no one would want to face the English army.

The Treaty was very clear about Scottish independence from England. It stated that Scots nobles, churchmen and parliaments were to be independent from England.

What were the results of the death of the Maid of Norway?

Margaret died on her way from Norway to Scotland in 1290.

The Scottish nobles were divided over who should rule Scotland next. Two important **factions** (the Bruce family and the Comyns/Balliols) faced each other. There was a real fear in Scotland of civil war.

The way these factions behaved led William Fraser, Bishop of Glasgow, to ask for the help of Edward I in choosing Alexander's successor on the death of the Maid.

The Treaty of Birgham was also at an end. There would be no marriage alliance.

Why did the Scots appeal to Edward I of England?

Edward had been friendly with Alexander. He had a reputation as a good lawmaker, but Edward I of England was a powerful ruler and the death of Alexander gave him an opportunity to establish **feudal overlordship** over Scotland at Norham in 1291.

What happened at Norham?

Edward demanded that the Scots who claimed the right to be king should recognise him as overlord of Scotland. Faced with the threat of English military intervention the various claimants for the Scottish throne agreed to Edward being their overlord. He now believed that he was in charge in Scotland!

What was the Great Cause?

The Great Cause refers to the task that Edward undertook to choose a new king for Scotland from thirteen claimants. There were only three serious claimants: John Balliol, Robert Bruce, The Competitor, and John Hastings. Edward decided to make John Balliol King of Scots in November 1292.

In legal terms Balliol had a better claim to the throne than Robert Bruce, The Competitor, or John Hastings.

Key people

Alexander III of Scotland – King of Scots from 1249 until his death.

John Balliol – King of Scots from 1292 until 1296. He is also known as Toom Tabard.

Edward I of England – King of England from 1272 until his death in 1307. He is also known as Edward Longshanks or 'Hammer of the Scots'.

Robert Bruce – 'The Competitor' was one of the claimants to the Scottish throne on the death of Alexander. He was the grandfather of Robert I of Scotland.

Margaret, Maid of Norway – daughter of King Eric II of Norway and Margaret, the daughter of Alexander III. She died in 1290 and this led to the Great Cause.

Hints & tips

Be careful not to fall into the trap of assuming King Edward I was a 'bad man' who was plotting to take over Scotland. Edward was King Alexander's brother-in-law and also a lawyer.

John Balliol and Edward I 1292–96

What you should know 👍

To be successful in this section you must be able to evaluate, identify interpretation and judge sources based on:

★ how and why Edward tried to assert his authority over King John Balliol
★ how John's defiance of Edward led to war between Scotland and England.

Context ❗

John Balliol was aware that he needed to impress Edward if he wanted to secure the kingdom of Scotland, but from the start Edward sought to control John and the way he ruled Scotland. Edward behaved like an overlord with John and this eventually led the Guardians of Scotland and King John to rebel against this control.

How did King Edward I of England treat King John of Scotland?

John's **inauguration** as the King of Scots was attended by English officials rather than the traditional Scottish nobles and churchmen.

Examples of Edward exercising rights as overlord include when the **Burgesses** of Berwick appealed to Edward over a court decision, made by the Guardians, that John had upheld. There was also the Macduff case. Macduff was a landowner who had been **disinherited** from his lands in Scotland. He appealed to Edward over this decision.

John was summoned, more than once, to northern England by Edward. King John of Scotland was humiliated when he travelled down to London to hear Edward listen to the Macduff appeal.

When war broke out between England and France in 1294, Edward demanded that, as he was overlord, Scotland should send troops to help the English.

How did the Scots react to the way John was treated?

English kings had previously claimed overlordship of Scotland, but this had generally been ignored by the Scots. Alexander III of Scotland, for example, had refused to do homage to Edward I of England.

The reaction of the Scots nobles shows they were not happy. The nobles elected a council of twelve Guardians in 1295 to help John stand up to Edward.

Key words

Burgess – the inhabitant of a town or burgh.
Disinherited – to cut someone off from what they own.
Inauguration – ceremony to crown someone as king.
Sack – to violently loot a town or city.

Key people

Macduff – the younger son of Malcolm, Earl of Fife. He famously claimed that he had been unjustly imprisoned by Balliol and deprived of his inheritance. Edward summoned Balliol to answer the charges.

A French–Scottish treaty was agreed in February 1296. Scotland was to wage war against England. A large Scottish army was raised and the north of England was attacked.

How did Edward react to Scottish defiance?

Edward invaded Scotland with a large English army in March 1296, marching first on Berwick, **sacking** the town and slaughtering many inhabitants. He then easily defeated a Scottish army at the Battle of Dunbar on 28 April 1296. Over 130 leading Scottish nobles and some of the Guardians were captured.

John surrendered at Kincardine but was publicly humiliated in a ceremony at Brechin. He was taken as a prisoner to London, but eventually ended up living in France.

Edward completed Scotland's humiliation with the removal of the 'Stone of Destiny' upon which all Scottish kings had sat while they were crowned. Edward also took away all Scottish royal documents. English officials were appointed to rule Scotland and Scottish nobles were forced to swear a personal oath of loyalty to King Edward.

Hints & tips ★

Do not assume King Edward was just a bully trying to grab Scotland. Under the feudal system, John Balliol had done homage for his right to rule Scotland. That means Balliol had accepted Edward as his superior and that he must do what Edward asked. Edward had the right to ask Scotland to send soldiers to fight in his army. When the Scots refused Edward had the right to punish Scotland!

William Wallace and Scottish resistance

What you should know 👍

To be successful in this section you must be able to evaluate, identify interpretation and judge sources based on:
★ why William Wallace and others rose up against English rule in Scotland
★ why the Battle of Stirling Bridge was so important
★ the importance of William Wallace
★ how Edward reacted to Scottish resistance.

Context !

If Edward thought that he now controlled Scotland he was mistaken. Rebellion broke out and the English were defeated at Stirling Bridge. However, Edward I reacted, marched north with a large army and defeated the Scots at Falkirk. Wallace was defeated, then captured and executed but resistance continued.

Who rebelled against Edward's rule?

The Earl of Carrick, Robert the Bruce (grandson of the Bruce who was 'The Competitor' in the Great Cause) and James Steward raised an armed revolt at Irvine in July 1297.

William Wallace was the first to rebel in the south-west of Scotland and Andrew Murray started his rebellion in the north-east of Scotland.

Wallace was a minor Scottish lord. He started his rebellion with the murder of Heselrig, the English Sheriff of Lanark. Andrew Murray was the son of an important supporter of King John. His rebellion from May to August posed a problem to the English in the north.

By late 1297 all English garrisons north of Dundee had been forced to leave or surrender. Murray's forces combined with Wallace's at the siege of Dundee.

The English reacted by gathering an army to meet this threat. The two sides met at Stirling.

Why did the Scots win the Battle of Stirling Bridge?

Wallace and Murray were at the head of the Scots army at Stirling. The English made an error in seeking to cross the narrow Stirling Bridge in order to reach the Scottish forces. This enabled the Scots to attack them before the English could organise their forces. The English caught on the Scots side of the bridge were massacred.

The Battle of Stirling Bridge proved that the Scots could defeat a superior English army in a pitched battle.

Andrew Murray was wounded in the battle and died in November 1297.

The Battle of Stirling Bridge

Key people

Hugh de Cressingham – the English treasurer of their administration in Scotland 1296–97. He was killed at the Battle of Stirling Bridge.

John de Warenne, 6th Earl of Surrey – prominent English nobleman. He commanded English forces that were defeated at the Battle of Stirling Bridge, but also commanded them to victory at the Battle of Falkirk.

Sir John Menteith – Scottish nobleman who was supposed to have betrayed William Wallace to the English.

Sir Andrew Murray – Scottish nobleman who jointly led the rebellion against the English. He died of wounds suffered at the Battle of Stirling Bridge.

Sir William Wallace – leader of the Scottish revolt against the English and Guardian of Scotland. His victory at Stirling Bridge showed the Scots could defeat the English army in pitched battle.

How was Scotland ruled at this time?

With victory at Stirling Bridge, Wallace and Murray became Guardians of Scotland. It is important to note that their rebellion was in support of King John. The important nobles worked with Wallace and supported him.

The English lost control of most of Scotland at this time and Wallace led raids deep into northern England.

How did Edward react to Wallace's triumph?

Edward gathered a large, experienced army and marched north. The two armies met at Falkirk. The Scots were decisively beaten by the English.

What happened to Wallace?

Wallace resigned from the Guardianship of Scotland. He was replaced by John Comyn and Robert the Bruce. By 1304 most Scottish nobles had accepted Edward's authority.

Wallace was eventually betrayed by Sir John Menteith. He was executed on 23 August 1305. Parts of his body were sent to Newcastle, Berwick, Stirling and Perth as a warning to those who would rebel against Edward I.

The rise and triumph of Robert the Bruce

What you should know 👍

To be successful in this section you must be able to evaluate, identify interpretation and judge sources based on:

★ how the ambitions of Robert the Bruce affected his actions
★ why Bruce faced such opposition from other Scottish noblemen and how he overcame that opposition
★ why victory at Bannockburn was so important to Bruce and the Scots
★ the importance of the Declaration of Arbroath and the Treaty of Edinburgh/Northampton.

Context ❗

Bruce became the King of Scots by murdering his rival in a church. For many years Bruce had enemies in Scotland and England but in 1314 he won a decisive victory at Bannockburn. In the years that followed he became known as 'Good King Robert' and eventually gained victory in the Scottish Wars of Independence.

Hints & tips ⭐

Be aware of how the Wallace rebellion caused Edward to change his strategy in controlling Scotland. Before Wallace, Edward treated Scotland like an occupied and defeated country. After the defeat of Wallace, Edward gave many Scottish nobles much of their power back in exchange for accepting Edward as their ruler.

Hints & tips ⭐

You may have seen the film *Braveheart*. Most of the film is inaccurate but it does give a feeling of how Scots were inspired by Wallace. However, do not assume that Scottish resistance ended with the death of Wallace. It did not.

How did Robert the Bruce become King of Scotland?

In 1306 Bruce met with his great rival John Comyn at the Grey Friars Church in Dumfries. Bruce murdered Comyn and as a result was **excommunicated** by the Pope.

Robert the Bruce declared himself King of Scotland in 1306 after a hurried ceremony at **Scone** with his supporters. He was later forgiven by his great supporter Bishop Wishart of Glasgow.

How did Bruce take control of Scotland?

To begin with Bruce was forced into hiding after defeat at Methven in 1306. In 1307 he returned to defeat an English army at the Battle of Loudoun Hill.

While Bruce was campaigning Edward took his revenge against his family. Leading supporters were executed and both Robert's sister and daughter were imprisoned in steel cages.

Robert the Bruce was helped by the death of Edward I on 7 July 1307 at Burgh on Sands. His son, Edward II, was no general, unlike his father.

Bruce then turned against his Scottish rivals, the Comyns. He launched a campaign against the Comyns in the north of Scotland. This is called the Harrying of Buchan or the 'Herschip of Buchan'. Those loyal to the Comyn cause were killed and their livestock slaughtered.

In March 1309, Bruce was confident enough to convene his first parliament in St Andrews. The Scottish bishops publicly supported Bruce as King of Scotland in the so-called 'Declaration of the Clergy' and there was a letter of support from the French king, Philip IV.

By 1313 most of the Scottish castles that were in English hands fell to Bruce's forces. Stirling was besieged by the forces of Robert's brother, Edward Bruce. Its commander, Sir Philip Mowbray, agreed to surrender the castle to the Scots if Edward II did not relieve the siege by Midsummer Day in 1314. Edward II could not refuse the challenge and the scene was set for the Battle of Bannockburn.

Why did Bruce win the Battle of Bannockburn?

Edward II brought a large force north with him. However, his army was poorly led unlike the Scots. The Scots army was significantly smaller than the English, but it was well led and by 1314 was very experienced.

The day before the main battle there were skirmishes between the two forces. The following day was a military disaster for the English. They were placed on boggy ground unable to manoeuvre their knights effectively.

Key words

Excommunicated – excluded from taking part in the rites of Christian worship. In a society that took heaven and hell very seriously, this was a dreadful punishment.

Fealty – where someone swears loyalty to a lord or king.

Schiltron – a battle formation of up to 2000 men carrying very long spears.

Scone – village in Perth and Kinross. Scottish kings were crowned here until 1651.

Key people

Edward II – son of Edward I. He led the English forces to defeat at Bannockburn.

Robert the Bruce – as Robert I he was King of Scots from 1306 until his death. He led Scotland to independence.

Robert Wishart, Bishop of Glasgow – Guardian of Scotland and a leading supporter of William Wallace and Robert Bruce during the Scottish Wars of Independence.

They were faced by three large Scottish **schiltrons**. When the English knights charged they were slaughtered.

Some English archers managed to fire at the schiltrons, but they were chased off by the Scottish cavalry under Sir Robert Keith. The English kept fighting, but fled when a new Scottish force appeared.

Thousands were killed as they attempted to cross the Bannockburn. The Scots had defeated the English king in battle. This secured Robert as King of Scotland in the eyes of most Scots.

An artist's idea of Robert the Bruce addressing his troops at the Battle of Bannockburn

What happened after the battle?

Robert the Bruce made laws forbidding nobles to hold land in both England and Scotland.

Bruce's forces repeatedly raided the north of England up to 1327. Scottish forces struck as far south as Yorkshire and also opened up another front against the English by invading Ireland and attacking English land holdings in 1315.

The English king refused to recognise Scottish independence. The Scots reacted with the famous Declaration of Arbroath in 1320. This document justified Bruce's kingship of Scotland and showed how the nobles of Scotland supported him.

In 1328 the Treaty of Edinburgh was signed. The English recognised Robert as King of Scots in an independent kingdom.

> ### Hints & tips ★
>
> *The Battle of Bannockburn did not secure Scottish independence. Another fourteen years passed before Scottish independence was accepted by the English. Be sure you understand what happened between 1314 and 1328 to secure that independence.*

For practice

The following sources and questions are for practice.

You can find a good model answer to the first question at the end of this section.

Examples of the other types of questions can be found at the end of the other Section 3 topics covered.

Question 1 – evaluate the usefulness

Source A is from *The Lanercost Chronicle* describing how Andrew Harclar, Earl of Carlisle came to an agreement with Robert the Bruce, January 1323.

> The Earl of Carlisle saw that the king of England neither knew how to rule his realm nor was able to defend it against the Scots who had just returned from northern England laden with stolen goods and with many prisoners and many cattle. Each year the Scots raided the north of England and laid it more and more waste. The Earl feared that he [the king] would lose his entire kingdom; so he chose the lesser of two evils, and on 3 January [1323] the Earl of Carlisle went secretly to Robert Bruce at Lochmaben and, after holding long conference and protracted discussion with him, at length came to agreement with him which led to his own destruction.

Evaluate the usefulness of Source A in illustrating the continuing hostilities between Bruce and the English after Bannockburn. (8 marks)

In reaching a conclusion you should refer to:
- *the origin and possible purpose of the source*
- *the content of the source*
- *your own knowledge.*

Question 2 – the two-source question

Source B is from Andy MacPhee, *The Scottish Wars of Independence, 1286–1328* (Hodder Gibson, 2010).

> According to Blind Harry's 'The Wallace', the rebellion began with Wallace's murder of Heselrig, the Sheriff of Lanark, in May 1297. This seems to have sparked a general uprising with Wallace at its head. His band of followers was significantly supplemented by men from all over Clydesdale and the addition of the forces of Sir William Douglas. Wallace and Douglas quickly moved north to Scone to confront the justiciar of Galloway, Sir William Ormesby, a man almost as hated as Cressingham. Although Ormesby escaped, Wallace and Douglas arrived at Perth in time to intercept messengers from Bruce, the Steward and bishop Wishart. It is unknown as to what extent these nobles had a hand in Wallace's rebellion, but English chroniclers make it clear that they believe that these powerful men were behind Wallace from the beginning.

Source C is from Michael Lynch, *Scotland: A New History* (Pimlico, 1991).

> The first outbreaks of resistance took place in the north rather than in Wallace's territory. The decisive move, which had turned a series of local stirs already threatening to fizzle out in July into a co-ordinated rising, was the linking of opposition in Moray with a rising in the shires to the east of the Spey and in the important burgh of Aberdeen. The leader of the northern rising was Andrew Murray, the son and heir of a leading baron. Together, Murray and Wallace were acknowledged as 'commanders of the army of the kingdom of Scotland and the community of the realm'. Their respective roles in the revolt have been obscured by the fact that Murray died in November 1297. Neither a general or a guerrilla by instinct, Wallace nonetheless deserves to be remembered as an unflinching patriot and a charismatic warlord. That is why the community entrusted him with sole Guardianship of the realm in the spring of 1298.

⇨

How much do Sources B and C reveal about differing interpretations of the roles of William Wallace and Andrew Murray in Scottish resistance? (10 marks)

Use the sources and recalled knowledge to explain your answer.

Question 3 – the 'How fully' question

Source D is from the Macduff case, 1293–95, *Record of the King's Bench, November 1293–95.*

> November 1293: It is said to the king of Scotland by his lord the king of England that he is his liegeman for the realm of Scotland for which he performed homage and **fealty** to him.
>
> The king of Scotland came before Edward the king and made a personal request of the king: 'Sire I am your liegeman for the realm of Scotland and I pray you to suspend this matter about which you have informed me which affects the people of my realm as well as myself, until I have spoken with them'. And Edward granted the king of Scotland his petition and assigned him a day to appear at the parliament after Easter. The same day was assigned to Macduff.

How fully does Source D illustrate the relationship between King John and Edward I? (10 marks)
Use the source and your own knowledge.

Question 4 – the 'Explain' question

Explain why the death of Alexander III caused the succession problem 1286–92. (8 marks)

Model answers to exam questions

This example is based on the practice question 1 on page 157, using Source A. This is not a perfect answer but it does show that by following the rules on how to answer this type of question, using your own knowledge and then linking it exactly to what the question asks you to do, you can easily gain full marks.

Example

Question

Evaluate the usefulness of Source A in illustrating the continuing hostilities between Bruce and the English after Bannockburn. (8 marks)

In reaching a conclusion you should refer to:

- *the origin and possible purpose of the source*
- *the content of the source*
- *your own knowledge.*

Here is a good answer

Source A is very useful in illustrating the continuing hostilities between Bruce and the English after Bannockburn. The source was produced by the Lanercost priory in Carlisle, which is useful in illustrating the hostilities as Lanercost was on the border with Scotland

and the monks there were educated and would have been able to give a detailed account of Bruce's actions. However, the source would be biased as it is from an English point of view, though this is still useful for showing that view. The fact the source is a contemporary source is also useful as the monks experienced Bruce's invasions of England and would also have had access to first-hand accounts of Bruce's activities. The fact that the source is a Chronicle is also useful as these are accounts of important historical events from the time period and the fact that the chronicler chose to include details of Bruce's actions shows the relevance of the content in showing the continuing hostilities.

The content is useful because it gives two clear illustrations of the continuing hostilities and their impact. The first is that Bruce kept raiding into northern England 'and laid it more and more waste'. This made English lords in the north unhappy with their king who 'could not protect them'.

The second reason is that English lords in the north began to reach private arrangements with the Scots in an attempt to stop the Scottish attacks. The source states, 'Carlisle went secretly to Robert Bruce at Lochmaben and, after holding long … at length came to agreement with him'.

The source however does have limitations in that it does not include all examples of hostilities between Bruce and the English.

It does not report how Bruce opened up 'a second front' against the English in Ireland to put pressure on Edward II to reach an agreement with Bruce. The source also fails to mention the success of Scottish raids in formal combat with the English, as at the Battle of Old Byland where a significant English army was defeated and King Edward II was almost captured.

Finally, the source fails to mention Bruce's ruthlessness in dealing with his Scottish rivals such as the Comyn family. His destruction of Comyn power at the Battle of Inverurie and the hership of Buchan made sure he was secure in his Scottish base.

Overall this source is useful in showing one or two reasons why the Scots won independence but does not give the bigger picture.

Why is this a good answer?

The answer deals effectively with origin, timing and type of the source. This gains 3/4 marks for assessing the provenance of the source. The only area that is not looked at is the purpose of the source. If this had been analysed then another mark would have been gained.

The content of the source is also used well. Two clear points are introduced, the meaning of the source extracts are explained well and the comments are supported by correct quotes from the source. This gains 2/2.

Finally the judgement on usefulness is well balanced by referring to things not mentioned in the source such as the attack on Ireland and the Battle of Old Byland. These points are used well to help evaluate the usefulness of the source and gain 3/3.

The three main parts in this answer combine to gain the maximum of 8/8 marks.

Chapter 10

Migration and empire, 1830–1939

The migration of Scots

What was the 'Highland Problem'?

The large population increase in the Highlands of Scotland led to the subdivision of land into crofts with each generation. Eventually tenants did not have enough land to survive.

Landowners wanted to 'improve' their land by creating profitable sheep farms. One way to do that was by raising rents to 'persuade' crofters to move or use non-payment of rent as justification for eviction.

Poor-quality soil and harsh weather conditions made for a difficult life in many rural areas of Scotland, especially the Highlands. Crofting families survived on a diet consisting largely of potatoes and when that crop failed hunger became more severe. The kelp and herring industries also failed.

Landowners encouraged **emigration** either forcibly or with inducements. For example, James Matheson, a landowner on the island of Lewis, paid for people to leave the land and even cancelled debts that were owed to him.

What were the effects of the Agricultural Revolution?

The introduction of machinery such as steam-driven threshing mills and more effective ploughs meant that fewer people were needed to work farms.

Decline of rural craftsmen whose products were replaced by cheap factory goods also meant people in the Lowlands lost their jobs and moved to the cities in search of work.

Key words

Emigration – the act of leaving one's own country to settle permanently in another.
Migration – movement of people from one place to another.

Why did some Scottish people move abroad?

By 1914 travel by steam ships across the Atlantic took one week. This meant less time for migrants to be not working and not earning wages.

A few Scots were transported to Australia as they were convicted criminals.

The Empire offered new opportunities for enthusiastic people as soldiers, administrators and businessmen. Scots were mostly well educated and frequently had money when emigrating so they were 'welcomed' as immigrants.

Some parts of the Empire, such as Canada, employed emigration agents to actively recruit Scots settlers. Canada's climate was similar to that of Scotland so it was attractive to Scots.

Help to emigrate was given by government, through the Colonial Land and Emigration Commissioners, as well as the 1922 Empire Settlement Act. Charities like the Highlands and Islands Emigration Society were also set up to help people to emigrate.

Why did some Scots move to the central belt and England?

People moved in search of a better life with greater opportunities. They were drawn to the attractions of the 'big city'. Employment in the developing factories was attractive as pay was often higher and the hours of work less. There were also shops along with a better social life with access to pubs, dancehalls and the cinema.

Improved transport links to urban centres developed throughout this period which allowed for easier movement of people from the country to the cities and from Scotland to England.

Hints & tips ★

Although the phrase 'push and pull' is no longer fashionable with some historians as a summary of reasons for migration, it is still very useful to use in this topic. People moved because they had to move (were 'pushed') or because they wanted to go (were 'pulled') by the attractions of a fresh start in life.

The experience of immigrants in Scotland

What you should know 👍

To be successful in this section you must be able to evaluate, identify interpretation and judge sources based on:

★ the experiences of Irish immigrant groups to Scotland and how these experiences differed between Catholics and Protestant Irish

★ what life was like for Jewish, Italian and Lithuanian groups in Scotland.

Context !

Between 1830 and 1939 immigrants to Scotland came from four main areas – the Irish (Catholic and Protestant), Jews, Lithuanians and Italians. Scots reacted in different ways to these groups while the ability and willingness of immigrants to assimilate into Scottish society also differed.

What was the experience of the Catholic Irish in Scotland?

Poverty in Ireland led to mass emigration in the mid-1800s, especially after the Irish Potato Famine of 1845–51. Most Irish emigrants were Catholic and Scotland was largely a Protestant country.

In the 1830s and 1840s many Scots were horrified by the poverty and disease of Irish immigrants. Irish immigrants were accused of bringing diseases with them and were blamed for their spread. Typhus was called the 'Irish fever', for example.

Irish immigrants often settled initially in the poorest areas of towns and cities. This meant the Saltmarket, Cowcaddens and Maryhill in Glasgow, Lochee in Dundee and the Cowgate area of Edinburgh. They were often blamed for being 'benefit scroungers', claiming poor relief after three years' residence.

The Scots often resented the Irish who competed for jobs. Catholic Irish workers were accused of being strikebreakers and of being willing to work for less money than Scottish workers. Later, members of Catholic Irish communities were involved – often in significant numbers – in strikes, trade unions and trade union campaigns. This participation was both welcomed and sought by Scottish workers.

The Catholic Irish developed their Catholic identity through expansion of the Catholic Church and its organisations, such as the League of the Cross, set up to oppose the evils of alcohol.

Mixed marriages between Catholics and Protestants became more common as the century progressed, particularly in smaller communities where the choice of marriage partners was less.

The Independent Labour Party and Labour generally gained much support from the Catholic population, especially after Catholic voters deserted Liberals after the **Easter Rising** in 1916.

What was the experience of the Protestant Irish in Scotland?

One in four Irish migrants was Protestant. Irish Protestants had a lot in common with the average Scot. There was a long-term cultural interaction between Ulster and lowland Scotland.

It was easier for Irish Protestants to fit in (**assimilate**) because of religion. Some employers, such as Bairds of Coatbridge, actively sought skilled Protestant workers.

Key words

Assimilate – to mix with and fit in with the society that immigrants joined.

Easter Rising – At Easter 1916 Irish nationalists tried to start a revolution with the intention of winning independence for Ireland. In the aftermath the Liberal government treated the 'rebels' with great brutality and lost political support from Catholic voters.

Orange Lodge / Lodge System – Irish Protestants formed local groups to protect their interests. The name came from William of Orange who became King of Britain after defeating Catholic King James II.

The first Scottish **Orange Lodge** opened in 1800 in the weaving centre of Maybole in Ayrshire. The growth of the **lodge system** in Scotland shows the spread of Irish Protestantism.

Most of the (sectarian) incidents did not involve Scottish workers, but were instead Orange and Green disturbances involving Protestant Irish and Catholic Irish immigrants.

What was the experience of Jews in Scotland?

The Jewish community was centred on Glasgow from the 1880s. Anti-Semitism was never that widespread, but some prejudice and discrimination did affect the Jews in Scotland. *The Daily Record* headline of August 1905 reported, 'Alien Danger: Immigrants infected with loathsome disease'.

Very few Jews received any help from local poor relief. It was members of the Jewish community that helped each other. For example, the Glasgow Jewish Board of Guardians and the Hebrew Ladies Benevolent Society in 1901 were dealing with 500 cases of needy Jews.

What was the experience of Lithuanians in Scotland?

Around 7000 Lithuanians settled in Scotland and changed their names to integrate more easily into Scottish society. They were attracted to Scotland by jobs.

Lithuanian immigrants were largely employed in the coal industry. At first Lithuanians were used as strikebreakers, but soon most Lithuanians joined trade unions and would strike with the local workers.

Scots complained about the Lithuanians being dirty and immoral, but Lithuanians were much fewer in numbers than Irish immigrants and were not seen as a threat to the Scottish way of life by native Scots.

What was the experience of Italians in Scotland?

By 1914 there were approximately 4500 Italians living in Scotland. Italians set up many businesses, such as ice cream parlours, cafés and fish and chip shops. The Italian cafés did not sell alcohol and were places for young people to meet.

However, there was some tension between Catholic Italians and Protestant Scots. Italian cafés were criticised by Scottish Protestant Church leaders for opening on the Sabbath (Sunday). The café owners also met with criticism from local people who claimed the cafés were sometimes the scenes of unruly behaviour.

There was very little integration between Scots and Italians for much of this period, as the intention of many Italians was to return to Italy once they had made money in Scotland.

> ### Hints & tips ★
>
> Be careful to answer the question you are asked. This section is about how immigrants reacted to their new life in Scotland and what happened to them. A later section deals with how they affected Scotland and Scots. Do not mix up your information.

An Italian ice cream parlour

The impact of Scots emigrants on the empire

What you should know 👍

To be successful in this section you must be able to evaluate, identify interpretation and judge sources based on:

★ how Scots affected the economy and culture of Canada, India, New Zealand and Australia
★ how the arrival of Scots affected the native population.

Context ❗

Scots migrated to countries all over the world. Most of those countries were part of the British Empire. Scots had a very big impact on the economy, culture, educational systems and religious customs of the countries they settled in. Scots also had a big effect on the local native populations.

What was the impact of Scots on Canada?

Scots played a very important role in the fur trade, especially in the Hudson's Bay Company. The Scot George Simpson was Governor-in-Chief of company territory in Canada between 1821 and 1860.

Sir John MacDonald, Glasgow born, was the father of the Canadian Confederation and the first Prime Minister of Canada. The Transatlantic Canadian Pacific Railway, an important piece of engineering, was also his idea. It was financed by Scots like George Stephen and its main engineer, Stanford Fleming, was another Scot.

The newspaper, the Toronto *Globe*, was founded and ruled by Scotsman George Brown.

There was religious development through the Church of Scotland's contribution to laws and learning and education (for example McGill University). Canadian universities developed Scottish-based broad, practical curriculums.

There was also a cultural impact in terms of literature and Canadians embracing their Scottish 'identity' through tartan, bagpipes and the fiddle.

What was the impact of Scots on Australia?

Australia had a large agricultural sector. Therefore, farming, sheep farming and the wool trade were all influenced by Scots. For example, the merino sheep was introduced into Australia by the Scot, John Macarthur. Scottish investment also helped develop agriculture. For example, Niel Back and Company was set up by three Scots and developed 44,000 acres of arable land.

Scots also invested heavily in mining. The gold rush of the 1850s brought to Australia a considerable number of Scottish miners and many gold camps were recognisably 'Scottish'.

Shipping and trade were other areas of enterprise in which Scots excelled. Examples are McIlwraith McEacharn & Co. and Burns Philp.

Robert Campbell from Greenock became known as the 'Father of Australian Commerce' due to his development of industries like shipbuilding and sheep farming.

Scots played a large part in creating the sugar boom of the 1880s in Northern Queensland.

The Church of Scotland played a role in developing education in Australia (for example, Australia College and Scots College in Melbourne). It also influenced the development of Melbourne and Sydney universities.

The treatment of the Aboriginal natives by the settling Scots was not always good (for example, the Hornet Bank massacre and the Warrigal Creek massacre).

What was the impact of Scots on New Zealand?

By 1891, 25 per cent of the UK-born population in New Zealand was of Scottish origin.

Scots had an impact on industries such as paper-making, shipbuilding, farming and commerce. Scots founded banks and financial institutions as well as having a political impact and influence on education.

The treatment of Maori natives varied. There were land grabs from Maoris, but there is also evidence of positive interaction, such as Sir Donald Maclean, who was native minister in 1877–80.

What was the impact of Scots on India?

Scots had an impact as Governors of India. For example, Lord Dalhousie ended traditions such as '**sutee**' and clamped down on the '**thugee**' cult of killers.

Scots also played a military role in putting down the Indian Mutiny. Scottish engineers developed infrastructure across the Indian sub-continent and Scottish businessmen contributed to the development of tea plantations and the jute industry.

Many Indian institutions such as elite schools, universities and press owed much to Scottish emigrants, for example, Reverend Alexander Duff and the University of Calcutta.

Key people

Sir Colin Campbell – Scottish general who is credited with ending the Indian Mutiny.

Robert Campbell – Scot from Greenock who was known as the 'Father of Australian Commerce'.

James Andrew Broun-Ramsay, Lord Dalhousie – Governor General of India between 1848 and 1856. He modernised and unified India, but also alienated many Indians by taking over Indian states when their leaders died.

Sir John A Macdonald – born in Glasgow. Prime Minister of Canada for eighteen years. The man behind the Transatlantic Canadian Pacific Railway.

George Simpson – born in Dingwall, Ross-shire. He worked for the Hudson's Bay Company. He became Governor-in-Chief of company territory in Canada from 1821 to 1860.

Key words

Suttee – Hindu practice where a widow would throw herself on the funeral pyre of her husband.

Thugee – organised cult of killers in India. They specialised in killing travellers quickly by strangulation.

The effects of migration and empire on Scotland, to 1939

Hints & tips ★

Do not assume that the impact of Scots on other countries was always positive. While there is lots of information about how Scots opened up new lands and developed them do not forget that the local people were not always well treated by immigrant Scots.

What you should know 👍

To be successful in this section you must be able to evaluate, identify interpretation and judge sources based on:

★ the effect of Irish, Jewish, Lithuanian and Italian immigrants on Scotland
★ how the British Empire affected life and businesses in Scotland.

Context ❗

Between 1830 and 1939 Scotland was affected in many different ways, not only by the immigrants who came to live in Scotland but also in the many ways Scotland's connection with the British Empire affected life and work for ordinary Scots.

What was the contribution of Irish immigrants to Scotland?

There was an economic contribution, including railway building and infrastructure, such as the Glasgow underground system, as well as the role they played in the jute industry.

There was also a sporting contribution, including the development of Celtic, Edinburgh Hibernian and Dundee United football clubs.

The Education (Scotland) Act 1918 allowed Catholic schools into the state system funded through education rates.

One in four immigrants from Ireland were Protestant and brought their own distinct culture which had an impact in Scotland, especially through the Orange Lodge.

What was the contribution of Jewish immigrants to Scotland?

Large numbers of poorer Jews arrived between 1880 and 1914 – by 1919 over 9000 lived in Glasgow alone. Most lived in the Gorbals and maintained their separate identity by speaking Yiddish, the Jewish language.

Jewish immigrants tended to work in particular jobs such as peddling and hawking (selling door-to-door), tailoring and cigarette making.

Key people

James Connolly – son of Irish immigrants, born in Edinburgh. He was one of the leaders of the 1916 Easter Rising in Dublin.

Thomas Lipton – descendant of Irish immigrants who created a successful retail business. Especially famous for Lipton Tea.

John Wheatley – born in Ireland in 1869. Member of the Independent Labour Party in Scotland. Became a Member of Parliament and is credited with the Housing Act of 1924 which saw the building of affordable housing for working-class men and women.

What was the contribution of Lithuanians to Scotland?

Lithuanians contributed to the economy through their involvement in the coal-mining industry around Coatbridge.

What was the contribution of Italians to Scotland?

Italians were usually found in catering trades, especially ice cream parlours and fish and chip shops.

In addition to catering, Italians became established as hairdressers. They set up the College of Italian Hairdressers in Glasgow in 1928, adding another distinct contribution to Scotland.

What was the impact of the Empire on Scotland?

The Empire played a role in making Scots rich – for example, jute and Dundee. Wealthy individuals such as Sir Charles Tennant, Sir James and Peter Coats and William Weir gained their wealth from trade in chemicals, cotton, coal and iron.

The Empire acted as a market for Scottish goods and emigrants as well as an investment opportunity. It helped the Scottish economy to develop, at least up until 1914, especially in production of shipping and locomotives.

The Empire was also a source of competition to the Scottish economy. Farm produce from Australia and the jute mill development in India were competition.

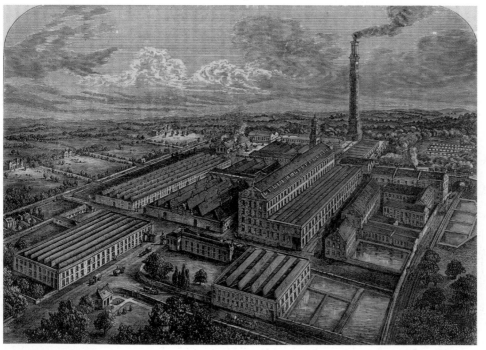

The jute mills of Dundee

For practice ◎

The following sources and questions are for practice.

You can find a good model answer to the second question at the end of this section.

Examples of the other types of questions can be found at the end of the other Section 3 topics covered.

Question 1 – evaluate the usefulness

Source A is from Reverend Alexander McIvor, minister for the parish of Sleat, Skye, in the *New Statistical Account of Scotland, 1834–45*.

> As their potatoes are planted in the end of spring, the young men go to the south in search of employment. The winter is almost altogether spent in idleness. There is no demand for labour in the parish. Oatmeal is a luxury among them, and butcher-meat is seldom tasted. Their poverty arises very much from over-population. There are 225 families in the parish who pay no rents, deriving their subsistence from small portions of land given them by the rent-payers for raising potatoes. Their abject poverty stands in the way of any stimulus that may be applied for enabling them to better their condition. The most efficient remedy appears to be an extensive and well regulated emigration.

Evaluate the usefulness of Source A in showing the economic reasons why so many Scots left Scotland. (8 marks)

In reaching a conclusion you should refer to:

- *the origin and possible purpose of the source*
- *the content of the source*
- *your own knowledge.*

Question 2 – the two-source question

Source B is from James E. Handley, *The Irish in Scotland* (John S. Burns, 1964).

> In general, the attitude of the majority of Lowland Scots towards the Catholic Irish immigrant was one of settled hostility. This hostility was due to economic, political and religious reasons, one or other of which dominated according to the rank and training of the native Scot, but all of which were to some extent present in the minds of those who objected to the settlement of Irish men and women on Scottish soil. On economic grounds, the industrial worker resented the immigration of labourers whose competition for employment would diminish the rate of wages available. For others there was a view that the Irish were not fit to associate on equal terms with the people of Great Britain. Holding such arrogant notions, they felt the presence of the Irish would exert an immoral influence on the Scots race and drag it down.

Source C is from Simon Wood, *Migration and Empire, 1830–1939* (Hodder Gibson, 2011).

> Economic troubles were frequently at the root of tension between Scots and Irish. Irish immigrants were competition for scarce jobs in the 1920s and 30s as economic depression hit Scotland after the war. It would, however, be wrong to paint the experience of the Catholic Irish in Scotland as one of constant conflict with the Scottish community. The Catholic Irish had a shared experience with the Scottish worker in that they were both affected by industrialisation and urbanisation, and they fought together during the First World War. In fact, any argument that the Catholic Irish had no loyalty to the British state was effectively ended during the Great War when Catholic Irish volunteered and fought for the British state, dying in large numbers.

> **How much do Sources B and C reveal about differing interpretations of the experience of immigrant Catholic Irish in Scotland? (10 marks)**
>
> *Use the sources and recalled knowledge to explain your answer.*
>
> ## Question 3 – the 'How fully' question
>
> **Source D** is from Allan Macinnes, Marjory Harper and Linda Fryer (eds), *Scotland and the Americas, c.1650–c.1939* (2002).
>
> Scots not only achieved personal success in Canada, but played a key part in shaping the country's development, as explorers, financiers and politicians. Sir John A. Macdonald – the product of a relatively humble home in Glasgow – became a lawyer, and went into politics, initially as an opponent of the colonial government in 1847. Conscious of the ever-present threat from Canada's more powerful neighbour to the south, and totally opposed to separation from Britain, Macdonald's strategy as first Prime Minister of the new Dominion was to promote a transcontinental railway which would join the Atlantic to the Pacific, open up the west to settlers, and in the process strengthen and unite the fledgling country.
>
> **How fully does Source D describe the impact of Scots emigrants on the Empire? (10 marks)**
> *Use the source and your own knowledge.*
>
> ## Question 4 – the 'Explain' question
>
> **Explain why migration and empire had a significant effect on Scotland, to 1939. (8 marks)**

Model answers to exam questions

These examples are based on the practice questions on pages 168–169. These are not perfect answers, but they do show that by following the rules on how to answer these types of question, using your own knowledge and then linking it exactly to what the question asks you to do, you can gain full marks.

Example

Question

How much do Sources B and C reveal about differing interpretations of the experience of immigrant Catholic Irish in Scotland? (10 marks)

Use the sources and recalled knowledge to explain your answer.

Sources B and C show differing interpretations of the experience of immigrant Catholic Irish in Scotland. Source B suggests that the Catholic Irish experience was almost completely negative as the Scots were hostile to them for several reasons ranging from the economic to the religious, whereas Source C suggests that the Catholic Irish experience was not entirely negative as there was interaction between Scots due to their shared experience of work and fighting in the war.

Source B explains that 'hostility was due to economic, political and religious reasons, one or other of which dominated according to the rank and training of the native Scot, but all of which were to some extent present in the minds of those who objected to the settlement of Irish men and women on Scottish soil'. This shows that prejudice against the Irish affected all groups in Scottish society, though for slightly different reasons. Source B goes on to explain that much hostility was 'on economic grounds' as 'the industrial worker resented the immigration of labourers whose competition for employment would diminish the rate of wages available', which illustrates the feeling that immigrant Irish were willing to work for less wages than the Scottish workforce, causing resentment. Source B also states that some had 'a view that the Irish were not fit to associate on equal terms with the people of Great Britain. Holding such arrogant notions, they felt the presence of the Irish would exert an immoral influence on the Scots race and drag it down', which explains the hostility as some Scots felt they were a superior people to the Irish and looked down on them.

On the other hand, Source C states that 'economic troubles were frequently at the root of tension between Scots and Irish. Irish immigrants were competition for scarce jobs in the 1920s and 30s as economic depression hit Scotland after the war', which agrees that economic problems caused tension, though it emphasises it was jobs that were the problem, not pay. Source C does disagree with B, however, in that it illustrates positive relations when it states that 'the Catholic Irish had a shared experience with the Scottish worker in that they were both affected by industrialisation and urbanisation, and they fought together during the First World War', which showed that the common experience of working together and fighting together meant that the Catholic Irish had a better experience in Scotland than Source B suggests.

However, Sources B and C leave out important points about the interpretations of the experience of Catholic Irish in Scotland as they do not give all the details about the experience. For example, the sources do not show that as many immigrant Catholic Irish were poor they tended to concentrate in the poorer areas of Scottish cities, such as the Lochee area of Dundee. Owing to poor pay and housing they were associated with drunken behaviour and blamed for criminality and even diseases like typhus, owing to the epidemic of 1847, which happened at the same time as Irish immigration. The source also misses out the interpretation that how they were treated led to the Irish Catholic community in Scotland creating a distinct identity owing to their religion and development of a separate education system. The sources also make no mention of the Irish Catholic experience politically as many supported Irish home rule. This led to the formation of Sinn Fein clubs in Scotland that sent money to help the cause of home rule in Ireland. The Irish Catholic community also became an important group supporting the Labour Party after the creation of the Irish state in 1922.

Why is this a good answer?

First, the student divides their answer up into recognisable sections that the marker can easily interpret when marking. There is an introductory paragraph, which recognises the issue in the question and identifies the overall differences between the two viewpoints with accurate outline knowledge about the two sources.

⇨

The answer goes on to interpret Source B and accurately develops the source points with explanation. Source C is then introduced, interpreted and compared to Source B. This student has chosen to quote directly and then explain the points. This is a good technique and shows accurate interpretation and understanding of the presented source points.

The answer then gives three very important points of recall, which give accurate information on interpretations not included in the two presented sources.

This answer would get 10/10: 2 overall marks, 5 source marks and 3 recall points.

Question

Explain why migration and empire had a significant effect on Scotland, to 1939.   (8 marks)

Migration and empire had a significant effect on Scotland to 1939 for a number of reasons. Firstly, migration had an effect on Scotland as it vastly improved Scotland's transport network. Irish labourers provided much of the hard, physical labour that helped build Scotland's railways and canals. Secondly, migration also had a positive effect on Scotland's commerce, making food more affordable. Thomas Lipton was the descendant of Irish immigrants who built up a retail empire that provided reasonably priced groceries and was famous for developing products like Lipton's tea. Migration also had a very significant impact on Scottish sporting culture as Catholic Irish immigrants formed football teams. The most famous of these include Glasgow Celtic and Hibernian in Edinburgh. There were also more important cultural effects from groups such as the Italians who had a significant effect on the Scottish diet and lifestyle. Italian immigrants were very involved in the catering trade, and the development of ice-cream parlours and fish and chip shops had an effect on Scots' spare time and diet as they gave people an alternative to the pub and provided affordable fast food.

Empire had a significant effect on Scotland due to the Scots who returned with money in their pocket from making their fortunes abroad. For example, the Forbes family made a fortune trading in India, which allowed them to develop their family estates in Aberdeenshire and improve the land. Empire also had a significant effect on Scotland as it was a market for Scottish products such as jute. The link between empire and Scotland can be seen in the way that the jute industry first developed in Dundee and became a successful export due to the production of hessian. However, it is also important to note that empire had a significant and negative impact on Scotland in the twentieth century as places like India developed their own industries, which provided competition for those in Scotland. This led to the decline of the jute industry, as it could not compete with the cheap labour that was found in India. Lastly, empire had a significant effect as it helped develop the view of the Scottish soldier as a skilful fighter. This is due to the fact that Scottish soldiers were distinctive in their highland kilts and proved themselves in actions such as the Indian Mutiny where the Scottish general Sir Colin Campbell and Scottish troops made a huge impact.

Why is this a good answer?

This answer is well structured with each point explained and illustrated with an example. This model of making two sentences per point is good. The answer also has a good start with a process sentence that directly answers the question. Each point is about a development that came from either migration or the empire and had an impact on Scotland. Overall, a full answer that would gain full marks as it makes eight detailed and supported explanations.

Chapter 11

The impact of the Great War, 1914–1928

Scots on the Western Front

What you should know 👍

To be successful in this section you must be able to evaluate, identify interpretation and judge sources based on:

★ why so many Scots volunteered to fight
★ the experience of Scots soldiers on the Western Front
★ the Scottish contribution to the Western Front.

Context ❗

From the outbreak of war, Scottish men volunteered in huge numbers. During the First World War the Scots suffered proportionately the most combat casualties of any nation involved in the conflict.

Key words

Battalion – military unit comprising 300 to 800 men. Commanded by a lieutenant-colonel.

Key people

Sir John French – Commander-in-chief of the British Expeditionary Force 1914–15. He resigned after the Battle of Loos in 1915.

Sir Douglas Haig – Commander of the British Expeditionary Force between 1915 and 1918. His period as commander saw the British army suffer huge casualties at the Battles of the Somme and the Third Ypres. A controversial figure after the war, he came under criticism for the scale of British casualties. More recently historians have pointed out that he had to deal with a unique set of conditions and a steep learning curve. He led the British army to victory in 1918.

Sir George MacCrae – born in Aberdeen, a successful Edinburgh businessman and politician. He famously raised the 16th Battalion Royal Scots. Many of those who volunteered were supporters and players for football teams like Hearts, Hibs and Falkirk.

Robert Cranston – successful Edinburgh businessman, politician and volunteer soldier. He raised the 15th Battalion Royal Scots.

Why did so many Scots volunteer to fight?

By July 1915 the average rate of recruitment for all males in Britain was 20 per cent, but in Scotland it was 24 per cent.

Scots joined up for a range of reasons: excitement, economic necessity, a sense of tradition and patriotism. Many joined up together, for example, Hearts players, McCrae's **Battalion** and Cranston's Battalion. In Glasgow the 15th (City of Glasgow) Battalion of the Highland Light Infantry was known as the Tramway Battalion as most of the men had been members of the city's transport department. The 16th Battalion was made up of Boys' Brigade members and the 17th from the city's Chamber of Commerce.

What was the experience of Scots soldiers on the Western Front?

The Western Front developed into a war of attrition between the Allies and the Germans. The need to protect troops led to the development of trench warfare.

The Scots' experience was the same as that of other troops in many ways. They ate the same food and fought in the same battles and were affected by things like shell shock, snipers and death. There were the common problems of lice, rats and disease. Conditions in trenches were not good – they were frequently damp.

The kilted regiments – Black Watch, Queen's Own Cameron Highlanders, Gordon Highlanders, Argyll and Sutherland Highlanders – were involved on the Western Front. Some men would remove their kilts to help them get through the flooded communication trenches as the mud weighed the kilts down and made it difficult to move.

What was the Scots contribution to the Western Front?

The kilted regiments were involved in the Battles of Loos, the Somme and Arras. They had a reputation as the 'ladies from hell' or 'devils in skirts'.

At the Battle of Loos in 1915, half of the 72 infantry battalions involved had Scottish names. One third of the 21,000 who died were from Scottish regiments. After Loos, the British commander-in-chief, Sir John French, was replaced by General Douglas Haig, a lowland Scot.

Scottish soldiers in the First World War

Three divisions, the 9th (Scottish), 15th (Scottish) and 51st (Highland) were involved in the Battle of the Somme, which launched on 1 July 1916. Other units had Scottish battalions in them. Sir Douglas Haig also played an important role at the Somme. His views that he could destroy the Germans and was willing to use attrition to do so were controversial. He was however willing to innovate – he used gas and introduced tanks.

By 1918 the British army was formidable and it was this army that counter-attacked after the great German offensive of March 1918 with great success.

Domestic impact of war: society and culture

What you should know

To be successful in this section you must be able to evaluate, identify interpretation and judge sources based on:

★ what sort of people opposed the war
★ how the government changed due to the war
★ how the war changed the lives of women
★ what the rent strikes were
★ how Scots commemorated and remembered their war dead.

Context

The First World War had a big effect on everyday life in Scotland. Scottish society and culture changed due to the war. Not everyone supported the war and when **conscription** was started opposition to the war increased. The war also led to an increase in government involvement in everyone's lives and one of the biggest changes was in the role of women in society.

Key words

Conscription – compulsory military service. It was introduced by Britain in 1916.
Politicised – people saw that politics was not something for far away wealthy politicians to control. The war taught many ordinary people that they could take action themselves to influence politics in the country. It is a word closely linked to **radicalisation**.
Radicalisation – the growing belief that people could take direct action to improve their own living and working conditions.
Quakers – a religious group. They believe in pacifism and non-violence so objected to fighting in the war.

Hints & tips

A question about the experience of Scots on the Western Front does not have to be limited to writing about ordinary soldiers in the front line only. Senior officers such as Douglas Haig were Scots involved on the Western Front, as were Scottish nurses such as Mairi Chisholm and Elsie Knocker. Unlike most nurses they really did work on the front line with the Belgian army.

Key people

Mary Barbour – a political activist who became involved in leading the Glasgow rent strikes. She went on to become a councillor and magistrate.
Helen Crawfurd – a Suffragette and socialist. She was an anti-war campaigner who was a leading light in the rent strikes in Glasgow.
Agnes Dollan – a Suffragette and pacifist during the war. She was a leading member of the Scottish Independent Labour Party. She was involved in the Glasgow rent strikes of 1915–16.
Elsie Inglis – a Suffragist and doctor. She was famous for setting up the Scottish Women's Hospitals for Foreign Service. These served in France, Serbia and Russia.

What sort of people opposed the war?

Voluntary recruitment was successful to begin with, but as the war went on demands for more men increased.

Conscription began in 1916 and men who refused to join up were conscientious objectors. The introduction of conscription in 1916 added to the anti-war feeling, especially from those who did not think it was right to be forced to fight.

Many objectors were members of the Independent Labour Party which was strong in Scotland. As a left-wing political party they objected to fighting a war for the bosses. Many socialists also objected as they believed passionately in peace and the brotherhood of all peoples. Some religious groups objected to war as well. Groups such as the **Quakers** would not fight, but would serve as stretcher bearers.

How did government change due to the war?

There was an expansion of government power to run the country in order to win the war with the Defence of the Realm Act (DORA).

Political parties joined together for the duration of the war to form a coalition government. The Liberal government was already facing difficulties about the amount of interference in people's everyday lives.

How did the war change the lives of women?

Women worked in industries such as engineering and munitions work. A purpose-built munitions factory at Gretna had 9000 women workers, 5000 male workers and a women's police force to keep order.

Some women served as nurses, such as Mairi Chisholm and Elsie Knocker who set up four Scottish Women's Hospitals in Europe and the Balkans.

Women did not get equal pay to men, but it did improve. Some women were granted the vote in national elections in 1918.

Mairi Chisholm and Elsie Knocker

What were the rent strikes?

Women were more **politicised** which means more aware and involved in politics. This was a result of rent strikes against rising rents that landlords tried to impose in places like Glasgow.

The Glasgow Women's Housing Association, Helen Crawfurd, Mary Barbour, Agnes Dollan and Jessie Stephens all played a role in resisting the rent rises and the threatened evictions to those who could not pay.

Direct action was taken against sheriff officers who were ordered to carry out evictions. Women used the media well by accusing greedy landlords of being like Germans hurting the people of Scotland!

The rent strike leaders had the support of business leaders who did not like seeing work disrupted and so the government introduced rent controls for the duration of the war.

How did Scots commemorate and remember their war dead?

Scottish war dead estimates vary but unofficial claims are that at least 110,000 died – that is 13 per cent of the total losses suffered by Britain. The greatest losses came from the Royal Scots – 583 officers and 10,630 men. The Black Watch lost 10,000 men and the Gordon Highlanders lost 9000.

Local memorials to the fallen exist all over Scotland. Sir Robert Lorimer's Scottish National War Memorial in Edinburgh Castle opened in July 1927. The roll of honour includes everyone of Scots birth, of Scottish parents, those who served in Scottish regiments or in others, for example, the London Scottish.

In 1921 the British Legion and British Legion Scotland under Douglas Haig were created to help care for veterans. The Poppy Appeal started at the same time. The act of remembrance with a silence at 11 a.m. on 11 November started in 1919.

Domestic impact of war: industry and economy

What you should know 👍

To be successful in this section you must be able to evaluate, identify interpretation and judge sources based on:

★ how Scottish industry was helped by the war
★ what problems in Scottish industry existed during the war
★ how and why Scottish industry hit problems after the war.

The war affected industry, agriculture and fishing. After the war, Scottish industry and the economy suffered problems which had either been caused by the war or had been disguised by the war. A large number of Scots emigrated to find a better life overseas.

Did the war benefit the Scottish economy?

Before the war the Scottish economy was based on traditional industries like coal mining, shipbuilding and the production of iron and steel. These industries were in trouble before the war, but war demands helped them.

Shipbuilding benefited from increased demand for warships and replacement orders for ships. When the war ended demand dropped and shipyards closed.

Steel benefited from increased demand to build the weapons of war. Ninety per cent of plate armour was produced in the west of Scotland. Coal benefited from increased demand to power the machinery and fuel the ships that were built on the Clyde.

War also benefited the jute industry in Dundee as demand for items such as sandbags increased. After the war competition from India led to a rapid decline.

The North British Rubber Company, based in Edinburgh, benefited as demand for waterproof wellington boots increased.

The fishing industry was severely affected by the war as Scotland's east-coast ports were taken over by the Admiralty and were just about totally closed to fishing.

Agriculture benefited as the government bought all Scottish wool for uniforms and Scots oats for feed for horses.

Were there any industrial problems during the war?

There was a tradition of powerful **trade unions**. As a result there were a series of strikes against what were seen as weakening trade union rights.

The Munitions of War Act led to restrictions in workers' rights, with munitions tribunals set up to deal with workers who did not comply with their restrictions.

There was determined opposition from the **Clyde Workers' Committee** to the introduction of unskilled labour (**dilution**).

There was also industrial unrest after the war with the 40-hour strike and the 'battle' of George Square in 1919 (see pages 179–180).

Key words

Clyde Workers' Committee (also known as the Labour Withholding Committee) – set up to oppose the Munitions Act. It was led by Willie Gallacher.

Dilution of labour – where complex industrial processes were reduced into a series of simple tasks. This enabled semi and unskilled workers to undertake the work.

Emigrate – to leave one's country and settle in another.

Trade union – organisation of workers set up to protect workers' rights.

Key people

Willie Gallacher – Scottish trade unionist, activist and communist. Chairman of the Clyde Workers' Committee. He was prosecuted for criticising the war and was sent to prison. From 1920 he became a leading member of the British Communist Party.

William Weir – Scottish industrialist and politician. He became director of munitions in Scotland in 1915. He came into conflict with the Clyde Workers' Committee.

What happened after the war?

Demand for heavy goods declined after the war and there was increased competition for the things that the Scots produced.

The fishing industry lost markets in Russia and Germany. Jute suffered from foreign competition, especially India, which developed its own jute industry.

Shipbuilding went into decline: between 1921 and 1923 the tonnage built on the Clyde went down from 510,000 to 170,000.

Soldiers returning from war faced poor prospects of getting jobs in agriculture, fishing and heavy industries and unemployment grew in the 1920s. Shortage of land in the Highlands and Islands caused problems including land raids.

Thousands of Scots decided to **emigrate** from Scotland in the 1920s helped by the Empire Settlement Act of 1922.

Domestic impact of war: politics

What you should know 👍

To be successful in this section you must be able to evaluate, identify interpretation and judge sources based on:

★ the effect of the war on Scottish politics and political parties
★ how the war damaged the Liberal Party
★ how the war boosted the Conservative and Labour Parties.

Context ❗

Before 1914 politics in Scotland was dominated by the Liberal Party. By 1929 the Labour Party and Conservative Party dominated. The war brought changes to the way government operated and led to new groups of people gaining the right to vote. These changes helped the Labour and Conservative Parties but damaged the Liberal Party.

Key people

Duchess of Atholl – Scottish **Unionist** politician. She was the first Scottish female to be elected as a Member of Parliament in 1923. She was a prominent anti-fascist before the war.

David Kirkwood – Scottish socialist and politician. He was an important leader of Red Clydeside. He became a Member of Parliament in 1922.

John MacLean – Scottish school teacher and revolutionary socialist. A passionate opponent of the war. He was personally popular, but this never translated itself into widespread political support.

John Wheatley – Scottish socialist politician. Wheatley was a member of the Independent Labour Party. He was originally associated with the ⇨

Hints & tips ⭐

A good way of understanding the effect of the war on the economy is to think of a graph like a triangle. In 1914 the economy was at the bottom left of the triangle. It was low because it faced problems. Then the triangle rises to its peak and that is the effect of the war boosting the economy. Then the triangle falls to the bottom right and that is what happened to the economy after the war. It crashed with the fall in wartime orders and the rise of foreign competition.

Key word

Unionist – in a political sense this means supporter of the union of British nations. In Scotland this meant supporting the Scottish Unionist Party (effectively the Conservative Party in Scotland).

⇨ Red Clydeside movement. He campaigned against conscription. He was elected as a councillor in Glasgow and then as a Member of Parliament in 1922. As an MP he is famously associated with the Housing Act of 1924 that saw a massive increase in local council housing.

What effect did the war have on the Liberal Party?

The war split the Liberal Party into those who opposed the war and the majority who supported it. Those who opposed the war formed the Union of Democratic Control which became one of the main anti-war organisations in Britain. The Liberal Party split more seriously with disagreements between Herbert Asquith, its leader up until 1915, and another Liberal called Lloyd George.

The 1918 Representation of the People Act gave the vote to all men aged over 21 and women over 30. Many of these new voters did not agree with traditional Liberal issues.

Liberals had been interested in little government intervention in people's lives, but the war had increased government control and intervention. People were used to it.

Old Liberal causes such as home rule became less important after the war. With the partition of Ireland into Northern Ireland and Eire in 1922, one old Liberal cause had gone. Many voters in Scotland who had voted Liberal now chose to vote Labour.

What effect did the war have on the Labour movement?

For many in Scotland, Labour meant the Independent Labour Party. The ILP was a socialist party that had helped create the mainstream Labour Party. Many of its members were involved in anti-war activities as well as the rent strikes.

Politically the mainstream Labour Party benefited from the war. They benefited from the extension of the franchise as well as the developments in government intervention. During the war Labour had been involved in the coalition government and had worked with the government on dilution of labour. Labour's vote went up from 800,000 in 1910 to over 2,000,000 in 1918.

In one sense the war caused Labour some problems. There were a series of industrial disputes during the war that led some people to think that part of Britain had become much more radical, even revolutionary.

Red Clydeside refers to the disputes and protests that occurred in parts of Glasgow and its surrounding area between 1915 and 1919. The rent strikes in Govan can be seen as part of this. 'Bloody Friday' on Friday 31 January 1919 saw 100,000 demonstrate in George Square in Glasgow in support of a 40-hour working week and the end of rent restrictions.

Fighting between police and demonstrators led to massive over-reaction by authorities, who moved 12,000 English soldiers to the city, supported by six tanks. They feared a revolution – Russia had turned communist in 1917. The strike ended swiftly as strike leaders were shocked at the violence.

How did the war benefit the Conservative Party in Scotland?

War also benefited the Conservative Party in Scotland (more accurately known as the Scottish Unionist Party). Middle-class voters feared the 'revolutionary' events such as the George Square riots and voted for the Conservatives as the party of law and order.

The Conservatives were well-organised with effective local party associations, junior sections like the Junior Imperial League and innovative campaigning methods, such as mobile cinemas. The party also benefited from support of newspapers such as *The Scotsman*. Newspapers like *The Sunday Post* were pro-Unionist.

Conservatives had a range of policies designed to attract a range of voters, from housing to pensions for war widows. They were especially 'friendly' to new women voters who tended to be middle class. After the war, pro-union, pro-empire patriotism led many to vote for the Conservatives.

> ### Hints & tips ★
> *Be aware that the word Unionist at this time means the Conservative Party. It has nothing to do with trade unionism.*

For practice ◉

The following sources and questions are for practice.

You can find a good model answer to question three at the end of this section.

Examples of the other types of questions can be found at the end of the other Section 3 topics covered

Question 1 – evaluate the usefulness

Source A is from the diary of Private Thomas McCall, Cameron Highlanders describing the attack at Loos, September, 1915.

> The soldier lying next to me gave a shout, saying, 'My God! I'm done for'. His mate next to him asked where he was shot. He drew himself back and lifted his wounded pal's kilt, then gave a laugh, saying, 'Jock, ye'll no die. Yer only shot through the fleshy part of the leg!'. We moved on towards the village of Loos, where machine guns were raking the streets and bayonet-fighting was going on with Jerry [slang for Germans]. Prisoners were being marshalled in batches to be sent under guard down the line. I came to a little restaurant. By the noise going on inside I thought they were killing pigs. I went inside and opened a door where blood was running out from underneath. I saw some Highlanders busy, having it out with Jerry with the bayonet.

Evaluate the usefulness of Source A as evidence of the experience of Scots on the Western Front. (8 marks)

In reaching a conclusion you should refer to:
- *the origin and possible purpose of the source*
- *the content of the source*
- *your own knowledge.*

⇨

⇨
Question 2 – the two-source question

Source B is from A. Dickson and J. H. Treble, *People and Society in Scotland: Volume III, 1914–1990* (John Donald Publishers Ltd, 1992).

Under a succession of able, and usually Scottish chairmen, Conservatives cashed in on the First World War. They were the patriotic party of the 'Anglo-Scottish' Empire – ex-officers as party agents with ex-servicemen in the British Legion, Orange Lodges tagging along. They fostered a kind of one-party state ethos that bridged businessmen, professionals and even those believing in collective action. This was in its own terms a 'principled society' such as the work that William Weir put into the National Grid – and owed a lot to the fears of industrialists about the problems caused by the post-war economic downturn. Some, at least, were alert to possible remedies; mixtures of free trade and government planning. They drew on a dense network of family and financial relationships and incorporated many former Liberals to form an interest group that filled many senior government advisory posts.

Source C is from I. G. C. Hutchison, *Scottish Politics in the Twentieth Century* (Palgrave, 2001).

One factor of considerable significance in the dominance of the Conservatives was their superior organisation, which easily outstripped Liberal and Labour in comprehensiveness and effectiveness. By 1927, only about twelve constituencies did not have a full-time agent/organiser, whereas the Liberals and Labour each had only a handful in total. Financially, the party was healthy: between 1823 and 1932 the conservative central organisation enjoyed an average annual income of £13,000. This contrasts with the virtually bankrupt Liberals and permanently cash-strapped Labour Party. In addition, the Conservative Clubs in Edinburgh and Glasgow continued their pre-war activities of raising regular large amounts to supplement the party's income. Party membership was buoyant: there were around 30,000 in Glasgow alone, a figure substantially in excess of the total of Labour in the whole of Scotland.

How much do Sources B and C reveal about the differing interpretations of the reasons for the rise of the Conservative party in Scotland after the First World War? (10 marks)

Use the sources and recalled knowledge to explain your answer.

Question 3 – the 'How fully' question

Source D is from a memoir by Major-General Richard Hilton, a Forward Observation Officer at the Battle of Loos, 1915.

The real tragedy of that battle was its nearness to complete success. Most of us who reached the crest of Hill 70 were firmly convinced that we had broken through on that Sunday, 25th September 1915. There seemed to be nothing ahead of us but an unoccupied and incomplete trench system. The only two things that prevented our advancing were, firstly the exhaustion of the 'Jocks' themselves and secondly the flanking fire of numerous German machine-guns, which swept that bare hill from some factory buildings to the south of us. All that we needed was more artillery, and some fresh infantry to take over from the weary 'Jocks'. But, alas, neither ammunition nor reinforcements were immediately available, and the great opportunity passed.

How fully does Source D illustrate the experience of the Scots on the Western Front? (10 marks)

Use the source and your own knowledge.

Question 4 – the 'Explain' question

Explain why the First World War had a significant impact on Scottish society and culture. (8 marks)

Model answers to exam questions

This example is based on practice question 3 on page 181. This is not a perfect answer but it does show that, by following the rules on how to answer this type of question, using your own knowledge and then linking it exactly to what the question asks you to do, you can easily gain full marks.

Example ⚑

Question

How fully does Source D illustrate the experience of the Scots on the Western Front? (10 marks)

Use the source and your own knowledge.

Source D partly illustrates the experience of Scots on the Western Front.

Firstly, the source states, 'most of us who reached the crest of Hill 70 were firmly convinced that we had broken through ... There seemed to be nothing ahead of us but an unoccupied and incomplete trench system'.

This shows that Scottish soldiers were often involved in battles on the Western Front. Hill 70 was in Belgium and a central part of the Battle of Loos. The extract also refers to trench systems and trench warfare was a major part of the experience of Scots on the Western Front.

Secondly the source refers to 'the flanking fire of numerous German machine-guns'. On the Western Front machine guns dominated the battlefield in 1915 and the German army had become expert in covering the whole Western Front with sweeping and crisscrossing machine gun fire, which were fighting conditions that the Scots experienced.

Thirdly the source states, 'All that we needed was more artillery, and some fresh infantry to take over from the weary "Jocks"'. This refers to the importance of artillery to attack enemy strong positions. Artillery barrages were commonly used before attacks on the Western Front and also to destroy enemy machine gun positions. The extract also mentions the weariness of 'Jocks' and lack of sleep was a main feature of the experience of Scots on the front line of the Western Front.

The source however does not give a full impression of the experience of Scots on the Western Front.

In the trenches the Scots faced all weather conditions and boredom when on duty all day and night while no attack was happening.

In the trenches Scots had to deal with rats that ate their food and lice that infested their clothes. This had a particular impact on the Scots as they wore kilts.

Scottish soldiers were not on the front line all the time. They were often rotated back to rest and get clean, usually every few days.

In the trenches Scots were not isolated. Unless a battle was raging, soldiers received hot food, fresh water and regular mail from home although their letters and cards sent home were censored by their officers.

⇨

Not all Scots on the Western Front were front line 'Jocks'. Scots such as Douglas Haig had a very different experience of the war, working and sleeping in comfortable houses behind the front line but having to take decisions that would lead to the deaths of thousands.

Scottish nurses such as Elsie Knocker and Mairi Chisholm served on or near the front line saving soldiers at great risk to themselves.

Finally Scottish soldiers found themselves being used as shock troops, first into battle at the Somme and Arras. It was believed that German soldiers were especially afraid of the fighting Scots, nicknamed 'ladies from hell' because of their skirt-like kilts.

Why is this a good answer?

First of all, you must make a decision. After all the question asks you to decide 'how fully'. The word 'partly' is a decision and later in the answer the student makes another clear decision by writing, 'The source however does not give a full impression of the experience …' This is a good link between using the source and moving on to using recall.

Students should always try to get at least three points (as up to four can be credited) main points from the source but remember it is never enough just to choose three to four quotes. Each source extract should be explained and linked to the question. This student does that (and makes it easy for the marker) by numbering each extract, therefore gets 3/4 marks.

There are also up to 7 marks available for using your own knowledge (called recall) to help answer the question.

This answer makes it easy for a marker by breaking up the recall into seven sections which each include a lot of new detail that is relevant to the question.

Overall this is an excellent answer that gains full marks just by following the rules of good answers.